Writer's Market Companion

2nd Edition

Writer's Market Companion

2nd Edition

JOE FEIERTAG, MARY CARMEN CUPITO,
AND THE EDITORS OF WRITER'S DIGEST BOOKS

WRITER'S DIGEST BOOKS
CINCINNATI, OHIO
www.writersdigest.com

Visit our Web site at www.writersdigest.com for information on more resources for writers.

To receive a free weekly e-mail newsletter delivering tips and updates about writing and about Writer's Digest products, register directly at our Web site at http://newsletters.fwpublications.com.

08 07 06 05 04   5 4 3 2 1

Library of Congress Cataloging-in-Publication Data

Feiertag, Joe, 1958-
    Writer's market companion / Joe Feiertag, Mary Carmen Cupito, and the editors of Writer's Digest Books.--2nd ed.
        p. cm.
    Includes index.
    ISBN1-58297-291-5 (alk. paper)
    1. Authorship--Marketing--Handbooks, manuals, etc. I. Cupito, Mary Carmen, 1954- II. Title.

PN147.F43 2004
808'.02'023--dc22

                                                        2004040289

Edited by Kelly Nickell and Michelle Ruberg
Designed by Clare Finney
Production coordinated by Robin Richie

About the Authors

Mary Carmen Cupito has worked as a reporter for *The Cincinnati Post*, *The Columbus Dispatch,* and *The St. Petersburg Times*. Since leaving full-time reporting, she has written many freelance articles for magazines, newspapers, and other publications. Mary teaches journalism at Northern Kentucky University.

Joe Feiertag is a public relations professional and former journalist who has built a highly successful career as a freelance writer and editor. He also has taught writing at the college level. He resides in Fort Thomas, Kentucky, with his wife, Kathy, and their two children, Alexandra and Michael.

Table of Contents

PART FOUR Protecting and Developing Your Work

Introduction

Since 1921, *Writer's Market* has helped writers navigate the sometimes-murky waters of the publishing industry. In our pursuit to assist you in reaching your personal writing goals, we've kept two primary goals in mind—to help you get published and to get paid. However, as more writing and publishing opportunities emerge, and the publishing industry changes, we have become more selective in choosing the markets that appear in *Writer's Market*. As a result of these choices, we have to sacrifice essential content, the nuts and bolts of publishing, if you will. To fill this gap, we're providing you with this *Writer's Market Companion, 2nd edition*. It is our intent that you use this book in conjunction with *Writer's Market*.

When the first edition of this book was written, the publishing industry had just started to embrace new technological advances, particularly as they related to the electronic world. If you are familiar with *Writer's Market*, then you know that we too have welcomed these changes with the creation of our subscription–based Web site, WritersMarket.com. It is our intent, through the Web site and its related print edition, *Writer's Market Deluxe Edition*, to provide you with the most comprehensive, up-to-date contact information for the markets to which you wish to submit.

Within this book, you will find that we've addressed these technological advances, providing you with new information, which covers formatting and submitting queries via e-mail, writing content specifically for the Web, and writing and creating e-books. We have also taken the time to explain electronic rights, and how they affect you and your writing.

To further assist you in developing a sound and functional writing plan, we've added a series of interactive worksheets to help you develop effective time management goals, write a winning sales pitch for your novel, and craft a savvy query letter. It is our hope that you use these worksheets as you see fit.

As you page through this book, you will find four distinct parts, along with four appendices. The topic covered in each part plays a significant role in helping you publish and sell your writing, and the appendices provide you with the resource information to help you fully understand and utilize the information presented in this book. Here's an overview of what you can expect to find inside:

Part I: Preparing Yourself for the Work Ahead looks at the various components of the publishing world, how the publishing world affects you, the writer, and how you can establish a solid writing plan that guides you toward publication. In this part you'll find answers to the following questions:
- What are the "hot" magazine topics and book subjects?
- Where can I find new topics to write about?
- What magazine and book markets exist for a beginning writer like myself?
- How do I find the best market for my work?
- How can I juggle my personal life with my writing life?

Part II: Building a Strong Foundation explains various research methods and provides resources for conducting the most accurate and up-to-date research. As a writer, you know that research is a key element in every type of writing. In Part II, you'll find answers to the following questions:
- How do I develop a research strategy?
- Where do I begin my research—the library or the Internet?
- Once I have the research finished, what do I do with it?
- How do I find the best sources to interview?
- What type of questions should I ask in an interview?

Part III: Taking Your Work to Market is one of the biggest sections in this book because it provides crucial information for how to find appropriate markets for your writing and how to prepare your materials for submission. You'll find information on a spectrum of topics, from preparing query letters and book proposals to selling your novel with and without an agent. We've also provided you with sample query letters, cover letters, and synopses, while sharing various resources for selling your work.

We know there is more than one type of writer who uses this book, and in this section, you'll find formatting and submission information for:

- articles and other short nonfiction
- nonfiction books
- short stories
- novels
- scripts
- corporate markets
- online opportunities

After reading this section, you will come away with answers to questions like:

- How do I handle rejection?
- How do I find a book publisher?
- What markets will buy my short stories?
- How do I find an agent?
- Is it appropriate to send a query by e-mail?

Part IV: Protecting and Developing Your Work covers five areas essential to establishing and developing your writing career:

- Rights
- Promotion/marketing
- Writing as a business
- Writing communities
- Finding extra money

As you read through the material, you'll notice that the information in the five sections above is indispensable to establishing and further developing yourself as a writer. You'll learn to understand the often confusing world of "rights" (including copyright), and how they affect most book and magazine contracts.

You'll also find concrete strategies for promoting yourself and your work. Besides, who better to promote your work than the person who wrote it! You'll discover how to use speaking engagements, bookstore visits, and media outlets to network with other writers and, more importantly, the people who buy your book or the magazine in which your article appears.

You'll also learn the keys to taking your writing to the next level by writing full time. You'll find information on how to set up a home-based office, track your writing income, and obtain health insurance. This portion also explains the essential tax issues you will encounter as a full-time freelancer.

As writers, we often hear that writing is a solitary pursuit. However, a writing community is an essential tool for writers as it provides a network of support (organizations, conferences, and colonies) and a learning tool (critique groups, writing programs, and correspondence schools). In this part, you'll learn ways to find and create a community of your own.

Finally, the last section of this part deals with something we all wish we had more of, but as writers, struggle to find: money. After reading this chapter, you will get answers to the following questions:

- How can a writing contest get me money and advance my career at the same time?
- How do I identify the contests, grants, and fellowships to which I should apply?

You'll also find valuable information in each of the appendices:

Appendix A provides you with the nuts-and-bolts of making money with your writing. This appendix includes interactive worksheets to help you calculate expenses, hourly rates, and project fees. It also provides you with the resources and tools necessary to set your pay rates and to negotiate higher rates.

Appendix B lists various writing resources, including books, magazines, newsletters, and Web sites, along with an additional list of Web sites categorized by genre. We hope that by providing you with this information, you can further research and develop your writing plan.

Appendix C contains a breakdown of the "Big Six," i.e., the major publishing groups that exist, including all of the major New York publishing houses. With this resource, you can develop a firm knowledge of the names and roles of the major players in the book publishing industry.

Appendix D is a glossary of common publishing terms you are bound to encounter you publish and sell your work. If you've ever wondered what a byline is or what desktop publishing is, you'll find the answers here.

We know that getting your work published, whether in a magazine or book, is a difficult task, especially when the publishing industry is constantly changing. However, we hope that this book, when used in conjunction with *Writer's Market, Writer's Market Deluxe,* or WritersMarket.com, will provide you with the key information you need to publish and sell what you write. It is our goal to help you achieve your dreams and, ultimately, publishing success.

—Kathryn S. Brogan, editor of *Writer's Market, Writer's Market Deluxe,* and *Guide to Literary Agents*

PART ONE

Preparing Yourself for the Work Ahead

CHAPTER ONE

The Writer's World

W hen the world of entertainment options exploded during the 1990s with e-mail, the Internet, video game consoles, cell phones, and more cable TV stations than anyone dreamed imaginable, some experts predicted that the world of book and magazine publishing would suffer. Who would have time for dead trees when there were so many new diversions?

It's true that publishing has faced more challenges in the digital age than ever before. By the end of 2003, magazine advertising had suffered its third consecutive year of decrease (partly because of the Internet, partly because of decreased circulations), and the number of magazines published in the U.S. and Canada is down by about 9 percent from 2000, according to the *National Directory of Magazines*. At the time this book went to print, major publishers in the UK, including HarperCollins and Time Warner, were cutting their acquisition of fiction titles by as much as 20 percent—perhaps a harbinger of U.S. cuts to come. But there are positive trends that you, as a writer, can capitalize on, and this chapter will discuss what's rising and what's falling, so that you can navigate the industry to your best advantage.

The Magazine Market Up Close

Getting a precise handle on the number of magazines in the U.S. is difficult. In 2003, the *National Directory of Magazines* listed 17,670 magazines in existence, which includes more than 14,000 print titles. Other sources put the number as low as 8,000 and as high as 20,000, depending on how you define magazines. Do you count scholarly journals, yearbooks, and club and association news magazines? For a writer looking for work, it doesn't matter how magazines are defined—it's simply encouraging to know there are a lot of markets for our work. Since 1993, more than 8,500 new magazine titles have premiered, but of the hundreds of new magazines emerging every year, not all survive. As with any business, only a small number of start-ups make it through those first tumultuous years. For magazines, the survival rate is about a third.

While thousands of start-ups have enjoyed newfound success, many of the top U.S. magazines have witnessed declines in circulation. In recent years, we've seen the demise of major magazines—including McCall's (which became the ill-fated *Rosie*), *Mirabella*, *Red Herring*, and *Book*. Some experts predict that the large-circulation magazines will lose the race against more niche publications, and that the market will continue to fragment into smaller and smaller niches.

Bo Sacks, a magazine industry veteran and expert, told *Printing News* in a March 2003 interview, "You name a successful magazine and I will tell you the special niche it fills. That is the secret to publishing today. Even very large volume magazines are now focused toward a special-interest group. If not, they are or will be in trouble. Even the long-revered Seven Sisters—the general-interest women's magazines of old—are changing or dying. The successful ones are not publishing with a broad appeal to all women, but rather to a specific segment of that population."

This may be bad news for the larger publishing houses, but the trend is not necessarily bad for writers—particularly those who are just starting out and looking for a foothold. It's usually easier to break into a small, niche publication than a national magazine.

Growing (and Declining) Magazine Categories

Magazine industry trends often reflect those of society. Nearly 150 years ago, as Americans were discovering bicycles, the novelty and excitement spawned an entire new genre of magazine—cycling magazines. New cyclists and those who dreamed of owning one were eager to learn all they could about these two-wheeled wonders. The phenomenon still occurs today.

Once again, the *National Directory of Magazines* lends some insight into where the growth is and isn't. In sheer numbers of titles, the top three rising categories include bridal, football, and dogs. Each have more than 100 percent title growth between 1993 and 2003. Other hot topics include interior design, golf, and college/alumni magazines. The largest magazine category is college/alumni, with more than 1,013 titles in 2003, followed by medicine at 937 titles. Those magazine categories suffering the largest declines include labor and general interest.

The picture changes if you consider where ad sales have grown. According to *Media Life* magazine, the greatest strength is in the travel and teen categories, with page growth at 16.6 percent and 13.4 percent respectively. These gains, however, are partially due to new titles in both areas. New niche travel titles have entered the market (*Arthur Frommer's Budget Travel*, for example), and titles with a small, targeted audience are faring better than more general-interest titles like *Condé Nast Traveler.*

Another strong category includes religious and spiritual publications—in both the book and magazine industries (we'll get to books later). According to MediaPost Communications, the top performing magazine in 2003, in terms of percentage growth, was *Guideposts*, with an 81 percent jump in pages. Of course, *Guideposts* has a much lower page count than other publications, and can't compare as far as sheer number of ads (think of how many ads you come across in a women's magazine like *Elle*), but it's important growth nonetheless.

Media Life also found that younger women with disposable income have proven to be a valuable demographic. Magazines such as *Lucky* and *Real Simple* have gained enormous ground in recent years, as have celebrity gossip titles, which are expected to continue in their proliferation. *US Weekly*, a general-interest magazine focusing on celebrities, saw impressive newsstand sales increases in 2003, and such increases are predicted to remain strong. Young men with disposable income, previously an untapped demographic in the U.S., now have their own section of the newsstand filled with magazines such as *Details* and *Maxim*. These men's titles are in various stages of growth, but certainly a market to which writers should pay attention.

The weakest categories continue to be business and personal finance, but with the descent of these categories came the almost parallel ascent of policy-laden magazines. As the country fell on troubled economic and political times, beginning with September 11, magazines with hard-core investigative reporting and political commentary became newsstand wonders. *The Atlantic Monthly, Mother Jones, The New Republic, Harper's Magazine,* and *The Nation* have seen sales surge, and, according to *The New York Times,* the "across-the-board ascent of policy-laden magazines represents a significant shift for publishing." *The New Yorker,* known for its long feature reporting, has seen overall circulation grow by 15 percent in the last five years.

Finally, magazines targeting an Hispanic audience have shown vitality in the market, and according to MediaPost, this niche category outpaced most others in 2003. Three of the strongest titles, in terms of ad pages and revenue, included *People En Español, Latina,* and *RD Selecciones.* Interestingly, in 2003, Procter & Gamble spent a greater amount of money advertising in Hispanic magazines than it did in other magazine categories.

While the newsstand is more competitive than ever, you can break into magazines by understanding their unique position in the market. Think about the type of reader each magazine is attempting to attract, and write a query that emphasizes how your piece will make that reader buy the magazine. Simon Dumenco, a media consultant and columnist, wrote in the April 2003 *Folio,* "Consider the amount of effort it takes to pick a magazine out of the morass of the newsstand—or, worse, go through the trouble of subscribing. Compared to surfing through one hundred-plus channels of digital cable or clicking around the Internet—well, if you're an editor, you better have figured out how to get your reader to crave your magazine like a stiff drink or a sweet soothing little pill." As a writer, that's your job, too.

The World of Books

In *So Many Books: Reading and Publishing in the Age of Abundance* (Paul Dry Books), author Gabriel Zaid makes the following observation: Every thirty seconds, a new book is published, and even if you were able to read one book per day, you would neglect four thousand others published that same day.

Despite living in this age of abundance—or perhaps because of it—book publishers have more to worry about than ever before. With more than 150,000 new books being published and marketed to bookstores annually (not to mention all those backlist titles that are still in print), it's becoming more and more difficult to gain attention for any book that doesn't already have instant recognition in the marketplace—through a celebrity author, an established brand name, or a television/movie tie-in.

Further exacerbating the problem are discount chains (e.g., Wal-Mart, Target, Costco) that often account for more than 40 percent of a best-selling book's sales, increasing the industry's dependence on hit books. Once a book takes hold in the discounters, the independent and chain bookstores often offer the same discount, thus influencing what gets sold at traditional stores, according to Paul Aiken, executive director of Authors Guild, in a *New York Times* May 2003 article.

In that same *Times* article, the chairman of AOL Time Warner's books unit, Laurence J. Kirshbaum, said that he decided to start a religious imprint because Wal-Mart buyers told him that half their sales were from Christian books. Following his lead, publishers Random House and Penguin both started new imprints for the "booming market for conservative books." Also, Bookspan, which operates more than thirty book clubs, including Book-of-the-Month Club, launched a new club based on conservative titles. Most authors for these conservative lines are likely to be well-known political pundits and celebrities, such as Ann Coulter and Bill O'Reilly, who both reached best-seller status in 2003 with their respective books slamming the liberal media and Democrats.

Even a January 2004 article in UK's *Telegraph* noted that publishers—at the expense of their relatively unknown midlist authors—are concentrating on big-name authors or attractive debut novelists who are more marketable.

How does an unknown writer break into a book publishing culture so infused with celebrity, and so driven by brands and appearances?

One area of hope is in small and independent publishers, which are growing and effectively competing with the big New York five (Random House, HarperCollins, Penguin, Simon & Schuster, and AOL Time Warner). R.R. Bowker's database puts the number of smaller publishers at about 73,000—a number that's doubled in the past decade. Often small presses cater to niche audiences, and know how to reach them outside of traditional bookstore outlets. Certainly very few of the books by small presses make the national best-seller lists (though some do, like the debut novel *The Time Traveler's Wife* by Audrey Niffenegger, published by San Francisco-based MacAdam/Cage). But authors who sign with independents can count on personalized attention and find themselves an important part of that publisher's catalog. It's a question to ask yourself: Would you rather be published by one of the big five and gain the prestige of the imprint, but receive no marketing attention; or would you prefer to be published by a lesser-known press, but have their dedication and loyalty?

Where's the Growth?

As you might have already guessed, the Christian market has become too lucrative to ignore. In 2001, for the first time, religious titles sat atop both fiction and nonfiction *Publishers Weekly* best-seller lists. Each new addition to the Left Behind series, by Tim LaHaye and Jerry B. Jenkins, hits best-seller status in its first weeks on the market. The first ten books in the series have sales of more than 55 million copies and comprise the fastest-selling adult fiction series ever. Several of the titles have debuted at No. 1 on *The New York Times* best-seller list as well as those of *USA Today*, *The Wall Street Journal*, and *Publishers Weekly*. Nonfiction Christian titles have also seen phenomenal success; *The Purpose-Driven Life* by Rick Warren was the longest-running nonfiction best seller on the *Publishers Weekly* 2003 charts.

But the secular life still runs strong. Movies and television are having a bigger impact on book sales than ever before and play a strong role in creating top sellers, according to *Publishers Weekly*. Books that received a surge in sales as a result of a movie tie-in include *Mystic River, Seabiscuit, The Hours* (and *Mrs. Dalloway*), *Cold Mountain, Master and Commander*, and, of course, *Lord of the Rings*.

But it runs the other way, too. If a book deal generates buzz before publication, Hollywood will snatch up the book's movie rights. The aforementioned debut novel, *The Time-Traveler's Wife*, was optioned to Brad Pitt's and Jennifer Aniston's production companies in association with New Line cinema only three months after the book deal was signed. No doubt news of the movie deal helped generate even more interest in the book—and more sales—than there might've been otherwise.

Debut novels like *The Time-Traveler's Wife* have seen dramatic success in recent years. In 2002, eleven debut novels held a total of 104 weeks on the 2002 *Publishers Weekly* best-seller lists. In 2003, the trend continued with eight more debut novels—still an impressive number. To look at it from another standpoint, in 2002, a record fifteen debut novels shipped more than 100,000 copies each. *Publishers Weekly* predicts that there will be more success on the debut fiction front, "where publishers work hard and spend lots to achieve that dream," so there's much hope for struggling novelists trying to break in if the work is considered marketable.

What is marketable these days? Thrillers, such as *The Da Vinci Code*, and commercial women's fiction are doing best. Any fiction for women in particular does well, perhaps because women are responsible for about 60 percent of book purchases in the United States. Romance adds up to more than half of all paperback fiction sold in North America, and more than a third of total fiction sold. That's double the sales of general literary fiction, and the category shows no signs of slowing down, growing at an average of 5 percent every year. Then there's "chick lit," which might be considered a reinvention of the romance novel for a younger audience and started with the sensational success of *Bridget Jones's Diary*—now a movie with Renée Zellweger. Such books typically feature single twenty-somethings who are looking for love while trying to succeed at a fast-paced career, usually in the media. Early signs indicate that chick lit will fragment into niches—for black women, for Christian women, for single moms, and so on.

With all the fuss over chick lit and debut novels, one would think there are no other areas of growth in fiction. There are—or at least there will be. Sessalee Hensley, who's been the Barnes & Noble fiction buyer for twenty years, told the *Wall Street Journal* in December 2003 that one of the new trends in her field is African-American fiction, which has seen its longest period of sustained growth in the last ten years. In 2003, six publishers' imprints are now dedicated to black books, and the lists aren't restricted to novels—they include nonfiction and children's as well. Yet very few black authors ever hit the best-seller lists—and this will remain a challenge for the category in years to come.

In general, though, ethnic/minority fiction is becoming an important publishing category. Latinos, as the fastest growing minority in the United States, are becoming one the nation's "hottest literary commodities" according a September 2003 *Denver Post* article. In 2001, HarperCollins launched a Latino imprint, and while no one has been quick to follow, 2003 was designated "The Year of Publishing Latino Voices for America" by the Association of American Publishers.

Also, gay fiction has become more mainstream and center (not relegated to its own shelf in the back corner), mainly because of the changing opinions of society and the popularity of television shows like *Queer Eye for the Straight Guy* (which already has a companion book on the market). Gay fiction is beginning to be perceived as fiction with a gay angle (an important distinction), and gaining ground in mainstream shelf display. Examples of this include best-sellers *Three Junes, The Hours*, and *Running With Scissors*.

In the nonfiction world, diet books, always a popular topic, were particularly strong in 2003 with the debut of *The South Beach Diet* and the continued interest in low-carb diets. Five hardcovers in the diet category racked up forty-two weeks in the No. 1 spot on the *Publishers Weekly* list in 2003. But this is hardly a category for a newcomer, since success often depends on a strong marketing platform and trustworthy credentials.

A more likely place for an unknown to break in is on the self-help shelf, another consistently strong category. According to an *Associated Press* article by Lisa Singhania in September 2003, "Boomers' desire to improve themselves as they get older and advance in their careers and families has substantially increased demand in the category. In recent years, the number of books, tapes, videos, and materials offering advice on everything from dysfunctional marriages to how to succeed in business has exploded into a multibillion-dollar industry." To give you an idea of just how big this category is, Borders bookstore says that self-help titles account for about 7 to 10 percent of total sales. Jenie Carlen, the spokesperson for Borders, told the *Associated Press*, "The primary motivator in self-help for the last five years has really been the media and what the media is covering, and they've keyed into prime demographics, which are baby boomers."

There's the key: What is the media covering? You can be sure that whatever trend you see consistently covered on television, in magazines, and on radio will be followed up by slower-paced book publishing industry. Pay attention to what's happening around you. Each type of media feeds into the other, and if you can pinpoint which way the trends are leaning, you might be able to pitch a nonfiction book that matches a publisher's needs.

With fiction, it does no good to follow the trends, since by the time you have your book ready, the trend may be on its way out. Instead, write what you're passionate about—or what you read.

Charting Your Path

Writing for magazines and books requires a different set of work habits, and each offers distinct rewards in terms of satisfaction and compensation. Whether you will do best pursuing magazine writing or a book contract depends largely on your personal style and the goals you set for yourself. For an overview of the relative advantages of each, consider the following points from Leon Fletcher, author of sixteen published books and more than seven hundred articles.

Books pay a lot more than most magazine articles. But unless you are an established author, or are lucky enough to have two or more

Category Growth and Decline in Trade Publishing

These numbers from R.R. Bowker indicate the number of titles published in each book category in 1992 and 2002 by trade publishers only. (Trade publishers sell their books primarily in bookstores.) University publishers are not included in these figures, but more information on total book production numbers can be found at the R.R. Bowker Web site, www.bookwire.com.

	1992	2002
Agriculture	113	62
Arts	393	317
Biography	639	799
Business	491	1,163
Education	171	430
Fiction	4,193	4,930
General	156	101
History	490	569
Home Economics	526	508
Juvenile	4,783	5,034
Language	230	378
Law	257	99
Literature	691	545
Medicine	442	561
Music	90	90
Philosophy, Psychology	659	798
Poetry, Drama	217	226
Religion	432	834
Science	854	1,032
Sociology, Economics	1,222	1,517
Sports, Recreation	450	476
Technology	692	1,101
Travel	389	526

publishers bidding against each other, the initial compensation is usually in the range of several thousand dollars. Typically this pay is in the form of an advance against royalties, which is paid over the course of a year while the book is being written and edited.

Comparing Books to Magazines

Advantages of Books	Disadvantages of Books
Pay is better	Harder to break in
More prestigious	Longer commitment
Spin-off benefits	Might have to hire agent

Depending on the initial advance, a book that sells ten thousand copies typically earns enough to cover the writer's advance and the publisher's other expenses. For many writers the initial advance is the only money they ever see because of poor sales. Even so, most books will probably earn you more than most magazine articles. If your book is even a modest success the rewards can mount quickly.

Of course, many book authors have to share a slice of their income with the agent who got them the book deal in the first place. That is because most book editors at larger publishing houses won't look at a manuscript unless it is referred to them by an agent. Four out of five published authors use agents, which says something about the difficulty of breaking into book publishing.

In the final analysis, books provide long-term benefits beyond the direct financial rewards. The prestige of writing a book can often boost your career. The research and expertise you gain from a book project can be spun into a variety of magazine articles, or other books.

The key advantage to magazine writing is that there are many more opportunities, based on the sheer number of local, regional, and national publications. Most publish anywhere from eight to twenty articles per issue. Unlike books, which have a longer shelf life, magazines continually need good articles. Additionally, magazine writing usually entails a brief commitment of a few days to a week—unlike books, which require a sustained effort for a year or longer.

Yet, depending on how you prefer to work, the transient nature of magazine writing can be a disadvantage. Every few days, or every week at most, you have to hustle to find more work. And you must juggle several projects at once.

Comparing Magazines to Books

Advantages of Magazines	Disadvantages of Magazines
More opportunities	Continual hunt for work
Easy to find a niche	Pay is less
Shorter time commitment	Opportunities to repurpose content

Getting Started

The way to approach a magazine editor, book publisher, or literary agent is through a query letter or a lengthier book proposal, as the case may be. (Both of these will be discussed in more detail in subsequent chapters.) In either case, think of your goal as not just getting your work accepted, but keeping it from being rejected. Understanding the difference can affect how well you compete in the marketplace.

Think of editors and agents with stacks of book proposals or query letters on their desks. Their goal is to get through the stacks as quickly as possible—a task that may seem insurmountable at times. They are looking for clues to determine whether you have what it takes to get published. The sooner they can determine this, the easier their job becomes. In short, you are trying to keep from being rejected because that is just what the agent or editor is looking to do. In this type of environment, every sentence should give them a reason to read the next sentence. Each paragraph should make them want to read the next.

Six Keys to Success

If the task seems daunting, it really need not be. You can make yourself stand out from the stack by simply arming yourself with the right skills and the proper research. The six pieces of advice that follow are cited by many writing instructors and published authors as the secrets to success. These points can go a long way towards making you stand out from the pack.

1. **Read and analyze good writing.** Writing doesn't come from a vacuum. You must read to understand what good writing is all about. You must read to inspire yourself. You should read as much as you can inside and outside of your chosen genre—books, articles, short stories, poetry, ad copy—anything that helps you develop a better awareness of style.

    As important as reading, you must analyze what you see on the page. Therein lies the art of writing. Study the details: the style of language, the dialogue, the narration, the structure of sentences, paragraphs, and the story itself. Ask yourself why they are written the way they are.

2. **Learn the mechanics and the essentials of the business.** Grammar, spelling, punctuation, proper formats for manuscripts, queries and proposals, how to work with editors, and how to read contracts—all of it matters a great deal in this business. (The list of books and other resources in chapter two can help.)

3. **Write every day.** What you learn from reading and studying, you must put into practice. "Many people want to be writers but they don't want to write. They want the name, the prestige, but they don't want the hard work—to sit down and write," author Leon Fletcher notes.

    The best way to write successfully is to develop a regular writing schedule. You must find the place and the time that works best for you and stick to it. (See chapter four for guidelines.) It takes discipline, as does any successful endeavor. Write until you know that your work is at least as good as what you see in print elsewhere.

4. **Study the writing markets thoroughly.** It's not enough to decide that you want to write mysteries and then scan *Writer's Market* or

Literary Marketplace for a publisher who produces that kind of book. You need to know what types of mysteries a publisher wants.

Think of a type of book you enjoy reading, say, mysteries. Would you walk into a bookstore and buy any or all mystery books? Of course not. You bring specific preferences—based on your own experience—to your choice of reading. A publishing company has its own preferences based on its experience. To be successful you need to learn those preferences. You can do this by reading as many books as possible by the publisher you plan to approach. Use the *Books in Print* directory to research what already has been published so you can differentiate your book concept. By all means, thoroughly study multiple issues of any magazine that you plan to query.

5. **Make sure you mean business.** As writers we are very fortunate to be in a business that allows us to aspire to a form of art. But publishing is still very much a business. "When a publisher takes on a title, he or she is, for practical purposes, betting that this manuscript will generate enough income to pay the author, to market it, to pay for the services of the people who will be working to get this manuscript into publication, to cover the production costs, to promote it upon production, and to have enough left for a reasonable profit," notes author Patricia J. Bell.

   If writing professionally is a business, successful writers must give thought to the kind of service that they offer. As a self-employed freelance writer, are you easy to work with? Do you make your editor's job easier by meeting deadlines and by keeping him abreast of your progress? Are you readily available to make revisions or answer questions? These are the value-added items that make editors want to do business with you.

6. **Be persistent.** "Persistence is the most typical, common trait of successful, published writers—even more typical and more common than writing skill," according to Fletcher. If, for instance, an editor rejects your proposal, that doesn't mean she is rejecting you

as a writer. It could be that your idea just didn't fit her needs at that time. Try again and keep trying until you succeed.

Writing is a skill you can only hone through practice. If you learn one thing from this book, know this: If you have talent and if you work hard enough and long enough to succeed, you will.

A Look to the Future

For much of the last decade, companies, and research organizations have been rushing to find the replacement for traditional books and magazines. The replacements have taken the form of hand-held video displays and PDAs that can hold more than 100,000 pages of text. MIT has added a new wrinkle to the paperless debate with its development of electronic ink. The concept involves microscopic black and white particles imbedded in paper-like sheets. The particles reorient themselves—forming letters and words—when an electric charge is applied. Bound into book form, these sheets could be "charged" with text and recharged whenever you want something new to read.

Other publishing experts see consumers walking into stores and custom ordering books, which are produced on the spot using high-speed printers and bindery equipment. A growing trend has consumers buying books and magazines online, downloading the data to their home computers and outputting the finished product on their home printers.

Books and magazines could take any of these routes or go in another direction altogether. But books and magazines will be around in some form. Whatever way books and magazines are produced, and regardless of how consumers choose to read them, society will need writers to produce the content. The idea of books and magazines going digital is opening whole new opportunities for writers and publishers. As words become data they can be easily transformed into multiple products, whether these are CDs, books, or some other format not yet envisioned.

"In the future, the pages may glow in the dark so you can read a book by its own luminescence," said Byron Preiss, book editor and multimedia producer, in an interview with *Publishers Weekly*. "But it will still always be a book, and reading will always be personal.

CHAPTER TWO

You,
the Writer

I f you write, there's really only one place to start. Look inward. Writers are storytellers. Discovering your own stories is an intensely personal process, like recognizing an old friend's face in a crowded waiting room. Consider first what you know and care about, and look there for stories to tell. Without some level of personal engagement, writing becomes drudgery.

While there is plenty of room on this planet for intimate personal essays, don't take this advice to mean that you should write only about yourself. Although the world's bountiful stories are any writer's to tell, all the stories in the world aren't right for every writer. So start with what you know and love when writing.

Betsa Marsh, newspaper and magazine writer and editor for twelve years before becoming a freelancer, put it this way: "It's just following what you really want, what your key interests are. Because we all know journalism doesn't pay very well, so you better do something you like."

The Great Idea

When it comes to writing, coming up with a great idea that translates well into an article or book can be tricky. One of the biggest keys to finding and developing such ideas involves staying tuned into the world around you, drawing inspiration from books, magazines, news reports, friends, strangers—in short, everything and everyone.

Marcia Thornton Jones, a children's book author and teacher, said that she and her writing partner, Debbie Dadey, never fear running out of ideas. "What we have trouble with is finding time to pursue them all," she said. In fact, the pair even wrote a book, *Story Sparkers: A Creativity Guide for Children's Writers*, on how writers can generate ideas.

Ideas, of course, are everywhere, and recognizing them is something to which both writers are attuned. At a book signing, for example, Jones and a mother of one her young readers named Jack were chatting about how many people they knew by that name. "Jacks are wild," the mother said.

"That sounds like the name of a children's book!" Jones said, pulling out her journal and jotting it down.

Part of the recognition process involves knowing where and when ideas are most likely to be spotted. "I do my most productive thinking about writing in the shower and emptying or loading the dishwasher," said author Jim Kraft. At those moments, said Kraft, who began writing children's books after a career writing greeting cards, the story often comes to him just out of the line of vision of the mind's eye. Approaching the topic obliquely "seems to work better than sitting at my desk thinking about it."

Chance remarks rouse ideas as well. On the way to basketball camp with his two sons and their friends, they suddenly all fell silent. Kraft's younger son commented, "Suddenly silence." The next minute, Kraft had an idea for a book. It became "Night Noises," a children's story about what happens when all the normal noises of the night suddenly stop.

The process isn't so very different for nonfiction writers. While you may not be inventing a new reality, you still must rely on your inner creativity to provide a fresh perspective or to spot a unique news angle. Pat Crowley, a newspaper reporter and freelance magazine writer, said ideas rush at him everywhere he goes. On the way to talk to a journalism class, the radio prompted two freelance story ideas. One was about whether lowering the legal blood alcohol limit, as lawmakers were proposing following a rash of drunken driving accidents, really makes any difference. The other idea involved the alarming side effects that advertisers calmly list in their commercials for drugs—an idea that hit him while listening to an ad for an anti-hair-loss product, which sounded great until the announcer mentioned it could cause inconveniences such as dry mouth, blackouts, or sexual dysfunction. "People would rather lose every hair they have than have sexual dysfunction," said Crowley, "and that's the way I'll sell it."

Eight Ways to Uncover New Ideas

By keeping your eyes and ears open to what's happening around you, you're likely to uncover original and salable ideas of your own. Use the following eight sources to uncover inspiration and ideas for your writing:

1. **Read.** The importance of reading can't be overrated. Good writers start with knowledge, and then move to understanding, even wisdom. While creative exercises can help generate ideas, there is no substitute for real, solid information in devising a story. Professional writers are also great readers, and their stories are grounded with information. Fiction writers can be inspired by history books and newspaper articles as easily as nonfiction writers can.

   Reading not only keeps you informed about what is going on, but also if you read carefully, you'll begin to notice what's *not* covered in stories. A story in a local newspaper about plans to build a new museum downtown, for example, mentioned the location would be right where a well-known hat shop has stood for decades. The fate of the hat shop, and the reaction of some of its loyal customers, might make a short item for your local city magazine. Read everything: posters, fliers, freebie publications, junk mail. Information seeds stories.

2. **Write.** A writer should keep handy a writing instrument. Whether you like notebooks and pencils or electronic gadgets, keep something to record ideas wherever they strike. Jot those stray notions that otherwise would evaporate and be lost. You don't know when or where an idea will strike you, and you

should never trust your memory to record it for you. Ideas are like dreams, which you can recall with clarity while supine, but which retreat into the ether when you get up to face the daily living. Write your ideas down.

3. **Listen.** The next time you're waiting in line, watching your daughter's soccer game, or waiting for the waiter to bring your dinner, listen—really listen—to the people around you. What concerns them? Parents at the soccer game may grumble about a coach's ill temper—could there be a story on how parents can tame a fractious coach? They may joke about the child on the field who is more interested in hunting for a four-leaf-clover—is there a story about pushing young children into sports too soon? They may talk about how their daughter has suffered yet another injury—a story on what coaches don't know about the importance of stretching and warm-ups? About sports injuries increasing among girls?

 While you're at it, make notes on the incident that sparked an idea—the appearance of the people talking, the sounds of their voices, the way they interact. Describe the day, its light, its warmth, its breezes. You never know when you'll need an anecdote.

4. **Watch.** On a tour of the local observatory with your kids, for example, you'll probably be spending a lot of time watching and listening to the tour guide. Allow yourself to wonder about him. Does he stay up nights watching the stars? Does his wife mind? Does he seem more enthusiastic about this nocturnal occupation than the kids do? Would he—or his job—make a good story? Colorful people and ordinary people with colorful or unusual occupations are everywhere. Mary once interviewed a man whose job was to analyze concrete. Her immediate reaction was pity—until he told her of the time his analysis had helped prove a man had murdered his wife and buried her beneath the basement floor, patching it with concrete from another house.

5. **Observe relationships.** With everything you see, remember to ask yourself, is there a story here? Let's say you're watching the neighborhood kids. You see ten-year-old Anita commandeering a crew of children, some older than her, into playing school. She is the teacher. They switch to a new game of exploring, and she is the fearless scout. They switch to kickball, and she's the coach, the referee, and the star player. This girl could spur ideas for several articles: teaching children to stand up for themselves; what to do if your child is bossy (or a bully); or looking at childhood leadership as a sign of giftedness.

6. **Talk.** Bat around your story ideas with friends. Preferably, writer friends. Sometimes you come up with the raw ingredients of an idea, but it isn't quite cooked until you talk it over. Such informal brainstorming, especially when warmed by good company and food, can generate far more ideas than you can dream up in your lonely room at night. Join a writers group. There's nothing like peer pressure to force you to come up with ideas and then write about them.

7. **Keep an idea file.** Clip stories from newspapers, newsletters, junk mail, advertorials, and the Web. Rip out the pages from your writer's notebook. Put these all in one place. Take them out periodically and look at them. Can any be expanded into a good story for a particular audience?

8. **Ask.** Allow yourself the freedom to wonder about things. The next time you hear something, see something, or read something that could be worth writing about, you'll probably have questions. Ask them. The conversation might produce a story idea.

Idea Generators

Use the following prompts to help you analyze your interests and expertise, and then generate your own stories from them. As with any idea-generating exercises, you'll probably come up with some unworkable notions. But the point of any creativity activity is to knock that interior editor, who's always telling you what you do wrong, off her perch for a while, so that the ideas percolating inside can tumble out. Don't criticize; don't revise. Just allow the ideas to flow. Only after you've jotted down some story ideas do you let the editor crawl back up and peer over your left shoulder to search for the gem that will become your story.

Narrow Your Ideas

Take the slice-and-dice approach to idea generation. For example, don't plan on writing 2,000 words on teenagers' drinking habits. Slice and dice it up into more manageable, focused ideas—how about warning signs of alcohol abuse among preteens? Or the failure of alcohol-abuse prevention programs among teen boys? Or the trend among parents to convene groups to prevent drinking among their children?

Robert Frost once said, "An idea is a feat of association." Bounce two topics off each other, combine several thoughts together, and watch what happens. You can use a grid to formalize this approach, as Cheryl Sloan Wray suggests in her book, *Writing for Magazines, A Beginner's Guide.* Down one side of the grid, list topics you're interested in—items in the news, hobbies, activities. Use *Writer's Market* to compile a list some of the magazine categories that appeal to you and list them along the top. Or try listing events in the news along the top, and human needs, such as shelter and companionship, on the vertical bar. Combine the topics in the rows and columns to create possible ideas. Take a look at the chart on page 28 to see what we mean.

A Day in the Life

Reflecting on the seemingly mundane events of your life also can uncover unlikely story possibilities. Cheryl Sloan Wray suggests writing down a few things that happened to you in the past few days. Then consider this: What can you tell others about these events? Unless you live an exceptional life, you will not produce stellar ideas for every event in your day. But if you practice looking for stories in ordinary places, you may well find them. What this exercise really does is helps you grow antennae to sound out everything as a potential story, the mindset of many a professional writer. Take a look at the example at the bottom of the page.

	Juvenile	Retirement	Career
Violence	Crimes committed by young girls	Crimes likely to be committed against those of retirement age	Employee assistance for victims of crime
Education	When children become the teachers	Returning to college following retirement	Planning a career in the sixth grade
Job Insecurity	Requiring students to sign ethics pledges before entering the workforce	Planning for retirement in an uncertain world	Employees' lack of loyalty and the bottom line

Write Short

Beginning writers have a better chance of breaking into the magazine market by writing short pieces of 100 to 500 words or so than by writing a 2,500 feature article. Read through the writer's guidelines

Event	Idea
Spent twenty minutes arranging carpooling for kids after school	Time management for parents
Daughter forgot homework — again	How to teach young children responsibility
Displayed our tacky plastic Christmas decorations	Decorating with natural items
Stayed up late helping daughter with homework while son finished his homework in fifteen minutes	The debate on how much and what type of homework is best
Watched daughter in full regalisa and makeup perform at dance recital	Have parents subverted childhood?
Fell asleep before my kids	Changing sleep patterns with aging

provided in directories like *Writer's Market* and look for descriptions of fillers, sidebars, quizzes, and other short items.

Use the following chart to help you think of a topic you want to write about and match it with one of the categories of shorter pieces. As with the pervious exercises, look in the *Writer's Market* for categories of magazines that might suit your topic and focus. For example, if you enjoy writing about the topic of cooking, fill in the blanks below to devise an idea and target category—you could write helpful tips focusing on cooking quick dinners for one person for retirement magazines.

You can make a more targeted list of shorter story ideas by analyzing the front-of-the book pieces in your favorite magazine over several issues. What tone do they use? How many sources are used? Are they informational? Do they perform a service for readers? What topics are typically covered?

Topic	Story Category	Focus	Magazine Category
Divorce	First person essays	Dating again	Women's/Relationships
Pet loss	Inspirational essays	Overcoming grief	Pet
Safety	Travel briefs	Traveling alone	Travel
Athletes	Short profiles	Daily training	Sports
Cooking	Helpful tips	Dinner for one	Retirement
Parenting	Instructional	Holiday activities	Child care

Take a look also at the magazine's preferences for its columns and departments, where stories typically run from several hundred to 1,500 words or so. Read the writers guidelines for descriptions of appropriate column or department topics, and study the style of these pieces in the magazine you are targeting. Then, come up with some ideas.

Look Inward

Think about ways to turn your personal experiences into stories—even if you don't write in the first person. Michael Bugeja, in his *Guide to Writing Magazine Nonfiction*, shows writers how to start with their own characteristics to come up with stories. For example, Mary's mother immigrated to America from Italy and her father was born here of Italian immigrants. She grew up on a street populated by aunts, uncles, and cousins. But it was in a solidly German-American neighborhood that now has become home to many races and ethnic groups. This experience suggests several possible stories: "Preserving Ethnic Cooking" (for a food or women's magazine); "How to Make Homemade Wine" (for a culinary magazine); "The Immigrant as Entrepreneur" (for a business magazine); "The Changing Face of America's Neighborhoods" (for a general interest magazine).

Also look at the expertise you possess. Most of us, even those who think their only hobby is reading books in comfortable armchairs, probably have wider interests and skills. Use the following prompts to examine what you have to offer:

- My family's heritage
- My (and my family's) health problems
- A crisis weathered
- Changes in my community
- My exercise habits (or lack of them)
- My volunteer activities
- My career goals
- My hobbies
- My expertise at work
- A celebrity or unusual person I know
- My passions
- My past success (and failures)
- Five things I wonder about

Be Alert for News

The news is full of potential article or story ideas—you just have to recognize them as such. To help you do that, try answering the following questions:

The last time I thought to myself, "I didn't know that," was

_____.

The last time I just had to tell someone something was

_____.

The last time I was really surprised was

_____.

Then ask yourself, would other people think the same way? Could you tell them something new?

Average Manuscript Word Count

Short-short story	250-1,500
Short story	1,500-10,000
Novella/novelette	30,000-50,000
Novel — hardcover	60,000-80,000
Children's picture book	150-15,000
Juvenile book	15,000-60,000
Nonfiction book	20,000-200,000
Query letter	1 full page, single spaced

Editorial Note: The average full double spaced type written page contains 250 words of pica typewriter type.

Freewriting

Often touted as a cure for writer's block, freewriting also can help you think creatively. The notion is simple. Sit down and write for a set length of time, say ten minutes. Don't edit. Forget what your English teachers told you. Ignore syntax, style, grammar, and spelling. Don't even worry much about content. You're not creating a piece for publication here. You're just allowing your thoughts to spill out and lead you where they will. Sometimes, this can create a story idea. Other times, it just feels good, and limbers up your fingers and your mind for the real work of writing. If you can't think of anything to write about, try using some of the prompts listed here:

- You've discovered you suddenly have no appointments, no duties, nothing to worry about for the next fifteen minutes. What do you do with your time?

- What do the people at your son's or daughter's sports games talk about on the sidelines?
- What do you like most about yourself? Least?
- What was your mother's most recent ailment?
- Do you remember an important first—first kiss, first car, first publication?
- What was your last argument about?
- Look at an old photograph. What does it make you think about?
- What bothers you about your family?
- What do you love to eat and why?
- Have you ever experienced a life-changing event, when you knew that things would never be the same for you or your family? What lessons did you learn from it?
- What was the biggest problem you had growing up?
- What is the biggest problem you face today?

Using Emotions as Prompts

Emotions can spur ideas. If they're strong, they also help guarantee you'll remain committed to finishing a writing project. Think about some of these emotions when considering what to write:

- What do you like most about where you live? Least?
- What story in the newspaper recently made you angry? Glad? Sad?
- What is your favorite possession and why?
- What was the most recent thing you cried about?
- What was the most recent thing you laughed out loud about?
- When was the last time you were embarrassed?
- What scares (worries, angers, gladdens) you? Your children? Your spouse? Your parents?

Lists

Sometimes lists can help you generate story ideas. If you keep a to-do list, analyze it. What do you spend most of your time doing? Is it the most important thing in your life? If not, maybe there's a story in how we squander our free time.

To Market

If you're writing fiction, poetry, or screenplays, it's usually necessary to complete the work before finding a market. However, this approach doesn't work as well for nonfiction, and may actually reduce your chances of success, since most publishers of nonfiction have very specific needs that must be met in order for them to buy an article or book. That said, finding the right market for your work remains one of the most crucial steps in the publishing process regardless of what you're writing. Let's take a look at the best ways to identify appropriate markets for both articles and books.

Finding Magazine Markets for Your Ideas

To get the nod to write for a magazine, you must match your idea to a specific market. This requires you to read the magazine before pitching an idea. In fact, many writers start with the magazine rather than the idea. (See chapter eight for more details on this process.)

If you don't already have a magazine in mind, try consulting a directory like *Writer's Market* to help you narrow your search. For example, in the table of contents of *Writer's Market*, look for the category of magazine that matches your idea (Romance and Confession? Personal Computers?), and then flip to the individual listings to find publications that seem to be suited to the idea.

Once you've identified a specific magazine, take some time to study its writers guidelines. Even with writers guidelines, it's essential that you familiarize yourself with any publication to which you plan to submit. But, in order to truly get to know a publication, you'll need to do more than just check out the table of contents in the most recent issue. You'll need to scan several months' worth of the table of contents to get an accurate idea of what stories the magazine's editors prefer. Reading through the letters to the editor also can generate ideas targeted to readers' concerns. When you read the articles, be sure to take note of the tone, sourcing, style, slant, and organization of each so that you'll know how to write yours. Finally,

Magazine Markets: A Sampling

What do some of today's hottest publications want? Here's a sampling from four popular magazines. Keep in mind that a magazine's needs and contact information can change. For the most up-to-date and complete guidelines, contact the publications, check their Web sites, or consult a directory like *Writer's Market* or www.WritersMarket.com.

Parade, The Sunday Magazine, 711 Third Ave., New York NY 10017, www.parade.com. A weekly publication, *Parade* publishes general interest (health, trends, social issues), interview/profile (news figures, celebrities, people of national significance), and topical pieces.

ParaBody & Soul, Balanced Living in a Busy World, 42 Pleasant St., Watertown MA 02472, www.bodyand soulmag.com A bimonthly magazine emphasizing "personal fulfillment and social change." *Body & Soul* publishes book excerpts, essays, how-to, inspirational, interview/profile, new product, personal experience, religious, and travel pieces.

American Baby Magazine, 110 5th Ave., 4th Floor, New York NY 10010, www.americanbaby.com. This monthly magazine focuses on the health, medical, and child-care concerns of expectant and new parents, and accepts essays, general interest, how-to, humor, new product, personal experience, fitness, and health articles.

Ladies' Home Journal, 125 Park Ave., 20th Floor, New York NY 10017, www.lhj.com. The monthly magazine focuses on issues of concern to women ages thirty to forty-five, and accepts investigative reports, news-related features, and psychology/relationships/sex articles.

Catholic Parent, 200 Nool Plaza, Huntington IN 46750, www.osv.com. A bimonthly publication with a primarily Roman Catholic audience, *Catholic Parent* accepts essays, how-to, humor, inspiration, personal experience, and religious articles.

(Source: Writer's Market Deluxe Edition at www.writersmarket.com)

taking a look at the ads will give you a good picture of who reads the magazine.

Once you're armed with the guidelines and a knowledge of the publication, think about how your idea can work within the magazine and how you can slant your idea so that it matches the tone and style of the magazine. If the magazine's recently covered a topic similar to the one you'd like to propose, think about new ways you can frame your story to make it different.

After you shaped your idea and written your query letter (which we'll cover in Part III), look at the magazine's masthead or in the guidelines to find the name of the editor who edits whichever section appeals to you, and then send a query with your idea. Your careful analysis of the magazine will be clear in your query letter by the way you describe how your proposed story idea will fit the magazine's standard contact and reach its target audience.

Finding a Book Market for Your Ideas

To find a publisher for your book, turn to the back of the *Writer's Market* for the Book Publishers Subject Index. There, you'll find lists of books arranged by topic, from adventure to young adult for fiction, and from agriculture to young adult for nonfiction. Then read the listing about each publisher, which will tell you such vital information as how it prefers to be approached, what percentage of books it publishes from first-time authors, and contact information. Write away or visit the publisher's Web site for catalogs and submission guidelines.

You'll also need to browse a bookstore to see what's selling, advises children's book author Debbie Dadey. But seeing what's not on the bookstore shelves can be a useful marketing exercise as well, as Dadey's experience attests. "You've got to write what you want to write, what really is important to you," she notes. Writing a series called The Adventures of the Bailey School Kids was important to her and co-author Marcia Thornton Jones. Both educators, they saw a need for books for primary school children who were reluctant readers, or who wanted to read but weren't yet ready for a novel and scorned picture books as baby books. They realized there weren't many books filling that need, and their series became immensely popular with just those children.

While you're at the bookstore, note which houses publish books similar to yours. Call the publisher and ask for the name of the person who edited the book. While you're on the phone, double-check the name and address of the publisher. (See chapters seven and eight for details about approaching a publishing house about your book manuscripts.)

Writer's Market is one of the most popular books for beginning writers to use to learn about markets. But if you can't find what you need there, more information about book publishers is contained in numerous catalogs and directories like *Books in Print*. Its *Trade List Annual*, for example, is a compilation of publishers' catalogs. Browsing through this book, available at many libraries, gives you a sense of which houses publish books like yours and provides you with an idea of the competition.

Resources for Finding the Right Market

Need more help finding markets for your work? Try the books and Web sites listed below:

Books

Some of the books and directories listed below are updated annually. Always check to make sure you are looking at the most current edition.

Bacon's Newspaper and Magazine Directory (Bacon Information Inc.): Lists magazines, newsletters, newspapers, and news syndicates.

Bacon's Internet Directory (Bacon Information Inc.): Lists online-only publications, as well as online-counterparts to print publications.

Books in Print (R.R. Bowker): The Subject Guide to this comprehensive annual compilation describes books according to topic. Forthcoming Books, a bimonthly, lists books printed between annual publications of BIP.

Top Book Markets:
A Sampling

Here's a look at four publishing houses. Keep in mind that, just like magazines, publishing houses have changing needs. For the most up-to-date and complete guidelines (including submission instructions), contact the publications, check their Web sites, or consult a directory like *Writer's Market* or www.WritersMarket.com.

Da Capo Press, Perseus Books Group, 11 Cambridge Center, Cambridge MA 02142, www.dacapopress.com. Publishes 115 titles yearly. Receives 500 queries per year; 300 manuscripts per year. 25 percent of books published are by first time authors; 1 percent are by unagented authors. Publishes autobiographies, biographies, coffee table books, general nonfiction, gift books, etc. in history, film, dance, theater, literature, art, architecture, sports and African-American studies.

Graywolf Press, 2402 University Ave., Suite 203, St. Paul MN 55114, www.graywolfpress.org. Publishes 20 titles yearly. Receives 2,500 queries per year. 20 percent of books published are by first time authors; 50 percent of books are by unagented writers. Publishes nonfiction, literary fiction, and short story collections for imaginative and contemporary literature essential to a diverse culture.

Paladin Press, P.O. Box 1307, Boulder CO 80306, www.paladin-press.com. Publishes hardcover originals and paperback originals and reprints. Publishes 50 titles yearly. 50 percent of books published are by first time authors; 100 percent of books are by unagented writers. Publishes nonfiction books covering military science, police science, weapons, combat, personal freedom, self-defense, survival.

Wizards of the Coast, P.O. Box 707, Renton WA 98057, www.wizards.com. Publishes 50-60 titles yearly. Receives 600 queries per year; 300 manuscripts per year. 25 percent of books published are by first time authors; 35 percent of books are by unagented writers. Publishes science fiction and fantasies and short story collections.

(Source: Writer's Market Deluxe Edition at www.writersmarket.com)

The Christian Writers Market Guide (Harold Shaw Publishers): Lists more than 1,200 markets. Includes publishers of books and periodicals, arranged by subject, as well as a host of other publishing information, including writers conferences, editorial services, and market analyses.

The Canadian Writer's Market (McClelland & Stewart/Tundra Books): Lists markets in Canada.

Gale Directory of Publications and Broadcast Media (Gale Group): Lists more than 37,000 newspapers, magazines, journals, and other periodicals. Markets are arranged geographically and indexed by subject.

International Directory of Little Magazines and Small Presses (Dustbooks): Lists editor names and addresses, and descriptions of topics published at thousands of small publishers. Listed by subject, region, and area of specialization.

Literary Market Place (Information Today, Inc.): This resource includes more than 15,000 entries listing names and contact information for book publishers, electronic publishers, literary agents, direct mail promoters, and more. Searchable online by subject area (for a hefty fee) at www.literarymarketplace.com. LMP's Industry Yellow Pages is a directory of names, addresses, phone numbers, and e-mails of people listed in LMP.

Ulrich's International Periodicals Directory (R.R. Bowker): This huge directory includes information more than 250,000 serials, arranged by 973 subject headings. Volume 4 of this multivolume set cross-indexes publisher information by subject. It also indexes serials available online. A Web site (www.ulrichsweb.com), available by subscription, features a database of more than 235,000 active and ceased periodicals, serials, annuals (regular and irregular), and newspapers.

Market Books (Writer's Digest Books): These annually-updated books include *Writer's Market* and *Writer's Market Deluxe Edition* (which provides access to www.WritersMarket.com), *Children's Writer's & Illustrator's Market, Guide to Literary Agents, Poet's Market,* and *Novel & Short Story Writer's Market.* Each book includes thousands of up-to-date market listings that include submission information, market facts, etc.

Web Sites

To learn about the business of book publishing, news, events, writers associations, online publishers, and more, start with BookWire online, www.bookwire.com, and the Book Zone, www.bookzone.com.

For links to publishers around the world and their catalogs, try the Publishers' Catalogues Homepage (www.lights.com/publisher). The Directory of Publishers and Vendors (http://acqweb.library.vanderbilt.edu/acqweb/pubr.html) also includes links to a publishers' e-mail address directory and Web sites.

For links to magazine markets, try the Internet Public Library (www.ipl.org/ar), which links to thousands of magazines' Web pages and *Writer's Market* (www.WritersMarket.com). Absolute Write (www.absolutewrite.com) and Writers Write (www.writerswrite.com) also are terrific sites for anyone who writes.

CHAPTER THREE

Your Writing Plan

Successful writers find the time everyday to hone their craft and meet their writing obligations—whether those obligations are external, from editors, or internal, from an incontestable desire to write.

Professional writers know there's nothing like a looming deadline to make them focus on their work. In fact, the real problem for beginning writers is usually not scrambling to meet a deadline, but simply organizing one's time efficiently enough to find time to write at a productive pace. As other commitments encroach on our days, writing is often pushed aside like an unpleasant chore.

Accomplishing your writing goals requires making a writing plan, a time schedule that lists what you need to do and when. This chapter explores some ideas on managing your time so that you find time to write. It also gives you tips on how to best use the time you have to produce a finished piece, and includes checklists on steps that should be taken to research, write, and rewrite.

Choose to Write

Everybody on the planet has the same amount of time every day. How we choose to use that time makes some of us writers and others of us short-order cooks. If you are a short-order cook who wants to write, however, you could probably take a bit of time to think about how you use your time—which is, after all, the stuff of your life.

Writing for publication demands a sincere commitment to the craft, in time and in effort. You have to want to do it, and you must be as dedicated to it as you are to the other priorities in your life.

Sandra Felton, who has written more than ten books on how to get organized, including *Neat Mom, Messie Kids* and *The New Messies Manual*, points to prioritizing and dedication as helpful organizational tools for writers. "I think the whole answer is focus," she said. "I think what focus means is you have to decide what you want to do and lob off other stuff that you also want to do. Because you want to write more."

Note that the choice is not between writing and doing something else that you don't want to do. The choice is among a nearly overwhelming array of things that seem appealing: reading and visiting friends and going to movies and to the theater and to the opera and to family get-togethers and on trips and watching way too much television. Faced with so many options, people tend to choose too many and feel like they're short of time.

Some people actually can use stray snippets of free time to write, penning novels on the back of envelopes while waiting in the checkout line at the grocery store. Such people wouldn't be reading this chapter. For most of us, writing for publication requires time to research, time to ponder, time to draft, time to rewrite, and time to polish.

Make Writing a Habit

Finding writing time requires a modicum of organization, but using it productively demands dedication. The theme of virtually every article about getting organized to write is straightforward: Just do it. Wanting to write and writing itself are cousins, not identical twins. Psychological research indicates that writing every day, whether your muse is whispering in your ear or has deserted you, produces not only more writing but more ideas for future writing. The writing habit, like the exercise habit, is its own reward. When you don't do it, you feel as if you're cheating yourself.

"The only thing I can tell you I do that's inviolate is when I have to

Time Management Tips for Busy Writers

Even people who write and publish regularly can have a hard time finding time to write. Web sites, books, and experts on organization can help you figure out how to get more organized, to find more time to write. The following tips can help you develop a personalized writing plan:

- **Publicize your writing goals.** Tell your friends, your spouse, your kids. Post your goals near your desk to remind you of them daily.

- **Do the hard jobs first.** It may feel great to cross off lots of little items from a to-do list, but if your goal was to submit an article in a month and you spent a week doing ten unrelated and minor tasks, then you'll feel little gratification, and you're really just wasting time. So start with the hard things.

- **Keep a time log for a week.** If you cannot figure out where your time goes or how you could possibly find time in your busy life to write, keep a log of everything you do for a week. (See the charts on page 60.) This step may force you to look closely at how you live and the commitments you've made to things other than writing.

- **Work toward your goal a little bit each day.** No matter what else is on your daily to-do list, make sure you do something to help you reach your writing goal every day. Remember the old saying, a writer is someone who wrote today.

- **Be flexible.** Nothing in a writing project, possibly nothing in life, goes entirely according to plan. People you want to interview may be busy. The report you want to read may only be available in an archive in Toledo. Somebody you love may get sick and need your attention. So adjust your plan. Expect some shuffling of items, and don't berate yourself for falling off your writing schedule. Just climb back on at the earliest opportunity.

- **Consider space as time.** When the place where you write disturbs you with its clutter, noise, lighting, or whatever, you're probably grumpily wasting time and energy when you're there. So change it to suit your writing preferences.

- **Set your priorities.** As important as writing is to most of us, other things rejuvenate us and make life worthwhile: family, friends, rest, and leisure. Set aside time for writing and for work, but leave time for people and play.

- **Listen to your body.** Humans live by diurnal rhythms. If you're a night person, work when everyone else in the house is asleep. If your IQ diminishes with the lateness of the hour, get up and work as the sun rises. Work with your nature, not against it.
- **Just say no.** Being busy has become a status symbol of sorts, but it's one that is ultimately debilitating to many of us. Your capacity for work will differ from a fellow writer's. Many of us are multitasking to the point of exhaustion, and many would benefit from learning to say, "No."
- **Feel free to ignore some or of all these tips.** The way a person finds time to write is as distinctive to the individual as the sound of the voice, the style of the gait. What works for one person, or even for many, may not for you.

write, I get up in the morning and literally go straight to the typewriter," said Stephanie Culp, who has written books on organization and time management. "Any little distraction that takes me away from my desk kills it. When I'm writing something large, it takes about three fitful days, and then I'm in the rhythm of it, and I write it. I can still write a book in three weeks."

Get into a writing habit. Start by setting aside an hour or a half hour every day to write. Or set a goal to write a certain number of words every day. Try to write at the same time every day so it will feel peculiar to do something else at that time. Write even if you feel uninspired, even if you don't feel ready to write. If you would be a writer, you must write. Just do it.

Your Writing Plan

Often, getting started on a writing project is the hardest part. Most writing jobs, however, can be viewed as a sequence of doable tasks that follow the same general path from beginning to end. If you accomplish each task in order, you can follow the plan to a finished piece.

The planning guidelines below are designed to help you write a non-fiction magazine article, but they can be modified to suit many writing projects. A book, for example, is made of chapters that are similar to magazine pieces. Break the book down into individual chapters, and break the chapters down into component parts. Schedule your writing project into your day at specific times, and, with a little luck but more hard work, you'll finish your pieces on time.

For people who resent and resist scheduling, remember that creating a writing plan is meant to relieve some stress, organize your life, and make your writing process more efficient. Meeting even mini-deadlines can lift your spirits and bolster your confidence. Simply crossing items off to-do lists feels so good that the act in itself becomes a reward and keeps you writing.

Take a look at the following guidelines. These, along with the charts on pages 50-52, will help you better organize your writing time and finish your projects:

1. **Set reasonable, measurable goals.** Let's say a magazine has expressed interest in your idea for an article and wants you to write it on spec (they'll only pay you the full fee if they like the finished piece enough to publish it). Let's also say the magazine has given you a month to write it. (If there is no such magazine, give yourself your own deadline and treat it seriously.) Because you understand the power of the written word, you should write down a specific goal, with due date: "Finish article by __ [whatever date]."

2. **Divide and conquer.** View your writing project not as an overwhelming monolith, but as a compilation of many smaller items. The reason hard jobs get bypassed is that they often seem too daunting if they're written as one entry on your list of goals. For example, "Write a book in the next year" can be overwhelming. The scope of the project is so big and the deadline is so far away, that achieving the goal seems impossible. Instead, focus on smaller tasks to do today, tomorrow, this week, and this month to help you reach that goal. You're likelier to accomplish smaller tasks in the near future than a vague goal in the abstract faraway. The tasks help you reach that distant goal step-by-step.

3. **Create a plan of ordered tasks.** Writing down tasks in the order in which they should be done keeps you focused, as well as frees your mind to concentrate on the important things—rather than wasting mental energy trying to remember all the niggling details that must be done each day.

4. **Select dates and stick to them.** "Some day, I'm going to write a book." How many times have we all thought this? Turn your lofty dream into an actual accomplishment by adopting a workable schedule. For example, choose a date on your calendar for beginning your writing project. Make it today.

5. **Work backward.** The most important step in planning the time for your writing project is this one: On your calendar, mark the story's final due date. (If you don't have a deadline from a publisher, give yourself a reasonable one.) Then, figure out when each of the specific items, in reverse order, must be completed if you are to meet that deadline. For example, if the story is due June 30, then the mailing deadline might be June 26, and the final fact-checking and polishing might have to be done by June 25, the second draft may have to be done by June 20, etc.

6. **Make a daily to-do list to accomplish the tasks.** Next to each item on your list, write the time you think it will take to accomplish it and the deadline for completing it. People commonly put far too many items on to-do lists, and, as a result, feel defeated when they have to copy uncompleted items from day to day. As William James once wrote, "Nothing is so fatiguing as the eternal hanging on of an uncompleted task." So, jot down what you can reasonably expect to accomplish in a day.

7. **Commit yourself to your writing.** Unless you make your writing plan formally part of your day, you run the risk of forgetting it when things get hectic. So transfer all your due dates to whatever organizing system you use to remind yourself of your

other daily duties. If you don't use a portable, personal organizer, remember that even primary school children use day planners these days. Mark your writing deadlines on the daily planner to make them an official part of your day, as important as your other work and your personal commitments. Also mark them on a central calendar in your home or office, as a reminder and to make them official.

Fourteen Steps for Meeting Your Goals

Here, listed in the general order you need to do them, are some specific and focused tasks you can do to finish your writing projects. You also can use this checklist to help you fill in the charts on pages 50-52.

1. **Do research in the library, on the Internet, and/or at the scene.** If you're writing a complex, informational magazine piece, you'll probably need many hours for research and interviewing. If you're writing a personal experience essay, you may not need any (but you do need time for reflection). Remember, most topics can be researched forever—especially if you use the Internet. Stay focused on your idea, and stop researching it when the information begins to sound repetitive. (For more on researching, see chapter four.)

2. **Read. Take notes. Make copies.** Read for content, but also read for what's not there—questions that you need to answer. Read for insight and understanding. Read for new ideas.

3. **File your notes immediately, labeling them for easy retrieval later.** Don't skip this boring but crucial step. Nothing is more frustrating than spending hours looking for an article you know you've copied but don't know where you've put.

4. **Make a list of which people you must interview.** Depending on your story, you might want to subdivide this list into official sources, who usually work in government or regulatory agencies;

expert sources, who know the topic better than most people; academic sources, who study your topic and may teach others about it; and real people, whose lives are affected by your topic. (For more on interviewing, see chapter five.)

5. **List your interview questions.** Most people begin with open-ended questions that the source will find easiest to answer and will make him warm quickly to the subject—and to you. End with questions that might annoy or anger the source, but must be asked.

6. **Set up interviews.** This step is often most difficult to manage, because your schedule must defer to those of your sources. So calling people early to set up interviews. But don't be surprised if a source says, "Let's do it now." If that happens, pull out your question list and shoot. Tell all your sources that you may need to talk with them again to check facts to make sure your article is accurate. Most people welcome such calls.

7. **Conduct interviews.** You will get better information, and more descriptive notes, by interviewing people in person. But doing so eats up great quantities of time. Budget according to your time and your story's needs.

8. **Read and reread your notes.** Highlight important parts. Think about what you've learned. This requires time, too.

9. **Make an outline.** Complicated stories may require formal outlines, with main points and facts to bolster them. One relatively easy way of doing this is to write main points on index cards, along with their sources, and rearranging the cards into a logical sequence. For simpler pieces, you may only need a rough image in your head showing where you want the story to go.

10. **Write a first draft.** Don't put absurd pressure on yourself by

expecting to write a lyrical masterpiece as soon as your fingers hit the keys. It's often easier to write if you get a draft down, and tell yourself you'll rework it later to make it sing.

11. **Edit or rewrite, as often as necessary (or until time runs out).** Often, the first draft is too long. Rereading it, or giving it to someone else to read, presents options for tightening it. Work at polishing the ideas, structure, and language.

12. **Double-check your work.** When you're satisfied with what you've written, check all the facts in your piece twice.

13. **Mail it.** E-mailing pieces may give you a few extra days to work on a piece. But if your publisher wants a hard copy, you must build in a few days for mailing so that it's delivered on time.

Scheduling Refined

Depending on the complexity of your project, you may want to further subdivide your writing project. Consider scheduling these mini-steps toward your writing goal:

- **The first interview.** It usually boosts your confidence to finish the first interview. After that, the remaining interviews seem easier to handle. Schedule the first one as early as possible. Getting this done early also allows you to better stop holes in your research, thus allowing you more time to gather additional information.
- **The note analysis.** Consider setting a deadline for having studied your notes and for having important parts highlighted.
- **A rough outline.** Scribble a rough outline as an exercise to start yourself writing something. You can always revise it after you've started work.
- **A deadline for writing the lead.** Deciding the beginning of your story also can help you plan the ending, helping you accomplish two writing tasks at once.
- **A second draft.** Many stories benefit by being revised, and revised again. If you have time, use it.
- **The halfway point.** Breaking up longer pieces into halves can keep you focused and give you an earlier sense of accomplishment. Ah, half done already!

14. **Work with editors to polish the piece.** Editors are paid to ask questions. Build in time for working with them to make changes on one piece as you're beginning this process again for another.

Organize Your Writing World

Once you've developed your individual writing plan and prioritized your goals, you can use the following checklists and logs to help solidify your agenda and record progress on various projects. By keeping careful track of each project's status and constantly updating your writing goals, you'll be better able to grow your writing plan.

Writing Schedule Checklist

Use this checklist to set up a writing schedule. Start with the due date, and work backward, filling in deadlines that must be reached to meet it. Transfer all deadlines to a central calendar or organizer, so they become part of your daily work plan.

Interview Source Log

Once you've done some research, list the people you need to interview. Include their category (official, expert, academic, etc.) or expertise (physicians, racecar drivers, politicians, ministers, etc.). Use this list to track whom you'll interview and when. Remember to transfer interview times to your daily calendar.

Weekly Activity Log

Fill in this chart if you want a good estimate of where you really spend your time. Under "Clock Time," write the time that you begin an activity. When you start something else, note the new starting time (round it off to the nearest quarter-hour). Subtract one from the other and put that answer under "Total time," how much time you spent on each activity. At the end of the day, rate each activity as 1, most important; 2, medium importance; or 3, not important. Then, ask yourself if you can delegate or simply not do the 3s.

Story Title:	Date:
Publisher:	
Final due date:	
Mailing date:	
Final date due:	
Grammar/spelling/punctuation checked	
Fact checking completed	
Polishing/lightening completed	
Second draft completed:	
First draft completed:	
Lead written:	
Final outline completed:	
Draft outline completed:	
Rereading notes completed:	
Interviews completed:	
Half of interviews completed	
First interview completed	
Interviews scheduled:	
Interview question listed:	
Source list compiled:	
Reading completed:	
Research completed:	
Research begins:	

Story Title:			
Publisher:			

Interview Date	Interview Time	Source's name and phone	Source's expertise/category

Time	Activity	Total Time	Priority Rating

Building
A Strong
Foundation

CHAPTER FOUR

Researching Your Ideas

The lengths that writers can go to understand their subjects may be best exemplified by James Alexander Thom, a former journalist who has written a number of acclaimed and best-selling books about the American frontier experience. When Thom decided to write the story of Mary Ingles for his book *Follow the River* he actually retraced parts of the route Ingles followed when she escaped Indian captivity in 1755.

Following the completion of the book, Thom said he could only write Ingles's story after he had walked in her steps. Thom couldn't trace Ingles's entire six-week trek through the woods along the Ohio and Kenawha rivers, but he made five separate trips to key spots along her route. At times Thom even ate what Ingles had eaten, and at one point he fasted for a week.

For the rest of his research, Thom visited Ingles's descendants, read detailed family accounts of her life, and studied historic documents. In the long run Thom's research only made his job easier, and it made his account more believable.

It is this kind of dogged pursuit of authenticity that can make your work stand out from the pack, whether you are writing a historical novel or an article on historic cars. To convince readers—and editors—that you know what you are talking about, you must first spend the time to understand the subject yourself.

As you outline your book or article, the idea of research may sound like drudgery, a necessary evil you must go through before you can get to your real work—the writing. Yet what many of us would consider drudgery is actually the most important step in the writing process. Consider, for a moment, that good research is what makes your finished work come alive with realism and truth. Each interview, each trip to the library is what adds excitement and authenticity to your finished piece. Research enlightens you and enables you to enlighten your audience. Research is nothing less than the heart and soul of what we do.

In reality, there are only so many subjects you can write from personal experience. And there are only so many subjects that you can learn firsthand, as Thom did. Fortunately, to learn everything else you can rely on others' expertise through interviews (which are discussed in chapter five). The Internet has made millions of information sources available to anyone who can afford a modem.

Whether your research is based on personal experience, interviews, document searches, the Internet, or any combination of the above, you should approach it with the same dogged professionalism. In the end, the quality of what you write will be based on the quality of what you know and learn. This is true whether you are writing fiction, nonfiction, or magazine articles. In all these cases research adds the critical element of realism. This chapter provides you with the tools needed to approach research in a time-efficient and thorough manner.

Deciding Where to Start

The quality of what you learn is determined not just by the quality of your source material, but also by the mindset you bring to the project. Approach your research with a real desire to learn. Find enough sources to obtain as many points of view as possible. Do not merely accept the things you read or hear. Ask questions and make your judgments based on factual information. At the same time, challenge your own assumptions as well. Be willing to consider other ideas and opinions even if it means reevaluating your work or redoing what you have done so far.

It's equally important to remember that the right mindset requires an open mind. Open yourself up to the unexpected directions your story may take as a result of your research. New angles reveal themselves constantly, and they may help your story stand out from others. Look at your story from every perspective in order to keep from researching in a vacuum.

Balancing Research and Time

While thoroughness is important, don't let your research become an end in itself. In Thom's case, his book required detailed accounts of events from another century. His reward was a lucrative book deal. You must tailor your research time to the size of the job at hand. To do this, keep these questions in mind:

- Who is your audience, and how much do they already know?
- Where can the material most easily be found?
- What is the projected length of the project?
- How much time do you have?
- How much are you being paid to complete the project?
- Can the research be reused later in another article or book?

Some writers hide behind mounds of books and papers, never actually writing a thing. Don't use research as an excuse not to write. Keep your goals nearby to help you stay on track.

Finding the Right Information

The task of research is somewhat like that of writing. More important than *where* to start is *the need* to start. You can't know exactly what an article or book will be until you write it. Similarly, you can't know all the information you need or where your search will lead you until it is underway. You can, however, narrow your choices with some foresight and good planning. From libraries and the Internet, to business and government sources, there's no shortage of places to find the right information on any subject. Begin with the places that will be of most benefit for your topic.

Libraries

For most topics, a library is a great place to conduct research. After all, libraries hold the cumulative written knowledge of our entire history and civilization. Practically nothing is known that cannot be found in a library somewhere. Best of all, there are guides (research librarians and reference librarians) to point you in the right direction. Thanks to inter-library loans, virtually no volume is beyond your reach. With directories on CD-ROM and the Internet, searching has never been easier.

There are three types of libraries: public libraries, college libraries, and specialized libraries maintained by industries or by special interest groups. The federal government is another leading source of information, but many of its publications are also available in larger libraries.

Main Public Libraries

These are usually the best places for conducting research. The selection of material is unmatched by any suburban branch location (though if you know what you want you can often have it sent from the main library to the branch near you). The reference librarian at your local library is a fine source of information. Many accept phone calls from patrons asking research questions, so long as the questions are specific and can be answered quickly.

College Libraries

A library at a large institution will have more resources available than most branches of your public library. Colleges and university libraries are usually open to the public, though you may not be able to withdraw a book unless you are affiliated with the school. In addition to the central campus library at most universities, many of the academic departments have their own specialized libraries, which may be open to the public.

Specialized Libraries

There are more than ten thousand special libraries throughout the United States. While their collections may be limited to certain subjects, many offer an unparalleled amount of information on their specific subject matter, be it medicine, engineering, history, or art. Most are open to the public at least on a limited basis, though you will probably need permission in advance to gain access. Even those that aren't normally open to the public likely will allow you access if you explain the nature of your research. You can find out about special libraries in the *Directory of Special Libraries and Information Centers* or in the *Subject Directory of Special Libraries.* Both volumes are available at larger public libraries. The Special Libraries Association (www.sla.org) also may be of assistance. You can reach the SLA by writing to 1700 18th St., NW, Washington, DC 20009, or by calling (202) 234-4700.

The Internet

The amount of information available on the Internet boggles the mind. Millions of Web pages are maintained by government agencies, universities, libraries, corporations, organizations, and individuals. Some experts estimate that the amount of information online is expanding at several pages per second. You can read and download government reports, newspaper and magazine articles, research studies, even the full text of books. While it can't supplant libraries and other sources of detailed information (at least not yet), using the Web for research is like shopping at a flea market. Every page is valuable to someone, but finding what is meaningful to you often requires sorting through a lot of junk. Knowing a few shortcuts can save you valuable time.

Search Engines and Subject Directories

No doubt you've already discovered the first major shortcut: search engines and search directories. These sites serve as partial directories of the Web, and you probably have a favorite one that you turn to again and again.

When you search using a subject directory, you browse through general information on topics such as art, business, computers, education, government, health, recreation, and science. Under each of these topics are layers of subtopics. Subject directories are similar to subject headings in the library. They direct you to a spot where more information is available. While far from comprehensive, they can give you an overview of the information available.

One of the most well-known search sites using this format is Yahoo!

Search engines help you find more specific information on a subject. They constantly scan the Web to create indexes of information. When you type in a word or phrase and hit the search button, the search engine creates a list of Web pages that relate to your subject. That list often refers to thousands of links. Some popular search engines and subject directories include:

AltaVista (www.altavista.com)

HotBot (www.hotbot.com)

InfoSeek (www.infoseek.com)

Lycos (www.lycos.com)

Google (www.google.com)

Overture (www.overture.com)

Yahoo (www.yahoo.com)

Metasearch Engines

Search engines are programmed in different ways, so you can get widely varying results from each engine. To search through many engines at once, you should use a metasearch engine (also called a metacrawler), which will send your request to several search engines at once, giving you a consolidated report of what is available. Although you may get better results, this also increases the chances you'll be deluged with thousands of sites. They're best used for simple searches, since many metasearch engines do not recognize advanced searching techniques and variables. They're most useful when individual search engines give you limited usable results.

Some popular metasearch engines include:

Dogpile (www.dogpile.com)

Ixquick (www.ixquick.com)

MetaCrawler (www.metacrawler.com)

Mamma (www.mamma.com)

Query Server (www.queryserver.com)

Vivisimo (http://vivisimo.com)

Search.Com (www.search.com)

WebCrawler (www.webcrawler.com)

Improve Your Search Results

You can greatly improve your search results by using various symbols as search tools. For example, to find sites that contain your string of words in the same order that you type them, enclose the words in quotation marks. Example: "New York Times." Or, if you use the minus (-) sign in front of a word, you can exclude pages containing that word.

Most search engines offer a special tip page on how to conduct more effective searches—or an advanced search page. Make use of them—they may save you valuable time.

Invisible Web

While search engines and metasearch engines can turn up perfect jewels of information, they don't even begin to scratch the surface of what's been called the "Invisible Web." This term refers to content that isn't tracked by search engines, such as databases and other sites that require direct queries (e.g., government census sites, library catalogs, and online newspapers). Usually such content is the most valuable because it is specific and of better quality. What's a writer to do?

Brilliant people already have created Invisible Web search sites. Here's a sampling of free tools to try when your search engine disappoints:

Invisible Web Directory (www.invisible-web.net)
Complete Planet (www.completeplanet.com)
Profusion (www.profusion.com)

Specialized Search Engines

There are also subject-specific search engines, like LawCrawler (legal) or Medline (medicine). They can help you hone in on Web pages more likely to cover your topic in detail.

Some popular specialized search engines and directories include:

Academic Info (www.academicinfo.net)
AskEric (www.askeric.org)
Infomine (http://infomine.ucr.edu)
LawCrawler (www.lawcrawler.com)
Medline PubMed (www.nlm.nih.gov)

Words of Caution

While the Internet is a great research tool, it is far from perfect. Consider the following points to steer past some of the pitfalls:

1. **Cross check information if you are not sure of the source.** While the Web opens the door to galaxies of information, you don't always know the level of expertise of the provider.

2. **Hyperlinks are handy, but they can be a time sink.** It's easy to spend hours searching the Web only to have little information to show for it when you are finished. One way to keep yourself disciplined is to set a time limit for your search. Sometimes the best and quickest source is an encyclopedia, a book, a magazine, or, better yet, a person.

3. **Some search engines accept payment from advertisers to list certain Web pages higher in the search results.** This can be especially true of some metasearch sites. When searching for information in which unbiased accuracy is paramount (health-related information, for example), choose a search site that indicates which listings are being sponsored by a third party.

Business Sources

Businesses routinely make information available through their public relations offices, customer service departments, and sales staffs. Many trade associations also can provide you with valuable material, including chambers of commerce and tourism offices at the state and local level. In fact, many exist primarily to disseminate information and are often eager to provide writers with information. So don't hesitate to contact these people; they can be an enormous help. Three books that list thousands of viable information sources include *Encyclopedia of Associations: International Organizations, Encyclopedia of Associations: National Organizations of the U.S.*, and *Encyclopedia of Associations: Regional, State and Local Organizations*.

Federal Government Information

There are several sources for government publications. You can contact the authoring agency directly, or use any number of government outlets that serve as information clearinghouses. In many instances the cost to purchase government documents can be prohibitive. Fortunately, many documents are available for free viewing at public libraries or at thousands of other depositories throughout the country. *The Monthly Catalog of U.S. Government Publications*, published by the Government Printing Office, is one way to find what you need. The GPO's Subject Bibliography Index lists thousands of publications by category. To inquire about government documents try the following agencies:

> **The Federal Citizen Information Center** (http://fic.info.gov) serves as a single point of contact for people who have questions about any federal agency. Its information specialists can also help you locate government documents and publications. For additional information, consult the Web site or call 1-888-FED-INFO.
>
> **The Census Bureau** (www.census.gov) has thousands of reports about the U.S. population and economy. It offers statistics on such diverse subjects as fertility, education, mining, ancestry, income, migration, school enrollment, construction, and international trade. You can access data through more than two thousand libraries and other locations that serve as data centers and federal depositories. For additional information, consult the Web site, write to U.S. Census Bureau, 4700 Silver Hill Road, Washington DC 20233, or call (301) 763-4636.
>
> **The Consumer Information Center** (www.pueblo.gsa.gov) may be the best known distributor of federal documents through its facilities in Pueblo, Colorado. It specializes in consumer-oriented materials and many of it documents are free or available for a minimal charge. For additional information, consult the Web site, write to Federal Citizen Information Center, Dept. WWW, Pueblo, CO 81009, or call (888) 878-3256.
>
> **The General Accounting Office** (www.gao.gov) is the investigative arm of Congress and compiles reports on all aspects of

government. All of GAO's unclassified reports are available to the public. For additional information, consult the Web site, write to Chief Quality Officer, General Accounting Office, Room 6K17Q, 441 G Street NW, Washington, DC 20548, or call (202) 512-4800.

The Government Printing Office (www.access.gpo.gov) is the largest distributor of government documents. The GPO provides information to designated libraries and other locations through-out the country, where you can view the information for free. For additional information, consult the Web site, write to Superintendent of Documents, Subscription Customer Service, Stop: SSOM, Washington, DC 20402, or call (866) 512-1800.

The National Technical Information Service (www.ntis.gov) dis-tributes scientific, technical, and engineering documents. The staff can perform searches by subject. For additional informa-tion, consult the Web site, write to National Technical Information Service, 5285 Port Royal Road, Springfield, VA 22161, or call (703) 605-6585.

Devising a Research Strategy

A research strategy will save you time and frustration by focusing your attention on the most valuable information sources, and by ensuring that you don't overlook important information. Depending on your topic, you should adapt the following steps to best suit your needs:

Develop Your Topic

State your topic as a question. For example, if you are writing about the effect of a food additive on the health of fetuses, pose your concept in the form of a question: "What impact does chemical *xyz* have on fetal health?" Next identify the key words in your question. In this case they are "chemical *xzy*" and "fetal health."

Test the key words by looking them up in the library catalog, in peri-odical indexes, and online. Be flexible. If you find too much informa-tion and too many sources, narrow your topic. Finding too little infor-mation means you may need to broaden your subject.

Select the Best Source of Information

To make the best use of your time, think ahead about which sources of information are best suited for your type of research. Planning ahead will help you choose from the vast amounts of information available in books, newspapers, magazines, journals, newsletters, and on the Internet. Let's take a closer look at the options:

- **Books** offer the most in-depth coverage of a topic, but the information may be more dated. The author is usually an expert, but the bias may be that of a single individual—the author.
- **Newspapers** offer up-to-date coverage and cover a wide range of subjects, but most reporters are generalists with limited expertise in the stories they cover.
- **Magazines,** like newspapers, offer current information. As with newspapers, the writers may not be experts in the subjects they cover, so be sure to check the bylines. Magazines are, however, more specialized, assuring that you are more likely to find the information you need. Magazines are more apt to openly represent an editorial bias (either conservative or liberal, pro or con) depending on the readership they are targeting.
- **Journals** are highly specialized—offering detailed case studies and analysis. Articles typically are written by a scholar in the field or by someone who has done research in the field. Scholarly or scientific journals are less likely to contain bias, but the material may be harder to digest due to technical language.
- **The Internet** offers a lot of information—so much that it can almost seem like too much. Using the search engines described in this chapter can help you stay focused. Also, remember that it's best to verify information found on Web sites, especially those maintained by individuals.ly publication with a primarily Roman Catholic audience, *Catholic Parent* accepts essays, how-to, humor, inspiration, personal experience, and religious articles.

Narrow your subject by asking yourself questions that will help you better define it:

- Do you want to focus on a specific country?
- What years should you cover?
- Are you more interested in the medical or social consequences?

Expand your subject by asking questions that broaden the scope:

- How safe are food additives in general?
- What are other safety concerns facing expectant parents?
- Are there any related topics to explore, such as food labeling requirements?

Gather Background Information

Reading entries in encyclopedias and articles in newspapers or magazines gives you a quick overview of your subject, and can save you time by helping you understand the broader context of your subject matter.

Use an online index or newspaper for an overview of more current topics. Use an encyclopedia for topics that are less current or for general background information. Better still, find an encyclopedia or similar source that focuses specifically on your area of study, such as *The Oxford Illustrated History of Medieval Europe*. You can find specialized encyclopedias and reference book in the library catalog or in a reference bibliography (a bibliography of reference sources broken down by subject).

Don't overlook useful sources that may be listed as "further reading" at the end of the encyclopedia entry. These can be good starting points for further research.

Find Books on Your Subject

You can use the library catalog or a bibliography to find books on your subject. Bibliographies are lists of works on a given subject. They can save you time, especially when they include annotations (descriptions of the works listed). When searching a library catalog, use key words for a narrow or complex topic. Use subject headings for a broader search. The *Subject Guide to Books In Print* is another great resource for finding books by subject. When you find the books you were looking for, scan the bibliography in the back of each for additional sources.

Find Articles on Your Subject

Periodicals are good sources for keeping up with the latest developments on a subject because articles are usually more up-to-date than books. Finding articles is a two-step process. You must first look in a periodical index to find listings of useful articles. You can search by subject, author, title, key word, or date. Next check the library's catalog or its list of periodicals to see if it stocks the publication that contains the article you need.

Periodical indexes may be in print or computer-based formats. The printed index *Reader's Guide to Periodical Literature* is one of the most common, and covers popular magazines from 1900 to the present. There are many others, such as the *Business Periodical Index and Abstracts.* Ask at the reference desk if you need help figuring out which index is best for you. Prior to searching through a periodical index, develop a list with more than one key word to describe each idea (for example, atomic energy and nuclear energy) so that you have several routes for researching your topic.

Another way to find useful articles is to ask an expert on the subject. She should know of useful articles and publications. Or, look at the bibliographies in books that focus on your subject and find out what sources those authors used.

Evaluating Your Sources of Information

As important as finding information is finding good information. The author's credentials as well as the timeliness of the book or article are factors to consider in evaluating the quality of the material you find.

Book Review Index and *Book Review Digest* are good sources for checking whether a book is well respected. *Who's Who in America, Biography Index,* or the biographical information in the publication itself are also useful in checking the author's expertise.

Also note whether the author or publication is closely aligned with an organization. If so, ask yourself what biases that might create?

Make sure that the information isn't too dated. Subjects such as medicine and computers require timely information because they are easily affected by changing technology. Is the source current enough for your topic?

If you're researching online, it's usually best to verify any information you uncover. Unless the site is being maintained by a reputable source, there's always a chance the creator made a mistake or let his personal biases influence the information presented.

Tips and Tricks for Effective Research

As you can see, it's fairly easy to write out a list of places to get information. What to do when you get there is another story. There is more than one path to the same point, and some are quicker than others. Think of unique ways to get the information you need, and think of unique ways to use the information you get. In other words, be as creative in your research as you are in your writing. Use the tips and tricks listed below to help you find the best research path possible:

- Work from the general to the specific. Look for general background information first. Use that to better define your search and begin to look for more specific information.
- Develop a rapport with the reference or research librarians at your local library. They live to help people find information.
- A quick check of an encyclopedia (for less current topics) or an online source or newspaper (for current topics) can provide a quick overview of your subject—saving you time in the long run.
- To get a quick overview of a large book or document, check the index for a list of illustrations, charts, tables, or graphs. Lengthy, complicated subjects are often summarized with charts and graphs. This is especially true of government and scientific documents. If you find a graphic that is of particular interest, scan the text pages around it for related details. Also look for an executive summary or introduction at the front of the document and conclusion statements at the end of each section.
- If you have trouble finding information on your subject, it could be you are using the wrong search words. For instance, instead of "Afro-American" try "African American." Check your words against the subject heading list in the directory you are searching, or use a thesaurus to come up with alternate words.
- When retrieving your books from the library shelves, browse

nearby books to see if any others might be useful. Library shelves are arranged so that books about the same topic are generally kept near each other.

- Keep a list of what you find and where you found it. You may need to go back to it later.
- A volume number usually refers to the year that a periodical was published. Volume 10 refers to a magazine in its tenth year of publication.
- When you need facts, assume that there is a reference source that has what you need. There nearly always is.
- Most books and many articles themselves have bibliographies that list additional sources of information. By following these leads you can amass a body of information quickly.
- A local college or university may have a professor who specializes in your subject area. If so, he or she will likely have a list of recommended reading on the subject. Call the public information office and inquire.
- Don't overlook that most ubiquitous of books: the *Yellow Pages*. Doing a story on home improvement and need an expert source? Open your *Yellow Pages* to remodeling and start dialing.

Resources for Conducting Research

The following Web sites are reference guides that can help you shave hours off your research time.

Web Sites

The majority of the Web sites listed below are maintained by private organizations, universities, or the federal government. The sites, many of which are updated regularly, can provide you with information on a variety of general and specialized subjects:

AllExperts (www.allexperts.com) offers free access to hundreds of questions and answers.

American Medical Association (www.ama-assn.org) contains information on health and fitness, including access to the *Journal of the American Medical Association* (JAMA). Also has links to other medical sites.

Argus Clearinghouse (www.clearinghouse.net) offers a collection of Web sites and directories searchable by subject. Categories include: art, business, engineering, health and science, etc.

Census Bureau (www.census.gov) maintains detailed information about the U.S. population and economy, much of which is accessible through its Web page.

Central Intelligence Agency (www.cia.gov) offers a publication section with maps and statistics for hundreds of countries, including information on heads of state.

Department of Health and Human Services (www.hhs.gov) allows you to browse through information on health and medicine, including such topics as disease prevention, pediatrics, elderly care, and health care fraud. Also has links to libraries, databases, online journals, and medical dictionaries.

Editorial Freelancers Association (www.the-efa.org) has links to dozens of government, medical, and library sites.

Electronic Text Center (http://etext.lib.virginia.edu) offers thousands of humanities texts in multiple languages. Many are available to the general public.

Encyclopaedia Britannica (www.britannica.com) indexes and reviews thousands of Web sites to provide a searchable directory of information sources.

Encyclopedia Mythica (www.pantheon.org/mythica) maintains a database of myths, legends and folklore with more than five thousand definitions of gods and goddesses, and legends from around the world.

Federal Citizen Information Center (www.pueblo.gsa.gov) specializes in consumer-oriented materials. Many of its guides are available free online.

General Accounting Office (www.gao.gov) is the investigative arm of the Congress. Many of the GAO's unclassified reports are available to the public online.

The Internet Archive (www.archive.org) acts as a "digital library" for Web sites, thus providing visitors with access to more than ten billion archived Web pages.

Ingenta (www.ingenta.com) is formerly known as CARL Uncover and provides access to thousands publications.

Internet Public Library (www.ipl.org) provides library-type services via the Internet, including a comprehensive list of online texts, a ready-reference collection, plus links to search engines and more than two thousand newspaper and magazine sites around the world.

Legal Information Institute (www.law.cornell.edu) provides information about Supreme Court decisions.

Library of Congress (www.loc.gov) presents American history in pictures, sounds, and text.

Library Spot (www.libraryspot.com) is a "vertical information portal" that provides hundreds of links to innumerable reference sites that have been "hand-selected" for their "exceptional quality, content, and utility."

Medscape (www.medscape.com) includes medical articles and a comprehensive database of articles in medical journals.

National Political Index (www.politicalindex.com) contains thousands of links to political Web sites at the local, state, and national levels.

National Writers Union (www.nwu.org) offers hundreds of links to search engines, Web directories, libraries, government sites, reference collections, newspapers, and databases.

RefDesk (www.refdesk.com) indexes, reviews, and links to various reference sites.

Books

Keep this list of popular references on hand as you research your subject. Some of these titles are expensive, or may be out of print. You may find that a library is the best place to find them. If you do find yourself using them all of the time, then it may be worth investing in your own copy.

Biography

- *Biography and Genealogy Master Index* (Gale Research)
- *Biography Index* (H.W. Wilson)
- *Contemporary Authors* (Gale Research)
- *Current Biography* (H.W. Wilson)
- *Dictionary of American Biography* (Scribner)
- *Dictionary of National Biography* (Oxford University Press)
- *Dictionary of Scientific Biography* (Scribner)
- *Encyclopaedia Britannica* (Encyclopaedia Brittanica)
- *Who's Who* (St. Martin's Press)
- *Who's Who in America* (A.N. Marquis)

Business

- *ABI Inform* (University Microfilms International)
- *Business Dateline* (University Microfilms International)
- *Dictionary of Business Finance and Investment* (Drake Publishers)

Current Events

- *Keesing's Record of World Events* (Longman)
- Periodical Abstracts

Education

- *Education Index* (H.W. Wilson)
- *The Encyclopedia of Education* (Macmillan)
- *Encyclopedia of Educational Research* (Macmillan)

Humanities (Architecture, Art, Drama, Film, History, Literature, Music, Mythology, Philosophy, Religion)

- *Encyclopaedia Britannica* (Encyclopaedia Britannica)
- *Humanities Index* (H.W. Wilson)

Maps

- *Demographics USA* (Trade Dimensions)
- *Information Please Almanac* (McGraw-Hill)
- *Times Atlas of the World* (Times Books)

Science and Technology

- *Applied Science and Technology Index* (H.W. Wilson)
- *Biographical Encyclopedia of Scientists* (Marshall Cavendish)
- *Concise Dictionary of Scientific Biography* (Gale)
- *General Science Index* (H.W. Wilson)
- *Handbook of Current Science & Technology* (Gale)
- *How It Works* (Grosset & Dunlap)
- *McGraw-Hill Encyclopedia of Science and Technology* (McGraw-Hill)
- *Milestones in Science and Technology* (Oryx Press)
- *Science and Technology Desk Reference* (Gale)
- *Van Nostrand's Scientific Encyclopedia* (Van Nostrand Reinhold)
- *World of Scientific Discovery* (Gale)

Social Science (Economics, Political Science, Government, Psychology, Social Work, Sociology, Urban Studies)

- *A Dictionary of the Social Sciences* (Oxford University Press)
- *Encyclopedia of American Social History* (Scribner)
- *Encyclopedia of Social History* (Garland)
- *Social Sciences Index* (H.W. Wilson)
- *World Quality of Life Indicators* (ABC-CLIO)

Speeches

- *Weekly Compilation of Presidential Documents* (National Archives and Records Administration)
- *Vital Speeches of the Day* (a biweekly publication)

Statistics

- *America's Top Rated Cities: A Statistical Handbook* (Universal Reference Publications)
- *The Gallup Poll: Public Opinion* (Scholarly Resources)
- *Information Please Almanac Atlas & Yearbook* (Houghton Mifflin)
- *Statistical Abstract of the United States* (GPO)
- *The World Almanac and Book of Facts* (World Almanac)

CHAPTER FIVE

Conducting Interviews

t's been said that a good interview is just like a good conversation. That's not so. In a good conversation, it's polite for the folks involved to ask questions of each other and to listen with equal interest to the answers. It's a time for mutual discovery and communication.

But an interview is, by definition, a lopsided interaction. The interviewee probably doesn't care much about the person popping the questions, and the interviewer is probably doing more than simply enjoying himself. Interviewing is, after all, work.

It shouldn't feel like work, however, and that's what the interviews-are-conversations theory is all about. If a person being interviewed feels as if she is talking to an old friend, the interview is more likely to produce powerful anecdotes, colorful quotes, and revealing information. Yet, before a source feels comfortable with an interviewer, the interviewer has to relax—a tough trick for many beginners.

In an effort to calm your nervous stomach, we've included in this chapter resources for finding people to interview, tips on how to interview, and some mix-and-match, interview-starting questions.

Preparing for an Interview

Nothing can take the place of doing your homework before an interview. There's no excuse for asking someone who's just been awarded the Pulitzer prize whether she's won any awards lately. Before doing the interview, head to the library or go online and look up background information on the topic and your interview subject. Research also helps to point out the controversies in a topic, and, importantly, helps you devise appropriate and engaging questions.

Don't think you have to know everything about the topic prior to interviewing someone. It's perfectly okay to tell a source that you've read his latest report on wastewater treatment options, but you need him to explain the finer details. (In fact, sometimes, playing dumb is the best way to get people to open up to you.) Most people are grateful that an interviewer has taken time to try to understand their business, and many enjoy assuming the role of a teacher to an interested pupil. Still, the more you learn about the topic, the less likely you are to be confused by a source's statements or bamboozled by someone who wants to evade controversial issues.

Figure out who you'll need to interview, what you hope to get from each of them, and what approach you'll need to take. Despite what you see on certain television interview shows, being unfailingly polite when requesting interviews, and thanking your source at the start and at the end of the interview, is the professional approach.

Don't overwhelm the source with questions. You want the source to do much more talking than you. Just ask questions and allow him to do the talking. National Public Radio's *Morning Edition* former anchor Bob Edwards once told a journalism professor that his two favorite interview questions were "Oh?" and "No!"

Jot down a list of questions that pertain specifically to your topic before the interview. You will probably need to ask closed-ended questions, designed to gather information or provide verification ("Did the dress really cost $10,000?"), as well as open-ended questions, designed to encourage the source to describe events, processes, thoughts, and emotions ("How did you know she was the woman for you?"). Start with the easy-to-answer questions, and end with the explosive ones. That way, if the source ends the interview after the touchy question, at least you'll have something in your notes to write about.

Finally, don't rely entirely on the questions in this chapter for your interviews. Think of them as catalysts. Add your own to the mix. Or, after you devise a list of questions based on your research, scan the list below and include those that you think will help flesh out the interview. Then turn to the back of this chapter for help in finding people to interview.

And relax. Interviewing can be the most fun part of the writing process, as you're free to approach people you never could hope to meet under ordinary circumstances. So, bring your notebook, pen, and tape recorder, and leave your antacid tablets at home.

Asking the Right Questions

A lot of interview prep work goes into coming up with the right questions. As we stressed earlier, research is crucial in helping you form smart and revealing questions. If they're available, read previous interviews your subject has done so you can get a feel for how he will respond to certain questions and what his stock answers might be. This way, if you get one of those stock answers, you'll recognize it and know that you'll need to dig a little deeper to get something fresh for your piece. That said, it's important to recognize that research alone isn't enough to pull off a successful interview. By exploring different types of questions, phraseology, and sources, you can come up with the right questions for any interview.

Who?

Who is the foremost question in the sextet of journalistic queries, followed by *what, when, where, why,* and *how*. When you write profiles, who is paramount, along with what that person does/did. However, finding out more about who you're interviewing is quite useful for many other types of stories. It's often a good idea to observe, as well as ask questions, to gather color to add to your stories. Try out some of these questions to help you learn about a source's personality:

- How did you decide to go into your profession/avocation?
- How long have you been doing this?
- What did your parents think of your decision? Your friends?
- What is a typical day like? Or, for the reticent, how does a typical

day start for you, how does it progress, and how does it end?

- Why do you think people believe your work is important? Why do you believe it is?
- When did you know that you would become what you are today? How did that knowledge change your life?
- What have you accomplished that makes you most proud?
- What mistakes did you make and what have you learned from them?
- How did you end up in this town?
- How did it feel when you reached your goal (or lost the battle)?
- How did you meet your spouse?
- How many children do you have?
- Do you own pets? What kind? How many?
- How do you juggle the demands of career and family life?
- What do you wish you could change about your life (career/cause)?
- What do you do to relax?
- Who was your mentor? What did you learn from that person?
- Who are your best friends? Enemies?
- What do you read for work? For fun?

Why?

The peerless follow-up question to so many answers is, of course, why. But the problem with asking *why* is that its single syllable can seem abrupt and provoking. It can jab the source like a poke in the ribs, inducing defensiveness. Try softening the thrust of this necessary monosyllable by cushioning it inside other words: "Do you remember why it was that you made that plan?" or "What an interesting idea. Why do you say so?" All those words really mean one: *Why?* They just sound nicer.

Emotions

Some television journalists have rightly earned contempt for pushing a microphone in the face of a grieving parent of a dead child and asking, "How does it feel?" Yet, our emotions tie us together;

they draw readers deeply into stories and books through a rush of recognition and understanding.

Observation and description can be better than quotes in conveying emotions in your writing. It's more powerful to write that tears trickled into the wrinkles in the elderly woman's face and dripped steadily on the bedclothes of her comatose husband than to quote her saying, "I felt sad." But if you're not there at the moment of turmoil, you'll have to ask how it felt. When you do, show respect for your sources who have experienced pain, and ask your questions gently.

Skim through the question list below for some ideas on wording difficult questions about emotions. You'll notice that some aren't questions at all. They're exclamations that often elicit a response, and they can be more natural, and less intrusive, than questions:

- I know this might be painful for you to talk about, but it will help people to understand your story. Can you describe what you were feeling at the moment when _____?
- What was your reaction? Your family's? How difficult was it?
- Can you please tell me about the emotions that you felt?
- How did you recover?
- How long did the feeling last?
- What an awful time it must have been for you.
- I'm so sorry.

Anecdotes

These little stories-within-stories add depth and interest to whatever you're writing. The problem is, there's no surer way of creating amnesia in another person than by asking, "Do you remember any good stories about this?" You can always leave your name and phone number, and ask the person to call you if they do remember any scintillating anecdotes. Or try these questions to prompt a person's memory:

- When did you realize that you were going to become a _____?
- When did you first meet?
- When did you make up your mind? How?
- When was there a turning point?

- When did it all begin?
- When did you decide to go ahead (or turn back)?
- At what point did things begin to go your way (or against you)?
- At what moment did you know that this organization (or cause) was special (or not worth your trouble)?

Information

You will rely on people to give you information, not just to describe emotions and reminisce about anecdotes. Often, the substance of the story can be elicited by four questions, suggested some years ago by LaRue Gilleland, a professor and former director of the University of Nevada's School of Journalism. They go by the acronym GOSS, for goals, obstacles, solutions, and start over:

- What were your (or your organization's) goals?
- What obstacles did you face?
- How did you find solutions to those obstacles?

The last S means that you often need to start over and probe for details and background. Ken Metzler, author of *Creative Interviewing*, suggested adding EY to the GOSS formula: E to ask the source to evaluate the information and Y as a reminder to ask why. Using these questions as the scaffolding, it's easy to sprinkle your own probes among them:

- If you knew then what you know now, what would you have done differently?
- What mistakes did you make, and what did you learn from them?
- Would you advise others to do it that way?
- Was it worth it?
- Who are the experts in this field (or the leaders in this endeavor or this industry), so I can contact them?
- What journals cover this field the best, so that I can go read them?

People on Personalities

People enjoy telling stories about other people. These anecdotes make personal profiles and other articles come alive. Here are some questions to help get you started:

- When did you meet? How?
- What was your initial impression of this person?
- How has that changed?
- If you were to describe this person to your next door neighbor, what would you say about him or her?
- Does he or she remind you of any one (or any thing)?
- When were you ever angry with this person?
- When did this person make you glad to know him?
- Why is this person's work (or actions) important?
- How will this person's work (or actions) affect the lives of others?
- How has this person's work (or actions) helped you? Hurt you?
- Who else should I talk with about this person?

Digging Deeper

Often, interviews help you discover new story ideas. If you find yourself finished with an interview for one story, and your source is friendly and willing, try fishing for a few other possible ideas by using following questions:

- What types of things concern you (or your group) most right now?
- What new projects are coming up?
- What trends will affect your business?
- How will the future bring changes for you (or your group)?
- If you could, what would you change about your organization?
- When people talk to you about this group, what do they complain about most often?
- What do they praise?
- Has your group won any awards lately?
- If something new happens on this, would you please remember to call me?

Follow-up Interview Questions

It's not clear whether novelist Gustave Flaubert, architect Ludwig Mies van der Rohe, or art historian Aby Warburg first said, "God is in the details." But whoever said it knew what he was talking about. And even though the saying has become corrupted to, "The devil is in the details," the meaning remains the same. Big things merely sketch an outline; little things color it in. After reading a story about a man who killed another during an argument about a bag of potato chips, a newspaper editor in Columbus asked the reporter, "How big was the bag?"

Few sources volunteer all the details you will need to make readers see and feel as if they are in your story. You'll have to prompt them with follow-up questions, of which only a tiny fraction is listed here. You'll have to make a point to look for the telling detail. Because these questions can become pesky, it's a good idea to let sources know what you're up to by stating first, "I'd like to know about that in much more detail because it's so interesting. Let me ask you some specific questions."

- At what moment did you know that this organization (or cause) was special (or not worth your trouble)?
- Exactly when did the problem start?
- How did it start?
- Can you describe everything in the room (at the scene)?
- Who was there?
- Where were they standing?
- What were they wearing?
- How did they behave?
- What did he (she/they) say?
- What did they do next? And after that?
- How many? How much? How long? How soon?
- What was the weather like? (Weather often makes a good metaphor, and you'd be surprised how many people remember the weather at important moments.)
- What color was it?
- What did it feel like? Smell like? Sound like? Taste like? Look like?
- What were you thinking at the time?
- How much did it cost?
- How much did it weigh?
- Where was it?
- Exactly when did it end?

Tips and Tricks for a Successful Interview

You never know what's going to happen when you sit down for an interview—your pen might run dry, the interviewee may be in a very bad mood, you may be coming down with the flu. This section provides you with some of the skills you'll need to keep your interviews from going astray.

Be Prepared for Anything

Prepare for interviews by assuming something will go wrong. Your tape recorder will tie the tape in bows. The batteries will die a silent death. Your pen will run dry or unleash a flood. These things don't always happen, but eventually, they all will. So, to borrow a term from computer systems people who know about backing things up, create redundancy. Bring two tapes, three pens, spare batteries, and several notebooks to every interview. You may not be ready for anything—a reporter at the *Cincinnati Post*, a daily newspaper, once had to interview a man in a sauna, sans everything. But you'll be ready for most.

The Silent Treatment

Some people just aren't garrulous. You'll ask a question designed to encourage them to expound on a life-altering event, and they'll answer in a five-word declarative sentence and stop talking. You have two options if this happens: Probe for details, asking multitudes of follow-up questions, or simply remain silent, pen in hand, a half-smile on your expectant face. Such silence can be so uncomfortable that reluctant sources may well start talking again.

Be Aware of Your Body Language

An interview is a form of interpersonal communication. If you sit hunched over your notepad, scribbling furiously and never looking up, the interviewee will never see anything except the top of your head. Look at the person you're interviewing every now and then. Smile. Nod. Appear interested.

You also can use facial expressions instead of questions: Often, a confused or doubting look on your face will prompt the interviewee to try to explain more, without even being asked.

Bring a wandering interview subject back to the point by waving a finger to get his attention, without speaking to interrupt him—which may feel rude.

Notice your source's body language, too. Did a question make him squirm? Laugh out loud? Stand up and pace? Describe his reaction in your writing.

The Waitress Routine

Asking questions is not enough. Listening to and understanding the answers is the whole point of an interview. So, particularly for complex interviews, adopt the technique most American waitresses have used for years, after they hear your order and then ask, "So you want a burger, with mustard, pickles, and no onions, super-sized fries, and a Diet Coke?" Turn your source's answers into reflective questions: "So let me see if I got this right. Are you saying _____?" If you get it wrong, the source is usually grateful for the chance to set you straight.

Do the Interview in Person

The best interviews are done in person. It's far easier for someone to cut short a phone interview, or worse, to be working on something else as he's absentmindedly answering your questions. E-mail interviews solve the problem of taking notes, but the answers you receive might seem overthought or too perfect, lacking the natural honesty that can come from a direct response. Plus, you can never be quite sure who has typed those marvelous responses (or terrible ones—some people just can't communicate in writing). It's also easier to ignore electronic questions than spoken ones, and it's harder for the interviewer to probe for details electronically. So try to do your initial interview in person, and then ask if you can follow up via phone or e-mail to check facts or pose questions that may occur to you later.

Admit What You Don't Know

Let's say you're interviewing a source and she uses a term that, despite your research, you've never heard before. Not wishing to display your ignorance, you decide to let it pass. She uses it again, and then later, again. In fact, you discover that this topic is of utmost importance to her. It's often painful for beginning—and experienced—interviewers, but you simply have to admit your ignorance sometimes. Do so, apologize, and ask her to explain.

But don't let sources intimidate you. Sometimes, people use jargon and multisyllabic words in an effort to impress or evade. One of the best interviewing questions ever asked is simple: "What does that mean?" One of the best, final questions to pose is, "Have I forgotten to ask something important?"

Finding the Right Person to Interview

Sometimes, you'd be surprised who is willing to talk with you— famous people, people who have just had the worst experience of their lives, people who don't like your profession or your looks, people who are tired of being interviewed, people who are busier than anyone ever should be. The big surprise is often simply how nice people are to interview.

When you think about people to interview, think first about the people you already know, and the people they know. Somewhere in that network of folks is somebody who might be willing to give you background on your topic. Ask for a chat, and remember to ask him for the names of other people to talk with and for the names of experts in their field. Also ask librarians, those marvelous people whose vocation is to find information for others.

Remember, too, that important people employ other people to arrange interviews. Organizations, universities, and businesses have public relations people—also called community relations people, marketing communications people, or public information officers—who want to get publicity for the people in their organizations. Call them.

Your library or Internet research will inevitably lead you to sources; simply call the people who wrote the encyclopedia entries, research papers, or government reports that you find. Often, the best route to finding a local source is to use the *Yellow Pages* to find companies or groups in your area. If you're unsure which state agency handles your topic, call the governor's office and ask for the name and number of the public information officer who can help direct you. Call the mayor's office for help in finding city personnel.

Books and Web pages also can help you find sources. You can post requests for interviews on electronic mailing lists or search the net for people you'd otherwise not ever be able to reach.

We've listed here some of our favorite sources for finding people. Of course, a few people will turn you down or won't return your calls, but frankly, if one person says no to an interview request, usually others will be happy to talk with you. Few sources are irreplaceable, and persistence is the key to getting to the source.

Books to Aid Your Search

Here are some handy reference books that can help you identify appropriate sources for whatever you're writing. Keep in mind that some of these reference books are rather expensive and/or difficult to find in stores, so it may be worthwhile to check your local library. Also, many of these books are updated regularly, so make sure you look at the most recent edition:

The Almanac of American Politics (National Journal Group), by Michael Barone, with Richard E. Cohen. This book is an oxymoron: It's an interesting reference book. It gives brief biographical information about senators, representatives, and governors, their records and election results, and presents information about their states and districts that is often fascinating. It also includes office locations, telephone numbers, and e-mail addresses.

The College Blue Book (MacMillan Library Reference), by the Gale Group. This lists almost 3,000 colleges in the United States and Canada, with the degrees they offer. It gives main telephone numbers, which you can call to ask for the public relations department for help in finding professors who are expert in various fields.

Congressional Directory (TheCapitol.Net), by Michael L. Koempel. This federal government publication lists members of Congress, from the vice president on down, with addresses and phones, brief biographies, and committee information.

Current Biography Yearbook (H. W. Wilson). This is a compilation of biographies about important people, often well written and interesting. It also includes contact information.

The Encyclopedia of Associations (Gale). This three-volume tome, indexed by subject, is a wonderful compendium of descriptions of groups of all types, with contact information. The encyclopedia lists more than 23,000 national and international organizations, trade and business groups, fan clubs, and other associations, and it seems as if every possible topic is represented.

Lesko's Info-Power III (Visible Ink Press), by Matthew Lesko. A helpful book listing experts in government and some organizations, along with good advice on how to find information through interviews. Among the information included are lists of about 11,500 experts, descriptions of government agencies and offices and their functions, and contact information for governor's offices, state libraries, and federal public information officers.

Newsmakers (Gale). This annual book gives short biographies of people in the news, indexed by nationality, occupation, and subject. It includes information about how to contact them, such as the name and phone numbers for celebrities' agents or publicists.

Polk City Directory (www.citydirectory.com). Available on CD-ROM, this resource gives people's names, occupations, and telephone numbers, along with street addresses, in virtually every city in the country. You also can look up who lives in each house on a street, which can be useful in finding neighbors of someone you're writing about.

Politics in America (Prentice-Hall), by Thomas R. Dye. This guide to senators and representatives touts itself as "primarily a book about people." Short biographical sections include key votes, committee assignments, offices, and phone numbers.

Student Contact Book (Gale). Don't be put off by the title if you're not a student. Each chapter in this small but useful book begins with ideas for research topics, such as "The attractions of young persons to cult organizations." It's chapters start with broad categories, such as Cults and Sects, and then breaks down into smaller categories, such as New Age or Occult. It also lists contact information for organizations dealing with that topic, such as the Parapsychology Institute of America, and names of free or low-cost publications of the group.

The Thomas Register of American Manufacturers (Thomas Publishing). This book lists alphabetically more than 152,000 companies and their capabilities, with names of company executives, phone numbers, and office locations.

Who's Who in America (Marquis). The venerable resource for finding important people. The 2004 edition includes brief bios of more than 100,000 people chosen for their positions or noteworthy achievements, along with contact information. It has a geographic and professional index. There are several other similar titles, not all published by the same firm, such as Who's Who Among African Americans and the International Who's Who.

Washington Information Directory (CQ Press). This book divides information sources into agencies, Congress, and nonprofit organizations. Chapters are arranged by broad topic, such as Environment and Natural Resources. It includes names, addresses, phone numbers, and the places the people work. A section on Congress gives extensive information on members, their committee assignments, and their staff people. Reference lists give information on federal regional offices throughout the country and top state officials. A subject index can help you find the department that handles that topic, where your sources work.

Yearbook of Experts, Authorities & Spokespersons (Broadcast Interview Source). This book lists sources for thousands of topics, arranged alphabetically and by topic and geography.

Web Sites to Aid Your Search

We have listed exact pages at Web sites to help you find people. But Web sites are often updated and changed, so these URLs may no longer be valid. If any of the following addresses do not work, try trimming everything but the main page name and searching from there. For example, if this address—www.gpoaccess.gov/cdirectory/index.html—doesn't take you to the Congressional Directory, start at www.access.gpo.gov/congress to begin your search.

Associations. Several sites give contact information for associations, often searchable by topic or geographical region. Sometimes, the *Encyclopedia of Associations* is faster and more comprehensive; sometimes the Internet will be. Here are some searchable sites:

- Associations on the Net: www.ipl.org.ar/ref/AON
- The Union of International Associations: www.uia.org/website.htm\
- World Directory of Think Tanks: www.nira.go.jp/ice/index.html
- Education World: www.education-world.com

Census data. Census experts can be publicity shy, but the government Web site (www.census.gov) lists public information officers for vast quantities of census data. (Sometimes, if you e-mail the public information officers with a question, they e-mail or call you back.)

Expert sites. Several sites on the Internet offer ask-an-expert services. ProfNet.com (www.profnet.com), a subsidiary of the PR *Newswire*, allows you to find an expert by typing in a topic. It pulls up experts' names, phone numbers, e-mail addresses, and URLs. *The Yearbook of Experts, Authorities & Spokespersons* also has a Web site (www.ExpertClick.com), where you can search more than 14,000 topics to find experts.

Government contacts. *The Official Congressional Directory* is online, with brief bios and contact information for members of Congress (www.gpoaccess.gov/cdirectory/index.html). A good starting point for phone numbers and web pages—and much more—about members of congress, is the Office of the Clerk's page (http://clerk.house.gov). For links to federal departments and agencies, go to the Federal Citizen Information Center at http://fic.info.gov.

To find state pages, type the state name into a search engine or start from the Library of Congress' State and Local Governments page (www.loc.gov/global/state). State and Local Government on the Net (www.statelocalgov.net) offers an even more detailed breakdown of state offices, with links to each.

The mother of all lists. Read electronic mailing lists and discussion boards to understand what people are thinking and talking about. Before posting a request for an interview on a list, however, check the frequently asked questions to see if it's proper netiquette. To find lists on various topics, try Google Groups at groups.google.com (formerly Deja.com). If you do an e-mail interview, be sure to check out who is responding, so that the teen mother from Philadelphia you think you're interviewing isn't in fact a male bus driver from Paducah. Ask for names of other people who know this person, check out their addresses and phones in the *Polk City Directory*, and ask for resumes to verify information.

People locators. Most search engines can find people's addresses and phone numbers. Many telephone and e-mail directories are available online, and some offer help in contacting celebrities. Try Yahoo's People Search (http://people.yahoo.com); Lycos (www.lycos.com); The Global Yellow-Pages (www.globalyp.com/world.htm); or the Internet 800 Directory (http://inter800.com).

Universities and colleges. Universities and research organizations have a strong presence on the Web and are chock full of experts. You can reach these people by contacting their institutions. A Web site like Scholarly Societies Project (www.scholarly-societies.org), with links to more than 3,000 scholarly groups, also may prove helpful.

PART THREE

Taking Your Work to Market

CHAPTER SIX

Selling Your Articles

The wonderful thing about magazines is that there are just so many of them. Those 18,000 magazines constitute 18,000 markets for a writer's work.

The terrible thing about magazines is that there are just so many of them. Those 18,000 magazines each have different audiences, different styles, and different voices—and different requirements of their writers.

The trick to selling your short nonfiction to any of these magazines is matching the article to the magazine. In other words, to sell an article to a magazine, writers have to do a little marketing. Now, before you argue that you are a writer and not a marketing professional, consider: The skills you use in marketing your story are not so very different from those you use in everyday life.

Say you're seated at a dinner party next to a woman in an evening gown, high heels, pearls, and a coiffure of perfection. Would you initiate a conversation by leaning her way and inquiring, "Hey, what'dja think about that boxing match on TV last night?" Rather than assuming she's a boxing fan, you'd probably invest a bit of time to learn her interests before plunging into such a conversation.

Yet would-be writers commit such gaffes with magazines every day. They try to sell stories on canoeing to backpacking magazines. They offer fiction to magazines that publish fact. They view themselves as writers whose work will be appreciated by whoever reads it, rather than as someone whose job is to figure out who they're talking with and to tell those people a story they'd be interested in hearing.

Professional magazine writers recognize that magazines are as individual as people are. They hold conversations with their readers every month, discussing their topics of mutual interest in their own style of language. Magazine editors know the people who read their magazines. They know their ages, their sexes, and their incomes. They know what stirs their interests and what bores them. So if you go to the trouble of learning about the magazine and its audience, you improve your chances of joining in its conversation with its readers.

Avoiding Rejection

Most editors expect to be approached professionally by writers. And professional writers do not write 2,000-word feature articles and blindly ship them off to random magazines. Most professionals (at least when they were getting started), first write a letter that proposes a story idea and that proffers themselves as the perfect person to write it—the query letter.

Queries are letters of introduction and sales pitches combined. While your query must explain in some detail what your story will be about, it also must be concise. Editors are busy people, and many figure that if you can't boil the story idea down to a page or so, it probably doesn't have a point.

In theory, querying doesn't sound so hard. But ask editors to describe the actual queries they receive, and you'll most likely hear sorrowful sighs. Many say they often receive what they delicately call "inappropriate" queries. And the single biggest reason for the inappropriateness is a writer's ignorance of their publications. Again and again editors complain that most people who write queries haven't even bothered to read the magazine.

"People haven't taken the time to study the publication to know what we're doing," said J.D. Owen, editor-in-chief of *Boys' Life*. "It's not kid-appropriate; it's too adult. The best advice for anyone wanting to write for us would be to look over some of our issues, see what we're doing and focus in on the kinds of things that are going to ring our chimes."

Understanding the Audience

Knowing who reads the publication is crucial if you want to write for magazines. That's why many magazine writers often don't start by thinking up ideas and then looking for a magazine to suit them. Rather, they study a magazine to devise ideas appropriate to its readers. So, before you submit queries to one magazine or many, do some market research. Here are a few steps to help you:

1. **Analyze the magazine's style.** When reading, don't allow yourself to be swept in by the stories or distracted by the content. Study it to discern the magazine's style—is it light or weighty, serious or flip? How do the features, the longer pieces, differ from the shorter departmental pieces in the front? Does the magazine just report the facts or encourage writers to comment on them? Does it use first-, second-, or third-person accounts, or all of them in different parts of the magazine? Are sidebars typically used? Are experts quoted, or is the author the voice of authority? Who reads this publication, and how does the magazine slant its stories to them? (Information about the audience often can be obtained by requesting a press kit from the magazine, or by looking at the publication's Web site and checking under the "Press" or "Advertiser" sections. This can provide specific demographics on the magazine's primary audience, including age, income, education, etc.)

    It's also a good idea to read more than one issue to get a feel for a magazine's true scope and consistently covered subjects. Take note of how a magazine is divided up—is the front portion dedicated to trends and gossip? How many full-length articles appear in each issue? Does the magazine use a lot of numbers—"8 Steps to a New You," or "12 Tips for Finding Your Soul Mate"? Also pay attention to the tone of the articles—are they playful? Revealing? Serious?

Once you've thoroughly studied a magazine, use what you've learned to shape your query letter and—once you get the assignment—your article.

2. **Read more than just the articles.** Read the table of contents in multiple issues to get ideas of the topics that are covered regularly, and note the angles that are taken for each topic, often explained in subtitles. Look carefully at the ads. Mary asks her students to count and categorize the ads (How many ads for upscale home furnishings? How many for discount stores?) to find out characteristics of its audience. Advertisers research an audience before paying big bucks to buy an ad—and writers can use this information to craft stories targeted to those groups.

Take a look at *Advertising Age*, a trade publication for advertisers, that often runs ads placed by magazines trying to define their readers. *Redbook*, for example, once used an ad called "Mothers & Shakers" that read: "There's no such thing as 'virtual motherhood.' If you're in it, you're on it, 24 hours a day, 7 days a week—at least in your heart. If ever I think I'm losing my balance between the me and the we, there's *Redbook* like a good friend on the other end of my see-saw."

Read trade publications about writing and marketing your writing. *Writer's Digest* is particularly helpful, offering advice on selling to markets and writing techniques.

It's also smart to find out if the magazine you're targeting has an editorial calendar that lists its upcoming themes and subjects. Using such a tool as a guide can help you shape your idea into a salable one.

3. **Find the right theme.** When you market your idea, you're

matching it to the specific target audience of a particular magazine, much like trying to find common ground for conversation with a guest at a dinner party. This usually means finding the right theme, and if you change a theme, you may just change the market for your work. For example, a story on divorce may focus on the theme of obsession for *Cosmopolitan*, on healing for *Parents*, and on commitment for *Guideposts*.

4. **Get the guidelines.** Now that you're really reading magazines, please hold off on writing your query a while yet. First, write to the magazine requesting its writer's guidelines, find them on the magazine's Web site, or check a directory like *Writer's Market* or its online counterpart WritersMarket.com, which offers more than 1,100 magazines' writer's guidelines. These guidelines (think back to the sample markets in chapter two) provide you with critical information, such as what topics the magazine covers, recommended word count, pay rates, which departments are open to freelancers, etc. So, for example, you discover from the guidelines that your dream magazine only excepts articles that average 1,500 words in length. Don't send them an idea for a 3,000-word article and expect them to bend the rules. Also, don't waste your time querying to departments that don't use freelancers—it's a waste of your time and the editor's time.

The guidelines for *Parenting Magazine* point out that the publication is "for mothers of children from birth to 12 and covers both the emotional and practical aspects of parenting." It advises writers to send their queries "to the specific departmental editor." It also stresses that "the best guide for writers is the magazine itself. Please familiarize yourself with it before submitting a query."

Highlights for Children offers very specific guidelines for submitting to its different areas, which include hidden pictures, cartoons, puzzles, etc. For articles, the magazine also stresses that it would rather receive a completed article than a query letter, and that stories should "teach by positive example, rather than preach."

A magazine like *Seventeen*, that bills itself as "a young woman's first fashion and beauty magazine," obviously has a unique focus all its own that smart freelancers will notice. For example, nonfiction articles must average between 1,200 and 2,500 words and are only commissioned after outlines are submitted and approved by the editors.

Such information is invaluable. Use it to mold your proposal to a particular market, or to find a market suited to your idea.

Stringing for Newspapers

Newspapers almost never have enough reporters to cover the stories in their areas, and many, particularly smaller papers, welcome freelancers. In the newspaper business, freelancers are called stringers.

Stringers may write feature stories, but they often begin by reporting on official meetings—school board meetings, town commission meetings, and the like. Some papers publish special sections, written by stringers, and some use feature stories from freelancers. If you want to string for a paper, it helps to have taken at least one journalism course to understand how to report accurately and write fast. A journalism degree will help you be even more qualified and marketable to string for newspapers.

Weekly community newspapers are often the easiest places to begin. But larger metropolitan daily papers also are traditionally understaffed and do hire stringers. To find such a job, write a simple business letter to the managing editor of a larger paper or the editor of a smaller one, asking if they need stringers. You may not have to come up with story ideas yourself, but include one or two if you know the paper hasn't covered them. Mention any writing experience you have and include clips, along with a résumé, and tell them you'll call to follow up if you don't hear anything within a month or so.

When you do call, the first thing to ask is if this is a good time to talk, since deadline pressure precludes phone conversations at certain times. If they need help, the editors will be willing to talk with you or direct you to another editor who handles stringers.

While it may be easier to win a newspaper assignment than one from a magazine, the financial rewards are usually far less. The range is from about $25 per story for small papers to $150 or more at larger ones. But you get more than money by working for a paper. You get published, and your clips can help you land bigger jobs. And if you're lucky, you'll also get a good editor who will work with you and with your copy.

Crafting a Query Letter

Reading the magazine and studying the writer's guidelines are the two biggest favors you can do for yourself before trying to write a story for any magazine. Once you've done those crucial steps, you're ready to craft a query letter.

Queries are one or two pages—editors are notoriously overworked and sensitive to demands on their time, so one page is ideal. They are at once brief and comprehensive—try to give the editor an idea of the breadth of your story, the sources you plan to utilize, and the angle you plan to take. And above all, they are interesting.

Put yourself in the editor's place. It's hard for her to take a chance on an unknown writer, particularly following multiple reports of journalists making up sources or entire stories. And even if a story is accurate, sometimes editors have to work hard to salvage a weak story, creating instead a mediocre story—and missing a chance to get a great story.

That's why your query letter must be an example of your best work. Your writing should be flawless—don't let little errors like spelling or weak sentence structure get in your way. Hook the editor in with a strong lead that arouses interest in the story your proposing—make the editor want to know more. More importantly, make sure that your query letter succinctly explains your idea—nothing's worse than a query letter that loses focus midway through and inadvertently proposes an entirely different topic.

Finally, don't forget to give your article a strong title—something that successfully communicates your unique angle or hook. This will give editors something to hold onto as they consider giving you the assignment.

To cut down on your chances of rejection, you might want to study a book on writing query letters and check out the sample query letters later in this chapter. But certainly consider the following tips:

Focus Your Idea

Think long and think hard about your idea. Perhaps because they lack experience in knowing just how many words it takes to tell stories, some beginning writers have trouble narrowing an idea into a workable notion. This can result in a scattered query that touches on five or six different story ideas without developing any of them, and can leave an editor scratching his head.

Focus is key. It's not enough to say you want to write an article about divorce. When devising your ideas, slice and dice a topic. Focus on an angle, one person in the news, one aspect of a larger debate. What unique angle will you take? What will make your article on divorce different from all those that have come before it? Will it be about surviving divorce? Deciding to get a divorce? Helping children cope with divorce? Understanding the divorce process? How will this article help readers? Why should they bother to read it? If there's no benefit, then the odds of the article getting accepted are slim.

Prove That You've Done Some Homework

No one expects freelancers to research an entire feature before asking an editor if she would be interested in buying it. But you have to know enough to convince an editor you've got a story. Read what your target magazine and similar publications have printed on your topic before querying, and look for a fresh angle. You also might name some of the sources—or at least give their occupations—you plan to contact. Including relevant statistics is another way to prove that you're well versed on your subject matter. For example: "Recent studies indicate that more than x (*insert statistic*) million children in the United States come from divorced families. I plan to talk with at least two noted children's psychiatrists in order to learn about the challenges these children face and what parents can do to help them."

Be Meticulous

Pay attention to spelling, grammar, and punctuation. Several editors say they would make exceptions for Sally Anybody, who made no pretensions about being a writer but who proposed an intriguing personal experience story. But all disapproved of a would-be writer misusing the tools of the trade. While a comma out of place probably won't sink your query, attention to detail is the hallmark of a good writer.

Write to the Right Person

Writer's Market lists the names of editors to query at thousands of publications, but people change jobs frequently. Call to check who should get your query. For example, simply ask the receptionist, "Who should receive a query for a piece in your Parenting Department?" And ask how to spell the editor's name. Or, check the magazine's masthead to stay current on changing positions.

Even if an editor doesn't care if you addressed your query to the wrong person, sending it to the right person makes querying more efficient—the letter is less likely to spend days bouncing from inbox to outbox.

And be careful if you're sending the same query to several magazines. No two magazines are exactly the same. Make sure that even if you're submitting the same idea to multiple magazines, you've tailored your query to make it specific for each publication.

Show Your Style

A query letter must convince the editor that you know how to write for the publication. Pitch the story with grace and verve. If a magazine adopts a particular tone of voice with its readers—a he-man voice for outdoor adventure magazines, for example—use that voice in your query. If the magazine allows different voices in its pages, let your own personality show through. If you've got a great anecdote or a quote, include it. Other writers could probably write the piece, but they might not be able to dig up your golden nuggets.

Sound Confident

If you've done your homework and you know your stuff, you will sound sure of yourself. Sounding confident and professional is a far better way to garner a sale than sounding like a beginner pleading for a break. Tell the editor, "I'll write [not "I hope to write"] about five ways mothers can help their daughters make friends, and keep them."

If you have any other nonwriting qualifications to write a particular story, note them. For a profile on a bookstore owner, for example, mention that you worked your way through college at a Barnes & Noble. If you don't have any relevant experience, don't dwell on it. There's no need to include lines like, "I've never published anything before, but I know I can do it." Let your query letter speak for itself.

Include Clips When Specified

Be sure to check a publication's writer's guidelines before sending clips. Some magazines want them with the query, and some don't. A safe bet is to include a short line at the end of your query saying, "Clips are available upon request."

If the magazine does ask for clips, be sure to use your very best. Some editors recommend sending only those clips that are similar to the article you're proposing. Thus, you should send clips from a children's publication if you want to write for a publication like

Highlights for Children. But others want to see what you've written, regardless of the subject matter. This gives editors a feel for your writing style and signals to them that you can start and finish the job.

If you do send clips, don't forget to include a self-addressed, stamped envelope so the editor can return the clips if he rejects your idea.

Choose Wisely

In the beginning, it may help to aim for small victories as you build your writing résumé. Once you've established yourself as a "published writer" by honing your craft with smaller or regional publications, you'll have an easier time cracking into national magazines.

It's also important to take into consideration that longer feature stories more often go to writers with a long-established working relationship with the publication, simply because a magazine is reluctant to risk $3,000 on an unknown.

So examine the shorter pieces in the magazines that you enjoy reading, and think about what you can offer. The pay will be smaller, the glory is less splendiferous, but it may be the easiest way to break in. Besides, you may be able to complete smaller pieces more quickly and do more of them than longer articles.

Wait Patiently

Waiting for a response can seem like an eternity. And sometimes it is. Writer's guidelines usually specify a standard response time, as well as indicate periods when the publication is closed to submissions. It's usually safe to add an extra month on to the specified response time. This allows for any number of delays, such a backlog at the assigning editor's desk, a sudden staff change that's slowed everything down, an intense debate about whether to buy your piece, etc. Don't get overeager or personally offended if you don't get an immediate response. And don't call the editor angrily demanding an on-the-spot decision about your query—the decision won't be in your favor. If you don't hear back, it's usually best to just move on to another publication. If your curiosity gets the best of you, a short, professional e-mail or letter is the best way to go.

Move Past Rejection

If you do get a rejection letter now and again, don't let it hold you back. Learn from it—even a form rejection can reveal a lot about what a publication wants and needs. If it's a subject you're passionate about, reshape your query letter and send it to a different publication. (Don't, however, try sending the same letter to a different editor at the publication that just rejected you—you'll get a reputation all right, but not the one you want.) Every writer gets rejected throughout his or her career; it's the nature of the business. But you shouldn't let it discourage you.

E-Queries

The number of magazines that accept e-mail queries is growing as more publications find that it saves them time and money. The e-mail format (see a sample e-query on page 201) is beneficial to writers in that it can improve overall response time and make it easier for writers to track their submissions.

The key is to first ascertain how a particular editor or publication prefers to receive electronic submissions, if at all. Some editors may only look at queries and work samples if they arrive neatly packaged as e-mail attachments. Conversely, the fear of viruses causes other editors only to consider queries and samples that arrive as plain text in the body of the e-mail itself.

Another alternative is to send an e-mail query that directs an editor to your personal Web site to view samples of your work. Many writers have found Web sites to be the easiest and most efficient way to showcase their work to prospective clients across the country. Some editors also find it preferable. Others don't.

Just as in print, when it comes to electronic queries you must do your homework to determine the best way to reach a particular editor. (For more information on e-queries, see chapter eleven.)

Querying Checklist

Before sending queries, ask yourself:

- Have I addressed the query to the right person at the magazine, and have I double-checked spellings, particularly of all proper nouns?
- Is my query neatly typed and free of errors?
- Is my idea to the point?
- Have I outlined the story or given at least a good idea of the direction the story will take?
- Have I included sources I have interviewed or plan to interview?
- Do I know which department or section my piece best fits, and have I told the editor?
- Have I included clips that show my talent or specified that they're available upon request?
- Have I noted why I'm the right writer for this story?
- Have I included a self-addressed, stamped envelope to ensure that I get a reply?
- Does my letter note my address, telephone and fax numbers, and e-mail address?
- Have I recorded the query's topic, the date, and the target publication in a log?

The Contract

Congratulations. You've written a query that has earned you an assignment to write for a magazine. Before you start dialing for your first interview, do one final bit of preparation: Read the contract before you sign it.

Good contracts delineate the story idea, the rights you're selling the publisher, the pay, the kill fee—if any—and the due date. Not all magazines use contracts, and those that do may not give so many breaks to the writer.

For more on contracts and protecting your rights, see chapter twelve.

Comments from Michael Embry, executive editor, *Kentucky Monthly*

Mr. Michael Embry
Executive Editor
Kentucky Monthly
P.O. Box 559
Frankfort, KY 40602-0559

Dear Mr. Embry,

Phantoms Don't Drive Sports Cars. Zombies Don't Play Soccer. Frankenstein Doesn't Slam Hockey Pucks. It's a safe bet that most third-grade kids in the country would know that these are some titles in a popular children's book series, The Adventures of the Bailey School Kids. Yet even some of her students and fellow teachers in Lexington don't recognize the name of Marcia Thornton Jones as the author of the popular series.

Catchy lead. It got my attention to read with interest.

Jones and fellow teacher and former Lexingtonian, Debbie Dadey, created The Bailey School Kids after a frustrating day in the classroom. Jones told Dadey that to make her students pay attention, she'd have to grow 10 feet tall, sprout horns and blow smoke out her nose. The two liked the idea so much, they wrote the first Bailey School Kids' first book, *Vampires Don't Wear Polka Dots,* during their lunch breaks. It quickly sold 250,000 copies. Still, they had to work hard to persuade Scholastic Inc., its publisher, that another Bailey School Kids book could be successful. Forty more books have followed.

Good background information about the authors.

The story I propose is a profile about the ebullient Jones, who is a consultant for gifted and talented students in a private school in Lexington, but who still writes a book a month with Dadey, using email. The authors also write two other series for Scholastic, and Jones travels the region as a teacher and speaker about writing.

Writer is specific about proposal —a profile.

Could you please let me know if you are interested in this article? I'm including a SASE and some clips. A former medical reporter, I have written articles for a wide variety of other magazines, including *American Health for Women, Health Management Technology and Curriculum Administrator.* I am currently co-writing a book for F&W Publications, *The Writer's Market Sourcebook.* I also teach journalism at Northern Kentucky University.

Writer provides pertinent information about her writing experience.

Thank you for your consideration.

Sincerely,

Name
Address
Telephone Number

Comments from Linda Vaccariello, senior editor, *Cincinnati Magazine*

Linda Vaccariello
Cincinnati Magazine
One Centennial Plaza
705 Central Ave., Ste. 175
Cincinnati, OH 45202

Dear Ms. Vaccariello,

Very engaging. →

Have you been to Oldenburg, Indiana? I'll take you there.

She knows our format! →

In a proposed 800-1,000 word *Weekend* article, I'll be your readers' guide to this old-fashioned German hamlet a little over an hour's drive from Cincinnati. Settled in 1837 by German Catholic immigrants, Oldenburg retains much of the old country atmosphere and charm, with today's residents still adhering to a founding philosophy of religion, family, and home.

Covers all the high points. →

Religion is integral to Oldenburg's history. There is such a proliferation of churches the community is often identified as the village of spires. The graceful, Gothic church steeples that thrust up through the trees and dominate the landscape will be the focus of my article. Along with quaint shops and restaurants, the spires are the main tourist attraction. Oldenburg is a fun-loving community that hosts a number of bazaars and festivals throughout the year, including a September Oktoberfest and a Christmas event. Community firefighters recently metamorphosed all the fire hydrants into colorful cartoon characters. Streets still designated by their original German names reflect the town's pride in their Teutonic heritage and visitors swear they still sense the pioneer spirit of bygone days. These features will make good sidebars for the article.

Has a track record with us— good! →

I believe cf2Cincinnati Magazinecf1 readers would like to be taken to "this old little town in the valley" in the hills of southeastern Indiana, for there they can find a day's respite from the citified chaos that all too often makes us weary, worried, and longing to escape . . . if for just a little while.

I have published several pieces in *Cincinnati Magazine* under "Ann Herold." Expenses for this article would be $25.00.

Very truly yours,

Address
Telephone Number
E-mail Address

Selling Your Nonfiction Book

An adage among writers is that you do your best work when you're writing what you love. It remains as true today as ever. But there is another truth about writing books today: If you want to find a publisher for your manuscript, you have to understand what will sell, and how to sell it. Simply having an idea that you love is the first step among many that must be taken before your wonderful notion is transformed into a book. This chapter will help you understand the steps to take to bring about that transformation.

Finding a Publisher

Because there are so many publishers, it's essential for writers to research a publishing house before sending in a proposal. Many smaller publishers specialize in certain topics, and, therefore, are limited in what they can accept and publish. Many houses—especially smaller ones—possess a deeply held philosophy of what they will publish, and you, as a potential author, are expected to know it. This is true even for university presses, which, in the face of shrinking budgets and declining library dollars for books, have become more sensitive to bottom-line issues and marketing.

"For writers, it means that they need to study their publishers and know what kind of a book they have," said Henry Y.K. Tom, executive editor of the social sciences division at Johns Hopkins University Press.

"They need to do their homework and be familiar with the lists of different publishers, so that they can identify a short list of possible publishers which are actively publishing the author's subject area."

Other editors echoed this notion. "Every time I get a fiction proposal, I don't bother to open it," said Kirsty Melville, publisher of Ten Speed Press. Her company publishes only nonfiction, and often "offbeat and quirky" nonfiction at that (some of its titles are *How to Be Happy, Dammit* and *What Color Is Your Parachute*). Writers, Melville said, who clearly are familiar with the types of books Ten Speed publishes and can state how their proposed titles fit within the existing line definitely improve their chances of acceptance.

The good news is that it's not that hard to do the research necessary to find the right publisher. Once you've chosen a topic, start looking for existing books that are similar to yours. Which houses are publishing these books? Take a look at a directory like *Writer's Market*, and begin to narrow down your search. Use the Subject Index in the back of the book to help you. For example, if your book has a strong regional angle, focus on "Regional" publishers like Coastal Carolina Press, Bright Mountain Books, or Minnesota Historical Society Press. If you want to write a book that focuses on the environment, then look under "Nature/Environment" for a publishing house that specializes in that subject. By directly targeting publishing houses you know publish your subject, you'll greatly enhance your chances of acceptance.

Once you've identified a specific house, take a look at its current line of books by checking the house's Web site or requesting a catalog. Compare your idea to the house's current line—have they recently covered your topic? If so, how will be yours be different and better? What books are included in the catalog's backlist—the section of the catalog that features the house's older books? Take a look at who the authors are, too—does the catalog feature books by first-time authors? Or do all the authors have multiple books?

At the same time you're evaluating a house's catalog, you also should be examining its writers guidelines (found online, by request, or in a directory like *Writer's Market*). Now, it's time to prepare your submission package.

Make Your Book Competitive

It is crucial for you to research titles similar to the one you plan to write. Doing this type of research before you actually start writing can help you decide what your book needs to cover in order to make it stand out from the pack. For example, take a look at the best-selling competing titles, and ask yourself how your book will be different—how it will be better. If you can't answer this question, then it might be time to ask yourself why you're writing the book at all. Eventually, all of this research will end up in the Competitive Analysis section of your book proposal. (We'll discuss the parts of a proposal shortly.)

It's easy to visit an online bookstore like Amazon.com, type in the title of a competitive book and then sit back and watch the computer pull up similar books. This will allow you to see how the other titles rank in sales. You can even read commentaries from other readers. But it's also useful to head to the library and bookstore to scout the competition. Browsing in a nonvirtual world gives you a look at covers, illustrations, and heft of the books, and it helps you visualize how your book will fit into the mix. You can even chat with bookstore owners about how books on the subject are selling or with the librarian about how often people check out similar titles.

If your topic is weighted down by a whole shelf full of books, don't despair. That may well be a good thing—it proves that editors believe many people are interested in reading about that topic.

When author Janice Papolos was preparing her book proposal for *The Virgin Homeowner* (see the proposal on page 117), she went to the *Books in Print* resource. She found that other books for new homeowners were massive, door-stopper books that advised readers how to haul out expensive tools to fix everything from the basement floor to the roof. Each had been reprinted multiple times. That, she believed, proved there was a strong market, an ever-renewing, reading populace.

She also knew her book would be different from other books on the market because it wasn't designed to show people how to fix things. Instead, it would be a fun and humorous book about her experiences learning about tending her house after living in apartments, her discovery of the meaning of such peculiar terminology as "flashing" and "phlange," and her realization of why it's important to know such things.

"I like to say there are 3,000 components to a house and I was clueless about 2,999 of them," she says. "I thought my boiler had a higher IQ than I did." But she learned important things about owning a house and worked this notion into a theme of her book that would appeal to readers—what you don't know can hurt you. Her proposal worked—*The Virgin Homeowner* was published by W.W. Norton & Co. in 1997, and it's still available today.

Crafting a Book Query Letter

Seldom will an editor read an entire unsolicited manuscript. Many won't accept unsolicited material of any kind. Even if a publisher does, it's often an editorial assistant or an intern who wades into the "slush pile" to read it. Agents can help by smoothing the way for writers by contacting editors they have worked with and whose tastes they understand, transforming the material from unsolicited to solicited.

It's your decision whether to approach an editor or an agent first, or simultaneously (see "Do You Need an Agent?" on page 110). But thankfully, both are looking for the same things: a fresh idea, evidence that you know your material, and an indication that you are the right person to write this book.

The best way to first approach an agent or editor is often with a query letter. As we learned earlier, queries are brief letters selling your idea and yourself. Aim for one page that piques the reader's interest. Mention the title of your book and explain what it is about, who its audience would be, and why they'd be interested in reading it. If you've drafted your first chapter, its lead might work as the first paragraph in your query. Also include a paragraph of your writing credentials and your expertise.

A word about voice: Allow your voice in the letter to display the same enthusiasm as it does when you're talking with friends about your book. Agents and editors like writers who believe their books are wonderful, but they dislike being told, "This will be a bestseller." Impart your ardor for your work more subtly.

If you decide to query an editor, try to find out who would be the right one for your book by reading the acknowledgments in similar books. Authors often thank their editors there. If they don't, call the publisher's publicity department to find out who edits books on your topic. You also can scan *Writer's Market* and read publications like *Writer's Digest* for mentions of specific editors.

Next, carefully research each possibility by learning more about the individual publishing houses. Check their Web sites for author lists and forthcoming titles. After your research is complete, follow each publishing house's submission guidelines (available by calling, online, or in a directory like *Writer's Market*), and submit your query letter.

To contact an agent, try the *Guide to Literary Agents* or online sites for organizations like the Association of Author's Representative (see the resource list on page 116). It may be more difficult to find an agent, so persistence is key. (For more information on agents, see chapter eight.)

And remember that all editors and agents are individuals. What strikes one as tired and derivative may strike another as a perfect entrant for a hot market. So if your query is rejected but you believe in it, don't hesitate to send it to someone else on your list. You can't consider one editor's opinion the only valid opinion.

It should go without saying that the query letter should be typed, free of errors, clean, and polite—but editors and agents agree that this, nevertheless, must be said. (One agent even pointed out how unpleasant it is to open an envelope that reeks of cigarette smoke.) So check, double-check, proofread, and have your spouse or best friend proofread to make sure the letter is perfect before you send it out. Otherwise, it will be a waste of your time.

End your query by asking the agent or editor if he would be interested in seeing more. Always include a self-addressed, stamped envelope for reply. But don't mail that letter just yet. The agent or editor could give you a happy answer: "We love it. Send in the proposal," and writing one of those requires a lot more work. If you

Do You Need an Agent?

While some publishers listed in the *Writer's Market* note that they accept material from writers who don't have agents, many editors prefer to work with agents who understand their house's needs and their own tastes.

"I think there's always a way for a talented writer to get published," said Tracy Carns, publishing director of the Overlook Press. But she advised beginning writers—especially those interested in working with larger publishing houses—to first find an agent. "This is a business of relationships," she said, "and agents have a relationship with the editor and publisher. They know what we like." She said she is far more likely to read first a proposal sent by a trusted agent than a cold submission. "I'll obviously look at everything, but not all submissions are created equal. Selling a manuscript is a specialized skill. That's what agents do. Why should a writer be expected to do that? You don't take out your own appendix. If you're a writer, you should write."

For each of the thirty books she acquires each year, Carns said she would rather deal with an agent. "If I'm going to deal on a business point, a financial point, it's good to have that professional intermediary."

Agent Kimberley Cameron noted that one author had who recently approached her kept a list of fifty to sixty publishers who had rejected his submissions, about 90 percent of whom simply said they don't read unsolicited manuscripts. "Maybe 10 percent did read it, but they still rejected him because the agent is the screening process," Cameron said. "That's what we do."

You can find lists of agents in many books and on the Internet (see the resource list on page 114). If you're worried about unscrupulous agents, note that the *Literary Market Place*, perhaps the most useful resource book for publishing, requires agents to submit letters of recommendation before they can be listed.

The Association of Authors' Representatives sets high criteria for those who may join its ranks, requiring them, among other things, to agree to abide by a Canon of Ethics. Its Web site (www.aar-online.org) also lists questions to ask any agent interested in representing you.

You can also meet agents (and editors) at writers conferences, excellent places to decide whether you'd make good partners.

don't have it ready to send out, then don't pretend like you do—that could lead to trouble.

Crafting a Book Proposal

Book proposals usually aren't something to dash off in a day or two. They can take months to write if you do a thorough job of researching. Some beginners might find it easier to simply write the book first, then use it to prepare a proposal—which editors say is not a bad notion since they want to be assured an unknown writer can produce an entire book before committing their house to the manuscript. However, doing the proposal first can give you a better idea of what your book needs to include in order to make it stand apart from other similar titles.

There isn't one right way to write a nonfiction book proposal, just as there is no one right way to write a book. That said, here are some guidelines: A proposal usually averages thirty pages or more. It contains a table of contents, an overview with a breakdown of potential markets, a competitive analysis section, an about the author section, a promotional plan, a detailed outline of what will be in each chapter, and two or three sample chapters. But keep in mind, the organization sometimes varies. Regardless, it should be concise, written in active voice, and generally in third person, regardless of the point of view used in the book itself.

The Table of Contents
The table of contents for your proposal should list what you've included in your submission. Each section of your proposal should start on its own page, so it's fairly easy to draft a useful table of contents for an agent or editor to follow as she reads through your proposal.

The Overview
The overview includes a strong title, a detailed description of what you plan to write, why it's important, who would want to read it, how it differs from other books on the market, how you'll research it, an

estimated length of the finished book, how long you'll take to write it (usually a year or less), and a description of illustrations, appendices, and other backmatter.

Spend time thinking of a good title for your book. It should intrigue and inform. Consider carefully who your readers will be and research them. Whether your book is for new parents or dog owners, find out how many of these people there are, because the more there are, the better your chances of selling your book.

The Competitive Analysis

While it's important for you to know what competition you are facing and how you can make your book unique, you also must convince an agent, an editor, and a publishing house of the same. Thus, the need for the competitive analysis section of your book proposal.

You basically are trying to allay an editor's fears about the inevitable competition that your book will face in the marketplace. You want him to be comfortable about bringing your title to print. Your skill at assessing the competition should show the editor that you are an expert in your chosen subject, that you are professional in your approach, and that you've found a fresh angle on the subject.

Begin with a short overview of the genre or category into which your book will fit. Show how the category is performing in general. Next, analyze no more than five leading competitors, looking at how those books have sold and why your title will sell. Don't bother to analyze out-of-print titles, self-published books, scholarly tomes or professional books. Editors are only concerned about the titles that will compete with your book in the consumer marketplace.

Formatting is similar to the rest of your proposal. Write concisely so that this section is no more than a couple pages. Whatever you do, avoid speaking poorly of the competition. It scores no points with editors, and it may backfire. Who knows? The person who reads your proposal may have edited one or more of the books you cite, or he may know the author.

You want to focus on how your book will be more timely, more comprehensive, and more up-to-date than those that have come before. Remember, all of this has to be backed up by the rest of your proposal. If you think your book will be better written or have more commercial appeal, your proposal must show how.

The About the Author Section

The about the author section of your proposal should tell an agent or editor why you're the right person to write this book. Go into detail about your experience and training, and stress any professional connections that may help you write and promote the book—for example, you're the leader of an organization that deals in some way with your subject matter. Also, even though you're writing about yourself here, this section should still be written in the third person.

The Promotional Plan

The promotional plan is the place to list what you plan to do to promote your book and ensure that it sells. For example, are you planning to speak at trade shows or conferences? Can you hold workshops that will help sell the book? (See chapter thirteen for tips on promotion.)

The Outline

The outline should be like a detailed table of contents of the book. Some experts advise condensing each chapter to a page or so. Michael Larsen, an agent and author of *How to Write a Book Proposal*, recommends a line of outline for every page of text in each chapter, so a twenty-page chapter would get twenty lines of summation. Note, however, that the chapter outline for *The Virgin Homeowner* (see page 117) provides sketchy, but catchy, lists for each chapter. In this proposal, the preface, which she submitted with the proposal, supplies more information about what the book will contain and how readers can use it.

The Sample Chapters

Finally, sample chapters should prove that you know how to research and write. These are critically important, so don't send rough drafts, and choose chapters that are representative of the content and style of the whole book. (Keep in mind that in most cases, it's best to send the first three chapters, so make sure those are especially strong.) Editors and agents will be looking for good writing, evidence of research, and your ability to keep readers interested.

Before You Send It Out

Before you send your proposal—with a stamped, self-addressed envelope so that it can be returned—keep in mind that agents and editors read all day. Anything you can do to make your letters and manuscripts easier on the eyes makes them more appealing.

- Don't type on both sides of the page.
- Do use standard fonts like Times New Roman.
- Do use wide margins of about 1½ inches.
- Do number the pages.
- Don't bind anything in your proposal.
- Do start each section of your proposal on a new page.
- Do double space the chapters, but single space the other parts of the proposal.
- Do triple-check the spelling of the editor's or agent's name one last time before you drop it in the mailbox.

Remember one last cliché about the publishing business: Even brilliant writers are rejected by publishers; some of them are even rejected several times. Some writers learn to appreciate rejection. If an editor tells you why she rejects your book proposal, don't let it crush you—let it teach you how to make it better. Then send it out to the next person on your list. Remember as you mail it off that as much as you hope to find a publisher for your beloved book, publishers are hoping to find a book they would love to publish.

Resources for Putting Together Your Proposal

Use the following books, organizations, and Web sites (many of which are referred to within this chapter), to help you put together a dynamic and salable book proposal.

Books

The following books can help you concept and develop the different aspects of your nonfiction book proposal:

Formatting & Submitting Your Manuscript, 2nd edition (Writer's Digest Books), by Cynthia Laufenberg and the Editors of Writer's Digest Books. Not sure how to put together your proposal package? Using dozens of real-life examples, this book tells you how.

Guide to Literary Agents (Writer's Digest Books), edited by Kathryn S. Brogan. This annual book by the editor of Writer's Market provides the most up-to-date information on literary agents, including their contact information, response time, submission guidelines, etc.

How to Get Happily Published (HarperCollins Publishers), by Judith Appelbaum. This book provides an informative overview of how to get your book published, including information on self-publishing.

How to Write a Book Proposal, 3rd edition (Writer's Digest Books), by Michael Larsen. This book covers every aspect of researching, writing, and submitting a nonfiction book proposal. Several sample proposals also are included and explained.

How to Write Irresistible Query Letters (Writer's Digest Books), by Lisa Collier Cool. The author uses her experience as a literary agent to tell you how to craft an attention-getting query letter.

International Directory of Little Magazines and Small Presses (Dustbooks), edited by Len Fulton. This annually updated reference includes contact information and submission guidelines for more than five thousand presses and journals.

Literary Agents: What They Do, How They Do it, and How to Find and Work with the Right One for You: Revised and Expanded (John Wiley & Sons), by Michael Larsen. As a nonfiction literary agent and author, Larsen shares his expertise on the ins and outs of getting an agent.

Nonfiction Book Proposals Anybody Can Write: How to Get a Contract and an Advance Before Writing Your Book (Blue Heron Publishing), by Elizabeth Lyon. This book includes the basics on how to put together a winning proposal.

Writer's Market (Writer's Digest Books), edited by Kathryn S. Brogan. This annually updated resource lists more than eight thousand book and magazine editors and their guidelines.

Organizations

The following organizations can provide you with additional guidance and resources as you prepare your proposal:

Association of American University Presses: www.aaupnet.org. This organization offers multiple resources about scholarly publishing including online discussion lists and a directory of presses. For more information, write to 71 W. 23rd St., Suite 901, New York, NY 10010, or call (212) 989-1010.

Association of Authors' Representatives: www.aar-online.org. Authors looking for an agent can search its member database. It also offers suggestions for topics you may want to discuss once you have found an agent. Contact the organization at P.O. Box 237201, Ansonia Station, New York, NY 10003, or call (212) 252-3695.

Web Sites

The Web sites listed here all include helpful information on crafting proposals:

Bookwire: www.bookwire.com. A comprehensive site about book publishing with good links to other useful sites.

Writers' Federation of Nova Scotia: www.writers.ns.ca. Advice on writing a nonfiction book proposal.

Writers Net: www.writers.net. Offers an online directory of literary agents along with advice for writers.

Publishers' Catalogues: www.lights.com/publisher. Lists catalogs of publishers everywhere.

Comments from
Literary Agent
Donna Downing.

THE VIRGIN HOMEOWNER

The Essential Guide to Owning, Maintaining

and Surviving Your First Home

BY JANICE PAPOLOS

We clearly know
what to except in
this proposal.

Proposal Table of Contents

- Concept, Style and Marketing Outline

- The Virgin Homeowner Table of Contents

- Annotated Table of Contents

- Preface to The Virgin Homeowner

- Sample 1: The Sorcerer's Apprentice: Or, Water, Water
  Everywhere (not reprinted here)

- Sample 2: Creosote is a Dirty Word (not reprinted here)

At least two sam-
ple chapters are a
must. (Please note,
chapters are not
reprinted here.)

CHAPTER 7 SELLING YOUR NONFICTION BOOK

THE VIRGIN HOMEOWNER

Overview

It is still the American dream to own a home, and according to the National Association of Realtors, home sales are surging to a fourteen-year high. Last year, some 4.2 million currently existing houses were sold in this country, and some 1,285,000 new houses were built.

For the first-time homeowner, however, understanding how a house works to keep you warm, supply your shower with hot water, and funnel all the unmentionables to leaching fields can be downright mystifying. Maintaining a house is a whole other problem. Once everyone's shaken your hand at the closing, who clues you in on everything that needs to be done? Years ago families lived within close distance of each other, and a parent or older sibling could come over and educate their novice homeowner. Today, we live in a very mobile society, and often the only resources lie between the pages of books.

The Style

All of the books currently on the market are written by men—men who are engineers or who could claim Bob Vila as kin. They are useful as references, but are dry and impersonal, written in a sort of medical-text style. None of them deal with the welter of feelings and insecurities that are aroused as you go through the first year or two with a new home.

The Virgin Homeowner differs from anything on the market because it will be written with humor, insight, and depth by a woman who actually is (or recently was) a virgin homeowner.

I haven't forgotten how frightening and confusing it is to make that transition from apartment renter to mistress of a house, and also how short your attention span is as you deal with the excitement and anxiety of this very major purchase, the move, and the change in lifestyle. Therefore, my goal would be to make the book lively and engaging, anecdotal and sympathetic. Just as Dr. Spock sits on the nursery shelf offering knowledge and comfort to fledgling parents, I expect *The Virgin Homeowner* will sit within easy reach of a new homeowner and educate with a light and memorable touch.

The Format

The book will be approximately 250 pages and chock-full of facts and rich stories of life on the new-home front. It will be fully indexed and include a number of elegant line drawings and humorous cartoons. Sidebar and boxed material will be included for easy reference, at-a-glance information.

In order to broaden the scope of the book and to add other voices and perspectives, I am scheduling focus groups with other new homeowners in

---

Sidebar annotations (left margin):

Proves that the market is growing. It's essential to prove how large the potential market is-and why this book is needed

Key difference with this book vs. the competition.

Any data ti support that women are making more family decisions (auto or home purchases)? Also, women make more purchases on the Internet (especially books).

All these words appeal to women.

This author gives an exact picture of what he finished book will look like-very impressive-she's done her homework.

Paplos/Homeowner Proposal

this area. I am a member of "New Neighbors of Westport," so my organization would help identify other "virgins" who could share their experiences. I also intend to interview men and women in California, Arizona, North Carolina, Wisconsin, and Vermont so that the book reflects regional specifics and concerns.

Among the accomplished craftsmen I intend to interview are: Americo Renzulli (the plumber featured in Martha Stewart's *This New Old House*); Jim Locke, author of *The Well-Built House* and owner of Apple Corps Construction; Don Fredriksson, author of *The Complete House Inspection Book*; and Duane Johnson, columnist for *The Family Handyman* magazine. A few of these preliminary interviews confirmed that anxiety and hysteria are pandemic among the first-time homeowner population and that there's a real need for this book.

The Competition

The books currently on the market are encyclopedic in their approach. Two of the best and most popular are *The New York Times Season-to-Season Guide to Home Maintenance* by John Warde and *The Better Homes and Garden Complete Guide to Home Repair, Maintenance and Improvement*. Both of these books run about 500 pages in length and teach the homeowner how to insulate his or her attic entrance as well as how to repaint crumbling brickwork, repair the roofing, and change toilets in the bathrooms. New homeowners, and particularly a majority of women, cannot—at this point—quite picture themselves in those scenarios. The Better Homes and Garden book was originally published in 1980, and is currently in its fifteenth printing.

Consumer Reports publishes *Year-Round House Care* by Graham Blackburn. It was originally published under another title in 1981 and revised in 1991. In April of '92 it had a second printing. This book is straightforward and helpful. I ordered it from *Consumer Reports* after reading its title in *Books in Print*. I have never seen it in a bookstore.

Two books with a different focus bear mentioning. They are Sunset Publishing Corporation's *Sunset Home Repair Handbook* and Henry Holt's *How Things Work in Your Home*. The Sunset book is 185 pages long and now in its ninth printing. Unfortunately, some very clearly written information is tucked amid many projects that are quite beyond the scope of many homeowners, especially first-timers. *How Things Work in Your Home* is beautifully written and illustrated. It covers the systems of a house, but its major emphasis is on the appliances used in a home—from vacuums to coffee makers to chain saws. This is a *Time-Life* revised edition that had five printings in hardcover and is currently in its fourth printing in trade paperback.

Important to include a cross section of homeowners.

Expert reinforcement-reminds reader of the need for this book

It's important to say how your book is better than the competition without being condescending to those other books.

There's a fine line between proving that other books in the category are succeeding, and the market seeming saturated-well-done here.

CHAPTER 7 SELLING YOUR NONFICTION BOOK

Paplos/Homeowner Proposal

Markets

This is the place for your marketing ideas and/or contacts. You are offering ideas and suggestions to the publisher's marketing department, which is becoming more of a powerful decision-making force in acquisitions.

While every bookstore has a "Home" section, and *The Virgin Homeowner* would fit easily within this niche, the book would also make a natural gift. There are many catalogs that target the homeowner, and a picture and description in the pages of Paragon, Lillian Vernon, The Safety Zone, Seasons, etc., would reach millions of people—first-timers and the people who know them.

Another excellent market would be the several hundred Home Depots and 800 Sears stores across the nation. The first thing my husband and I did after our closing was to drive to Home Depot, and this store or a Sears is an excellent place to come face-to-face with *The Virgin Homeowner.*

Surely one of the best markets for this book is the realty business. Professional realtors are the very people who can identify first-time homeowners and who almost always buy them gifts after the closing. Therefore, it seems a custom fit for a large national franchise corporation such as Century 21 to purchase this book in quantity and distribute it to its more than 5,000 offices across the country.

The National Association of Realtors (NAR) has over 800,000 members, and the organization publishes a monthly magazine called *Real Estate Today.* An ad in its pages would reach an impressive number of realtors quite handily.

Don't forget to include an About the Author section.

Another possible outlet would be a flyer distributed through Welcome Wagons of America. Typically, new homeowners call this organization and a representative comes to the home with all kinds of pamphlets and gifts to help them get settled in their home and community (I found my chimney sweep and handyman through Welcome Wagon).

Time Frame

Should be no more than one year.

I am currently researching and writing the book, and it should take about ten months to complete the manuscript.

She's clearly thought this through completely. there is little left to speculation.

Catchy phrases and chapter titles prove this will not be a dry reference manual. We get a good sense of her intelligent humor!

TABLE OF CONTENTS

Preface
Acknowledgments
"But First, a Word About Money..."
1. What I Should Have Learned From the Home Inspection
2. The Inner Mysteries: Heating and Electrical and Plumbing Systems
3. To Ridex or Not to Ridex: You and Your Septic System
4. Creosote is a Dirty Word
5. Ventilation is the Name of the Game
6. The Sorcerer's Apprentice: Or, Water, Water Everywhere
7. Where Has All the Gravel Gone? Driveways, Pathways, and Parking Areas
8. The Uninvited Guest I: Ants, Subterranean Termites, and Other Creepy Crawlies
9. The Uninvited Guest II: Security Systems and Burglary Alarms
10. The Healthy House
11. The Age of Innocence: Childproofing a Home
12. Finally Home

Appendices
• The "On-Track" Calendar
• House Doctors Directory
• Paint Palette Page (or: How Can We Touch Up That Room If We Can't
• Remember What We Used?)
• Notes of a New Homeowner
• Bibliography
• Indexes

ANNOTATED TABLE OF CONTENTS

1. **What I Should Have Learned From the Home Inspection.** The future was in front of me, and I took lunch orders instead; what does the inspection accomplish? How do you find a reputable inspector? The inspector as teacher; your role as student, check-list of prepared questions, how to read and understand the report, follow-up on the recommendations; an "Inspection Follow-Up Page" that lets the reader extrapolate the recommendations, notate them in this book, and check them off when attended to, the radon report.

2. **The Inner Mysteries: Heating and Electrical and Plumbing Systems.** Thank God I got a service contract! Anatomy of a heating system, ducted or gravity: gas-or-oil-fired furnaces, hot water/forced hot air, radiant heat, heat pumps, solar, electric, the pluses and minuses of each one; servicing each system before the heating season, how to reset a furnace, how I overcame my fear of bleeding radiators, budget plans, Move Over Sharon Stone! How I Failed to Flag My Fuel Line, Let the Snow Plower Bury It Beneath a Mountain of Ice, and How I Had to Attack It All Morning With Ice Picks Because We'd Run Out of Oil. Discussion of flagging methods. Anatomy of the water supply system, how to locate the main shut-off valve, hot water heaters, understanding a well, drips and running toilets and other things that drive you crazy, when to turn the garden water supply off so the pipes don't freeze.

3. **To Ridex or Not to Ridex: You and Your Septic System.** The World Beneath Our Feet: Anatomy of a septic system and leaching fields, the fascinating work of bacteria and the filtration of viruses, pump-out maintenance, the argument over a monthly treatment with Ridex

4. **Creosote is a Dirty Word.** What is creosote and why is everyone saying such terrible things about it? The anatomy of a fireplace, how do you find a chimney sweep and what does he or she do? How my friend Marshall does the job himself. How to build a fire that would make a boy scout weep.

Again, the challenge here is to keep this material interesting to the reader-give us ideas we can relate to. You don't need to much detail in the chapter outline

5. **Ventilation is the Name of the Game.** Why do I keep hearing about this concept and what are those holes in the side and roof of my house? How proper ventilation protects your house and performs the important functions of comfort control and moisture control, passive ventilation: gable ridge roof, soffit vents, and turbine vents, electric attic fans opening and closing vents in the crawlspace, cleaning vents.

6. **The Sorcerer's Apprentice: Or, Water, Water Everywhere.** Anatomy of a roof, the impregnation of shingles, how the roof might let you down and leak, "Is There a Problem with Your Flashing?" Guttertalk, Damn Those Ice Dams, locating the leak and getting it fixed, water in the basement: sump pumps, cracks in the foundation, regrading around the foundation.

7. **Where Has All the Gravel Gone? Driveways, Pathways, and Parking Areas.** Reviving gravel after the winter, repairing cracks and holes in blacktop, driveway sealers, costs.

8. **The Uninvited Guest I: Ants, Subterranean Termites, and Other Creepy Crawlies.** How to tell who's visiting (diagnosing diagrams), the best defense systems, how to find professionals to deal with the problem, discussion of yearly service contracts.

9. **The Uninvited Guest II: Security Systems and Burglary Alarms.** The "False Step" and other early-warning systems, your options other than a full-scale moat, how long do they take to install? How much do they cost? Safety Tips if You Go Away.

10. **The Healthy House.** Environmental concerns: radon, asbestos, lead, water quality; discussion of toxic materials and outgassing, carbon monoxide and alarms that detect its presence.

11. **The Age of Innocence: Childproofing a Home.** Modifying the environment, gates, cords, wires, electrical shields, hazardous household products, and plants, the 1 and ⅜" diameter test, the high toll of untempered glass, Are Glass Coffee Tables in the Picture? Safety Tips in the Kitchen and Bathroom, A Safer Out-of-Doors, Check Chart.

12. **Finally Home.** A psychological look at the moving and the new homeowner experience: interviews with other "virgins," what concerned them, what parts of the process they found overwhelming, how they got comfortable with their new role in life, and how they put down roots in their new communities.

Gives us a good sense of how the book will read—her voice comes through, and it's warm and reassuring.

PREFACE

In 1993, after the birth of our second child, and after living in New York City apartments for over twenty years, my husband and I joined the grown-up world and bought a house. While every now and then funny and disastrous scenes from "The Money Pit," "Mr. Blandings Builds His Dream House," and "Baby Boom" would surface to conscious levels, we tamped them down with assurances to ourselves that these were merely Hollywood's comedic exaggerations. We were so busy figuring out how to finance the house and negotiate this major move—physically and emotionally—we had little energy left to figure out the mysterious workings of a house and what our part would be in maintaining it. As I look back now, I am stunned that I didn't know what a new homeowner was supposed to do, not only to keep the house comfortable and running economically, but to keep disaster from coming in from every crack and crevice! I think I thought it would all sort itself out gradually while we found our sea legs and got more comfortable in our new surroundings.

Not likely! There is no honeymoon with a house. There are things we should have been learning and doing right from the time of the inspection, that would have resulted in less mishap and panic-filled moments.

Part of the problem was that I had this mystified awe of the house. I swear, there were times (thankfully rare) when I viewed it as more intelligent and more powerful than we were. And while I'm in a confessional mode: There was a time or two in which I felt the house was being downright vindictive. (If you own your own home, you may understand this paranoid fantasy.)

Little by little, though, we began to learn from the plumber, the electrician, and the oil burner service men. And our friends. I kept bumping up against new vocabulary and concepts like "flashing," "creosote," and "ventilation." Since I thought flashing had something to do with elderly gentlemen in raincoats, and I'm still a little unsure as to why my furnace is not breathing enough oxygen, I'm afraid we were rather amusing to our house "doctors."

One day, while sitting in front of the fireplace I had fortunately found out I was supposed to have cleaned (see chapter five, "Creosote is a Dirty Word"), I sighed and said to my husband, Demitri: "Somebody should write a book for the virgin homeowner." He laughed and pointed a finger my way.

All right, I thought. Let me look into it. Gingerly, I broached the subject with friends and family. They were amused and enthusiastic and proceeded immediately to tell me all the funny and perilous situations they had encountered—and survived—as first-time homeowners. It turns out that none of us are very enlightened. And we're all so very anxious.

So that's what these pages are all about: helping new homeowners level the playing field, so to speak, and become knowledgeable about and comfortable with their new habitat. Even if you haven't been lucky enough to have inherited the "Bob Vila" gene for home repair, my objective in this book is to prove to you that taking care of a house does indeed fall under the category of "totally do-able." (After all, this is all coming from a woman whose greatest victory on the mechanical front prior to owning a home was the successful changing of a halogen lightbulb!)

How to Use This Book

In the best of all possible worlds, readers would come across this book just before they begin house hunting. Starting with "What I Should Have Learned From the Home Inspection," they could read it straight through and tour all potential homes with an informed and educated eye. Then, when the right house appears, they could choose the right home inspector and do a bang-up job at the home inspection. Weeks later, and after the moving van departs, they would be comfortable with the systems of a house and clued into its maintenance routines.

But life doesn't work like that. Many of you will pick this book up in the hectic days just before the move or some months into your adventures on the domestic frontier. The ungodly time crunch of this settling-in period may not afford your reading every word from beginning to end, in one or two sittings. So let me highlight some of the important safety issues you need to take care of first.

Before you spend a night (or another night) in your new home, make sure you have working smoke detectors in all the right places and an emergency plan for escape in the event of a fire (read pages 00–00) and install two carbon monoxide detectors (see page 00 of "The Healthy House"). If your chimney doesn't have a chimney cap, call a chimney sweep and have one made for it without delay (see page 00 of "Creosote is a Dirty Word"). Have the chimney checked and cleaned at the same time. Then make sure all heating equipment is tuned-up and checked before the start of the heating season (read about this on pages 00 to 00).

If you have municipal water and didn't have your water tested for lead during the home inspection, run a test according to the directions in chapter ten, "The Healthy House," and while you're open to that section, scan the elements of a healthy, nontoxic home so that you make informed decisions when choosing paints and any new furnishings. And by all means, if you've got a toddler or two, read "The Age of Innocence" and secure windows and stairways, check the automatic garage doors, and order any other safety paraphernalia before you even think of letting your little roadrunners loose in their new and unfamiliar environment. (And while you're checking doors and windows, make sure that they're are providing the appropriate level of physical security as discussed in the first half of chapter nine, "The Uninvited Guest II.")

Once you're all relatively safe and sound, familiarize yourself with the major systems of your house by reading chapters two, three, and four. This way, if the circuit breaker trips, a fuse blows, or a leak develops there'll be no cause for panic. You'll also understand what a delicate flower your septic system is and how best to keep it healthy.

And if—when all the chaos subsides—you get hit with a bit of "Post-Parting Depression" and keenly miss your friends and former lifestyle, I hope that the last chapter, "Finally Home" is heartening as well as helpful as you go through the emotional experience of turning a house into a home and carving out a niche for yourself in a new community.

So sit down on your packing boxes, or in a corner of your probably underfurnished new home, and delve into this volume. Then get ready to appreciate what a marvelous facility a house is. Think of it. Physics and chemistry and electricity combine to give you and your loved ones shelter, warmth, comfort, and convenience... A house is a goodly thing. You keep the house; the house will keep you.

But First a Word About Money ...

Before we begin, let me say a few words about the eye-popping estimates for home repairs you're going to see scattered throughout this text. They may be a bit on the high side because many of them are quotes from a metropolitan area, but house repairs are not cheap, not in Arizona, not in Alabama. As my friend David Wright from the tiny town of Edenton, North Carolina likes to say, "My house accepts contributions only in denominations of one hundred dollar bills."

So, accepting that home repairs are expensive and that they're a fact of life, we need to ask ourselves two questions: How much money do we need to have in reserve to pay for annual repairs and maintenance, and,—here's the biggie—where is all this money coming from?

Much depends of course on how old and needy the house is when you move in. If you know the roof is going to have to be replaced in five years and the quote was $6,000 for the job, you've got some serious saving to do. If the old oil tank has to be excavated and a new one installed in your basement, start scanning the horizon for that $3,000 now. Beyond the imminent projects you already know about, are the miscellaneous repairs that crop up all the time. They may always be different, but you can count on them to occur. As my mother is fond of saying, "Once you own a house, you'll never have to wonder where your next nickel is going."

I spoke with Elizabeth Lewin, author of Your Personal Financial Fitness Program (Facts on File), and she told me that, depending on the age and location of the house, a homeowner should budget between 1 and 2 percent of the value of the house for major annual home repairs (a new roof, a driveway repaving, the curing of a leaky basement, the outdoor paint job, falling trees that don't hit the insured roof and so the homeowner pays for their removal, and other major repairs). Ouch! This easily translates to a couple of thousand dollars a year, and with mortgages, monthly bills, 401 (K) contributions, college savings plans, and crooked little teeth to straighten, what is a homeowner to do (besides pray avidly)?

Elizabeth suggests a more rational approach. She advises that a homeowner set up a savings account marked "House Reserve" and make a fairly frequent, routine deposit into it. For example, when you pay your mortgage, make a deposit in the house account. A money market account or short-term mutual bond fund (money could be automatically withdrawn from your checking account monthly for this) are other ways to save. Eventually you'll build up a nice little nest egg for your nest egg.

Elizabeth Lewin made a point to say that very new homeowners (she laughed and called them "extra virgin" homeowners) will probably not establish this savings account in the first months or year of homeownership. There are just too many set-up costs to allow much savings to take place.

Somehow we all manage, and you won't be the exception, but there's definitely a period of adjustment while you figure out where to spend less money in some areas because you have a big, new, superhungry category called "The House." Try to strike a balance where you don't deprive yourself, but you don't get caught out by a total lack of planning.

You know, sometimes the house serves as a goad or a motivator, even, and you just might find more economic opportunities coming your way because you are more focused and you simply have to create them in order to feed your house.

Bring it all together. ←

Once you adjust your thinking and begin to enjoy your home, the pride of ownership will make taking care of it more of a tonic and less of a bitter pill. This is your corner of the world now. Tend it well. And remember, the house and its maintenance and repairs and improvement are just a transferring of assets. What you give out, will come back to you.

CHAPTER 7 SELLING YOUR NONFICTION BOOK

CHAPTER EIGHT

Selling Your Fiction

After ten years of writing, Janet Evanovich decided to get serious about getting published. She had three novels written, all of which "had been sent to and rejected by a seemingly endless round of publishing houses and agents," she said. So she decided to abandon those projects—"big, bizarre books"—and try her hand at genre writing. Her first effort was rejected, but the second manuscript was accepted, and she was on her way to becoming the best-selling author of the Stephanie Plum mystery series. Rather than viewing the similarities of genre fiction as restrictions against creativity, Evanovich saw them more as the parameters of publication, and now her books regularly debut at the top of the best-seller lists.

Science fiction writer Walter C. Hunt waited fourteen years for his novel, *The Dark Wing*, to see publication. Written in the late 1980s, the book was sent to several speculative fiction houses—Ace, Baen, Warner, and others—and rejected, usually because the timing was wrong. "We like it the book, but it isn't what we're doing right now," was a frequent comment from editors. But Hunt's patience paid off. "I waited fourteen years for the same editor to get a position at science fiction publisher Tor books," he said. *The Dark Wing* was published in 2001, followed by *The Dark Path* in 2003, and Hunt has finally found his readership.

As both Evanovich's and Hunt's experiences demonstrate, there are few straight paths to getting your fiction published. The process is fraught with circumstances a writer cannot control. Editors change publishing houses. A short story from the slush pile too closely resembles another one just acquired. Imprints fold. Editorial focus changes. All of these circumstances and more can conspire to keep a manuscript from finding an editorial home. To increase your likelihood of success (publication!) it is important that you focus on the elements of the process a writer can control—the mechanics of fiction submission.

Selling Your Short Stories

As you probably know, the competition for publishing short fiction is fierce, and the days when a fiction writer could earn a respectable living writing short stories are long gone. Only a select few "slick" magazines today publish literary short fiction (think *The New Yorker, Harper's, GQ, Esquire, Playboy,* and *The Atlantic Monthly*), and to get an acceptance letter from one of these publications you'll need to be writing at the level of John Updike or Alice Munro. Traditional markets for more mainstream short fiction—swamped by a heavy volume of submissions—either do not accept unsolicited submissions or have quit publishing short stories all together.

On the other hand, magazines that do publish fiction are always hungry for new voices, and if you're willing to investigate the field, you'll find there are still healthy markets out there for all types of short fiction, including short shorts and the interactive fiction called hypertext. Another encouraging development in the field is the proliferation of online magazines and journals. Finding paper costs high and subscription numbers too low to sustain production costs, many periodicals have either developed Web sites to complement their print publications or moved online all together (see the sidebar on page 130 for more information on online markets).

Research

One main key to selling to magazines and literary journals is reading them. You can tell a lot about an editor's sensibility by spending time reading the short stories he chooses to publish, and in so doing discern

The State of Online Markets

As production and distribution costs go up and subscriber numbers fall, more and more magazines are giving up print publication and moving online. Relatively inexpensive to maintain and quicker to accept and post submissions, online fiction sites are growing fast in number and in legitimacy. Betty Almond, the editor of *EWG Presents*, said, "We have the means to reach a universal audience by the click of a mouse. Writers are gifted with a new medium of exposure and the future demands taking advantage of this format."

Writers exploring online opportunities for their short fiction will find a rich and diverse community of voices. Genre sites are strong, in particular those for science fiction, fantasy, and horror. Mainstream short fiction sites are also growing exponentially. Writers can find numerous online literary journals with a regional bent, and journals that range from the traditional to those highly experimental sites that publish hypertext (the first literary form indigenous to the Internet).

Online journals are gaining respect for the writers who appear on their sites, and more and more publishers are going to online journals to find talented writers. Jill Adams of *The Barcelona Review*, said, "We see our Internet review like small, independent publishing houses—as a means of counterbalancing the big-business mentality of the multinational publishing houses. At the same time, we want to see our writers 'make it big.' We hear from more and more big houses asking about some of our new writers, wanting contact information, etc. So I see a healthy trend in that big houses are, finally—after being skeptical and confused—looking at it seriously and scouting online."

While the medium is different, the traditional rules of publishing apply when submitting to online journals. Writers should research the site and archives carefully, looking for a match in sensibility among the various sites publishing. They should follow submission guidelines exactly and submit courteously. True, these sites aren't bound by traditional print schedules, so your work theoretically may be published more quickly. But that doesn't mean a larger staff, so do exercise patience with editors considering your manuscript. Just as writers who publish online are no different than other writers, online editors are still editors who have a job to do.

whether or not your work is a good fit for that publication. There are three reasons it's important for a writer to do this: (1) It saves postage cost and time (both the writer's and the editor's); (2) it's a simple way to vastly increase your chances of publication because you won't be trying to sell the wrong story to the wrong publication; (3) doing your research gives you an opportunity to personally connect with an editor in your cover letter. Mentioning that you've taken the time to read a particular magazine or journal, and have found your work similar to the types of fiction they publish, will give you a definite edge over your competition in the slush pile.

It's also important to read several back issues of a publication you want to submit to, and keep track of editorial changes. Several years ago, the venerable *North American Review* underwent a changing of editorial guard, and incoming fiction editor Grant Tracey set out to significantly change the tone and feel of that magazine. So a short story that may have been welcomed by Tracey's predecessor may not have made it past the first reader on a new *NAR* staff.

You can also find out what a magazine is looking for in fiction by checking its Web site. In addition, you can find detailed guidelines in market directories such as the annual *Novel & Short Story Writer's Market*. But your work is not finished once you've determined whether a publication wants romance, mystery, or literary short stories. It's not just what but how. With competition as fierce as in today's market, editors need methods for shrinking the slush pile, and one quick way is to reject outright any submission that doesn't follow guidelines. Writers are creative spirits, but in the submission process it's best to be an utter conformist and follow to the letter what an editor asks for in submissions. There are no bonus points for clever, attention-getting gimmicks. Pay attention to the details: What is the maximum word count? Does a publication accept multiple or simultaneous submissions, or neither? Will a journal accept electronic submissions? Does the editor want a disposable copy of the manuscript, or will she return yours? Do you need to enclose a self-addressed stamped envelope? The full list of particulars is long and important.

Adams, editor of *The Barcelona Review*, said, "The best advice I can give is to read the guidelines carefully and take them seriously." Adams said she gets frustrated when writers ignore her electronic literary review's maximum word length of 4,000 words and send 10,000-word manuscripts, saying that they couldn't possibly cut the piece and retain its integrity. "Maybe not," Adams said. "But then it's not the story for our review, and my time—and the writer's—has been wasted."

Revise

Another major key to getting your short fiction published is remembering to revise. It can be easy in the afterglow of a finished story to want to rush it out into the world, to share your enthusiasm for your creation with readers. This is never a good idea. Phil Wagner, editor of the literary journal *The Iconoclast*, said "Do all rewrites before sending a story out. Few editors have time to work with writers on promising stories; only polished."

Know that once you've finished your short story, what you have is a first draft, which Michael Seidman in *The Complete Guide to Editing Your Fiction* calls "your attempt to quarry a stone." A story can require an unlimited number of revisions to reach its full potential. Joyce Carol Oates is known to revise work of her own that has *already been published*. Give the manuscript time to become as polished as you can make it. Joining a writer's critique group can also be helpful. Also, entering contests is a good way to get feedback on your writing. In addition to honors and, quite often cash prizes, contests offer writers the opportunity to be judged on the basis of quality alone, without the outside factors that sometimes influence publishing decisions. New writers who win contests may be published for the first time, while more experienced writers may gain recognition for an entire body of work.

Submit

When the story is ready and you've targeted a publication, clip a brief cover letter to your short story and send it to a specific editor, making sure your submission is addressed to the appropriate person. Because reading a flat page is simpler than one that's been folded in thirds and squashed into a business envelope, send submissions in a manila envelope, with a stamped, self-addressed return envelope. If the publication accepts e-mail submissions, follow the instructions carefully; sending an unreadable file is, obviously, self-defeating.

Cover letters are polite pieces of business correspondence, simply acting as an introduction to your story. They should include the name of the story, a sentence or two on what it's about, its word count, a mention of why you're sending it to a particular magazine, and a paragraph about who you are. The cover letter won't make the sale. That depends on your story. But a sloppy or typo-ridden one can easily kill it.

As with all written correspondence, the cover letter should be typed, checked for typos, and sent with a stamped, self-addressed envelope, unless the magazine says it cannot return submissions or you mention that it's a disposable manuscript.

Be prepared to be persistent, because magazines, online and on paper, report being inundated with submissions for fiction. At *The Barcelona Review*, only about one of the two hundred submissions it receives each month is accepted, and sometimes not that many. If your short story is sent back, send it out again. Always keep a copy for yourself and a record of where and when you sent it. A submission log can help you keep a record of stories were sent where and when, which were returned, editor's comments, and other pertinent information.

Selling Your Novel

Finding a publisher for a novel is in many ways like finding a home for your short fiction—it's a matter of persistence, talent, and luck. It involves first writing well, then researching publishers and agents, and then sending and resending material until it reaches someone who appreciates it as much as you do. Novelist Jeanne M. Dams attested to this. Dams is now the author of twelve mysteries, including the Dorothy Martin series, but it took drive and determination to get there.

Frustrated in her job in education, Dams took up writing because "I had some silly idea there was an easier way to make a living than what I was doing." It took five years to finish her first novel, about an American woman and her cat who solve a murder mystery. Eventually, she quit her job and devoted herself to finishing and then selling the novel. "Everybody tells you not to do that, and everybody's right," Dams said. "There were times I really wasn't sure how we were going to pay the electric bill."

It would be two years before she found a publisher for the novel *The Body in the Transept*, a "cozy" mystery so named because it's an Agatha Christie type of book, one to cuddle up with in an armchair on a rainy day with a cup of tea. "I obeyed the rules and sent it to one publisher at a time," she said. "Then I got sick of the time lag." So she began sending queries, synopses, and/or sample chapters to several publishers and agents at once.

Dams attended writers conferences to learn her craft and to make contacts. She submitted the manuscript for critiques. Eventually, she attended a Mystery Writers of America conference called "Of Dark and Stormy Nights" because her work could be critiqued by an agent or editor rather than other writers. Her manuscript landed in the hands of Michael Seidman, who was then an editor of mysteries at Walker & Co.

Knowing that Seidman had a reputation for disliking cozies, Dams determined that she would simply have to steel herself and learn from the experience. But she was flabbergasted when Seidman simply looked at her and asked, "Why hasn't this already been published?" It soon was. Armed with Seidman's comments, Dams found an agent. *The Body in the Transept* was the first of her Dorothy Martin series, and won the Agatha Award for best first mystery novel of 1995.

The Outlook

The good news for novelists is that the industry is very receptive now to new voices. Before the book publishing industry became consolidated in the later part of the last century, editors established relationships with writers and cultivated their work. An editor had the time to recognize potential, and coax out of the writer the best book he could produce. The writer-editor relationship was usually a long-term proposition, with the publishing company looking for its payoff later in the arc of a writer's career—on the third or fourth novel, say, when the writer began to fully realize his talent and develop a following.

Since that time, publishing houses have consolidated into the Big Six, five of which are in New York, (Simon & Schuster, Random House, HarperCollins, Penguin Group USA, Holztbrinck Publishers and AOL Time Warner Books). Lots of analysis has been devoted to how these changes have altered the face of publishing, and to the reasons behind these changes, but one thing is certain: Editors do not have nearly the amount of time to spend with their writers as they used to. The result is what you may have heard called "the death of the midlist author," or a phenomenon in which blockbuster novelists continue to publish, and first-time authors are highly sought after as the next "big thing," but an author with a modestly selling first novel may well not get a second chance, at least not with her original publishing house. The publisher may want to make room in the list for a new author with break-out potential. Hence the opportunity for writers with talent, determination, and no track record, or, first-time authors.

With an Agent

That said, it is increasingly difficult for a first-time writer to get a reading at one of the Big Six houses without an agent. Unwieldy slush piles have caused the majority to decline unsolicited, unagented submissions, so in many cases you have to have an agent to get in the door. There are obvious advantages to working with an agent. First, she will give you a leg up on finding the right editor for your manuscript. Agents are industry insiders who know the tastes of editors at both independent publishers and imprints of the big houses. Acting as business manager, an agent also handles contracts, rights negotiations, and royalties, which frees an author's time for writing. But of course it's a service you'll pay for—the average contract stipulates the agent earns 15 percent of your book's domestic sales, and the foreign sales percentage may be higher.

And Without

Many authors do choose to work without an agent, and even with the closed nature of New York City's publishing houses, they can still succeed in going this route. Best-selling author Janet Fitch (*White Oleander*) chose to go it alone, and sold her manuscript to the first editor she approached at Little, Brown. So it can happen either way. If you do choose not to work with an agent, remember you are your own business manager. You'll want to distance yourself from the passion of your writing, and approach the submission process as completely different from the creative. You will need to precisely meet the submission specifications of each publisher you're sending your work to. This will accomplish the first and most important goal—it will increase your odds of getting your manuscript read. Don't make the novice's mistake of believing an editor will overlook sloppiness or inattention to detail to find the author is actually the creative heir to James Joyce. It just doesn't happen.

Research

When selling your novel, it is imperative that you research the markets thoroughly. Make a point to familiarize yourself with the industry by getting closer to it. Regularly visit publishers' Web sites and review what titles are currently on their list, what titles are upcoming, and whether or not there is news of a new imprint, folding imprint—any changes that may affect how you submit your work. Visit your public library and regularly read *Publishers Weekly*. Bookstores also hold a wealth of information. Browse the stacks and familiarize yourself with the fiction being published today. What are you seeing a lot of? What is consistently popular? What trends are emerging? Booksellers can be wonderful resources for information about publishing trends. As you gradually become more familiar with the industry, you'll develop a sense of the sorts of fiction different publishing houses are looking for—their publishing "personalities"—and discover new opportunities as well. And don't forget to do your online research. Web sites such as Maud Newton (www.maudnewton.com/blog) and others are great resources for timely information on changes to and issues affecting the publishing community.

Submit

Some book publishers want to see only a query first, but many want a letter with sample chapters, an outline, or sometimes even the complete manuscript. As we saw earlier, a query letter is the introduction of writer to editor or agent, but it is also a sales pitch. It tells enough about the book to intrigue the reader, mentions the title, offers the author's credentials and expertise, and asks for a chance to send in more of the manuscript.

Editors and agents say they look to the query not only for the idea but also for a sense of how a writer uses words, and they say they usually can tell if a person cannot write simply by reading their letters. When writers send an interesting query, Judith Shepard, editor-in-chief of The Permanent Press, said she also asks them to send the first twenty pages of the manuscript. "So, if someone wants to send me a query with the first twenty pages, that's more practical," she said. "What I prefer not to have, but what I get, are full manuscripts."

Before mailing anything, put yourself in the place of an editor. The Permanent Press, which publishes about twelve books a year, receives about seven thousand submissions annually. "We get so many submissions I almost hate to see the postman come," Shepard said. "But if someone is completely unknown, it's the letter that gets me. I'm very taken by the words that people use ... how people express themselves. I'm not as interested in the story line."

See pages 148-151 for a sample "pitch," query letter, and synopsis worksheets to help you prepare your work for submission.

Your Query Letter

A query letter is your letter of inquiry. It serves two functions: to tell the editor what you have to offer, and to ask if they're interested in seeing it. Many editors prefer that you send the query letter either by itself or with a synopsis and a few sample pages from your novel (not more than twenty). This is called a blind query or a proposal query, because you're sending it without having been asked to send it. No matter what you call it, it's your three-minute chance to hook the editor on your novel. If he likes your query, he'll call and ask for either specific parts of your novel proposal (a synopsis and sample chapters, for example) or the entire manuscript. Then he will make his decision.

Remember, your query letter is vital. You must make it compelling and interesting enough to hook your reader. Although every winning query works its own magic, all good queries should contain the following:

- A "grabber," or hook sentence that makes the reader want to get her hands on the actual novel.
- One to three paragraphs about your novel.
- A short paragraph about you and your publishing credentials (if you have any).
- A good reason why you're soliciting the person you're soliciting. Why this publisher instead of another?
- The length of the novel.
- A sentence or two about its intended audience.
- An indication that an SASE is enclosed.

Your Synopsis

If you will also be sending a synopsis along, you're lucky—you have another opportunity to hook an editor. The synopsis supplies key information about your novel (plot, theme, characterization, setting), while also showing how all these coalesce to form the big picture (your novel). You want to quickly tell what your novel is about without making the editor read the manuscript in its entirety. There are no hard and fast rules about the synopsis. Some editors look at it as a one-page sales pitch, while others expect it to be a comprehensive summary of the entire novel. Many editors prefer a short synopsis that runs from one to two single-spaced pages, or three to five double-spaced pages. On the other hand, some plot-heavy fiction, such as thrillers and mysteries, may require more space, and can run from ten to twenty-five double-spaced pages, depending on the length of the manuscript and the number of plot shifts. If you opt for a longer synopsis, aim for one synopsis page for every twenty-five manuscript pages. But try to keep it as short as possible.

When compiling your synopsis, be sure to include the following:

- A strong lead sentence.
- Logical paragraph organization.

- A concise expression of ideas with no repetition.
- An introduction of your main characters and their core conflicts
- Plot high points.
- Narrative (third-person) writing in the present tense.
- Transitions between ideas.
- Strong verbs and minimal use of adjectives, adverbs.
- Correct punctuation and spelling.
- The story's conclusion.

Your Outline

An outline is often used interchangeably with a synopsis. For most editors, however, there is a distinction. While a synopsis is a brief, encapsulated version of the novel at large, an outline makes each chapter its own story, usually containing a few paragraphs per chapter. In short, you're breaking down the novel and synopsizing each chapter individually. Try to keep each chapter to about a page, and begin each new chapter on a different page.

Never submit an outline unless an editor asks for it. Fewer and fewer agents and editors want outlines these days. Most just request a cover or query letter, a few sample chapters and a short synopsis. Outlines are most often requested by genre fiction editors, because genre books run for many pages and have numerous plot shifts.

In compiling your outline, keep in mind:
- Your outline is an extended, more detailed and structural version of your synopsis.
- Remember to explain the gist of the chapter.
- Highlight pivotal plot points.
- Write in the present tense.
- Reveal how the chapter opens and ends.
- Make sure the chapters follow sequentially.
- Do not include extended description and dialogue.

The Basics of Contacting Literary Agents

Once you and your manuscript are thoroughly prepared, the time is right to contact an agent. Finding an agent can often be as difficult as finding a publisher. Nevertheless, there are four ways to maximize your chances of finding the right agent: Obtain a referral from someone who knows the agent; meet the agent in person at a writers conference; submit a query letter or proposal; or attract the agent's attention with your own published writing.

Referrals

The best way to get your foot in an agent's door is to be referred by one of his clients, or by an editor or another agent he has worked with in the past. Because an agent trusts his clients, he will usually read referred work before over-the-transom submissions. If you are friends with anyone in the publishing business who has connections with agents, ask politely for a referral. However, don't be offended if another writer will not share the name of his agent.

If you don't have a wide network of publishing professionals, use the resources you do have to get an agent's attention.

Conferences

Going to a conference is your best bet for meeting an agent in person. Many conferences invite agents to either give a speech or simply be available for meetings with authors. Agents view conferences as a way to find writers. Often agents set aside time for one-to-one discussions with writers, and occasionally they may even look at material writers bring to the conference. If an agent is impressed with you and your work, she may ask for writing samples after the conference. When you send your query, be sure to mention the specific conference where you met and that she asked to see your work.

Submissions

The most common way to contact an agent is by a query letter or a proposal package. Most agents will accept unsolicited queries. Some will also look at outlines and sample chapters. Almost none want unsolicited complete manuscripts. Check the agent's submission guidelines to learn exactly how an agent prefers to be solicited. Never call—let the writing in your query letter speak for itself.

Because a query letter is your first impression on an agent, it should be professional and to the point. As a brief introduction to your manuscript, a query letter should only be one page in length.

The first paragraph should quickly state your purpose—you want representation.

In the second paragraph, mention why you have specifically chosen to query him. Perhaps he specializes in your areas of interest or represents authors you admire. Show him you have done your homework.

In the next paragraph or two, describe the project, the proposed audience, why your hook will sell, etc. Be sure to mention the approximate length and any special features.

Then discuss why you are the perfect person to write this book, listing your professional credentials or relative experience.

Close your query with an offer to send either an outline and sample chapters, or the complete manuscript—depending on your type of book.

Agents agree to be listed in directories such as *Writer's Market* to indicate to writers what they want to see and how they wish to receive submissions. As you start to query agents, make sure you follow their individual submission directions. This, too, shows an agent you've done your research. Like publishers, agencies have specialties. Some are only interested in novel-length works. Others are open to a wide variety of subjects and may actually have member agents within the agency who specialize in only a handful of the topics covered by the entire agency.

Publishing credits

Some agents read magazines or journals to find writers to represent. If you have had an outstanding piece published in a periodical, you may be contacted by an agent wishing to represent you. In such cases, make sure the agent has read your work. Some agents send form letters to writers, and such agents often make their living entirely from charging reading fees, not from commissions on sales.

However, many reputable and respected agents do contact potential clients in this way. For them, you already possess attributes of a good client: You have publishing credits, and an editor has validated your work. To receive a letter from a reputable agent who has read your material and wants to represent you is an honor.

Occasionally, writers who have self-published or who have had their work published electronically may attract an agent's attention, especially if the self-published book has sold well or received a lot of positive reviews.

Recently, writers have been posting their work on the Internet in hope of attracting an agent's eye. With all the submissions most agents receive, they likely have little time to peruse writer's Web sites. Nevertheless, there are agents who do consider the Internet a resource for finding fresh voices. Only the future will show how often writers are discovered through this medium.

A Note on Promotion

Today more than ever an author needs to be ready to take a very active role in selling her book. Some authors report being surprised by a lack of promotion and publicity for their new books, but increasingly this is the norm in book publishing. Best-selling author Terry McMillan (*Waiting to Exhale, How Stella Got Her Groove Back*) sold her first novel, *Mama*, to Houghton Mifflin in 1987, and was largely responsible for its success. "As soon as I found out the publicity department wasn't going to do anything other than send out the standard releases, and I wasn't going on a book tour, I said, 'What is going on here?' " she said. McMillan wrote bookstores, colleges, and universities, setting up readings and promoting the book, and sent her publicist her itinerary. She ended up selling about ten thousand books.

A publisher may or may not be interested in your level of willingness to promote your book before a contract is signed, but it's important that you as an author know going into the process what may be required of you once your book is published. For her part, Shepard at The Permanent Press said, "It really doesn't have any influence on me (in a proposal). However, if we accept the book, the possibilities for promotion that the author can generate along with us are very useful.

In fact, more and more authors are trying to promote their own books. There just isn't a tremendous chance otherwise." (See chapter thirteen for more on promotion.)

Handling Rejection

Nobody likes rejection, but it's a fact of life in publishing. For some writers, rejection letters become a perverse point of pride, and you can find some Web sites entirely devoted to them (with some very entertaining entries). And a California-based literary journal has chosen at its title *The Rejected Quarterly, A Journal of Quality Literature Rejected at Least Five Times.*

Do be aware that in publishing short and novel-length fiction, there are good and bad rejections. Bad rejections are either no response whatsoever or a one- or two-sentence form note. Good rejections are those in which an editor comments personally on your manuscript. (For more information on coping with bad rejections, see chapter six.) Take those as encouragement—editors rarely have time to pen such notes, and if they have taken the time to do so, that's a positive sign. It can also be helpful to include the editor's comments in your submission log, so if you submit to that publication again you can make specific reference to the earlier communication. Above all, persevere.

Resources for Selling Your Fiction

The books, magazines, and Web sites listed here can provide you with additional information on all aspects of writing and selling your fiction:

Books
Most of the books listed below come from top literary agents, respected authors, and noted editors. Let their years of experience give you the extra edge you need to get ahead:

> **Book Editors Talk to Writers** (John Wiley & Sons), by Judy Mandell. In a Q&A format, more than forty editors offer up suggestions for improving your work, submitting it to publishers, and more.

The Complete Handbook of Novel Writing (Writer's Digest Books), edited by Meg Leder and Jack Heffron. This 400-page book offers writing instruction, submission tips, author interviews, and more.

Fiction: The Art and Craft of Writing and Getting Published (Pomegranate Press), by Michael Seidman. This author and editor tells you what the common submission stumbling blocks are and how to avoid them. He also offers writing tips and exercises to help you improve your work.

The First Five Pages: A Writer's Guide to Staying Out of the Slush Pile (Fireside), by Noah Lukeman. The author draws on his experience as a literary agent to show you how to identify and correct bad writing and get your novel read.

Guide to Literary Agents (Writer's Digest Books) edited by Kathryn S. Brogan. This annual book provides listings, guidelines, and contact information for more than a thousand literary agents.

How to Get Happily Published, 5th edition (HarperResource), by Judith Appelbaum. This book provides information on working with editors and agents, tackling publicity, self-publishing, and more.

How to Write a Damn Good Novel (St. Martin's Press), by James N. Frey. For beginners and experienced writers, this book focuses on the basics of storytelling and shows you how to improve and correct your work.

How to Write & Sell Your First Novel, revised edition (Writer's Digest Books), by Oscar Collier, with Frances Spatz Leighton. This guide uses case studies to reveal the keys to writing and publishing a successful novel.

Novel & Short Story Writer's Market (Writer's Digest Books), edited by Anne Bowling. This annually updated resource directory provides listings, writing guidelines, and contact information for more than a thousand book and magazine publishers.

The Novel Writer's Toolkit (Writer's Digest Books), by Bob Mayer. From a successful novelist, this book takes you step-by-step through the process of novel writing, including information on developing a story idea, revising your work, submitting it, etc.

The Marshall Plan for Novel Writing (Writer's Digest Books), by Evan Marshall. This book covers all aspects of novel writing. Other books in The Marshall Plan series include *The Marshall Plan Workbook* (Writer's Digest Books), which offers detailed worksheets to take you through the entire process, and *The Marshall Plan for Getting Your Novel Published* (Writer's Digest Books), which focuses mostly on the submission process, including detailed instruction for putting together a winning synopsis package.

The Plot Thickens (St. Martin's Press), by Noah Lukeman. In this follow-up to *The First Five Pages*, Lukeman teaches you how to correct common plot problems and improve your novel.

The Weekend Novelist (DTP), by Robert J. Ray. This mystery novelist shows you how to write your novel by following fifty-two weekend writing sessions.

The Writer's Digest Writing Clinic (Writer's Digest Books), edited by Kelly Nickell. Learn how to edit and revise your novels, short stories, query letters, and synopses through real-life examples of critiques by professional editors.

Writing and Selling Your Novel (Writers Digest Books), by Jack M. Bickham. This author of more than eighty novels shows you how to write publishable fiction by presenting a professional approach to all facets of writing.

Writing the Breakout Novel (Writer's Digest Books), by Donald Maass. This experienced literary agent and author shares to the secrets to crafting a great novel. *Writing the Breakout Novel Workbook* (Writer's Digest Books), expands on the principles behind the first book by taking you step-by-step through the fiction writing process and teaching you how to read like a writer.

Magazines

Use the following publications to stay ahead up on what's happening in the publishing industry, learn about your craft, and more:

Publishers Weekly: This weekly magazine provides the latest on the industry news. 360 Park Avenue South, New York, New York 10010. Tel: (646) 746-6758. Web site: www.publishersweekly.com.

Writer's Digest: This monthly magazine features interviews with authors, writing instruction, market information, etc. F&W Publications, 4700 E. Galbraith Road, Cincinnati, Ohio 45236. Tel: (800) 221-3148. Web site: www.writersdigest.com.

Pages, The Magazine for People Who Love Books: This bimonthly publication features industry news, author interviews, and more. Pages Magazine, 5880 Oberlin Dr., San Diego, CA 92121. Tel: (858) 812-6488. Web site: www.ireadpages.com.

Locus, The Magazine of the Science Fiction & Fantasy Field: This monthly magazine includes news, interviews, book reviews, market listings, convention coverage, etc. Locus Publications, P.O. Box 13305, Oakland CA 94611. Tel: (510) 339-9196. Web site: www.locusmag.com.

Web sites

The Web sites listed here can provide you with additional information for preparing your synopsis:

Authorlink: www.authorlink.com. An excellent site for news about publishing and articles about writing.

Booktalk: www.booktalk.com. Connections to publishers and agents; some news about the industry.

Eclectic Authors: www.eclectics.com. Offers discussion board and advice on writing.

Poets & Writers: www.pw.org. Offers links to workshops, services, and publications of interest to writers.

Sisters in Crime: www.sinc-ic.org. A good site for mystery writers, male and female.

Writer's Weekly: www.writersweekly.com. Offers articles, markets, and more.

Writers Write, The Internet Writing Journal: www.writerswrite.com. Offers reviews, interviews, and articles on craft.

Work It Out Before You Send It Out

To help you organize your thoughts and condense the unwritten proposals that are already running through your head, we've included several worksheets here for writing a hook (or pitch), and for your synopsis and query letter. Before you start, you should photocopy each of them several times. That way, if you digress from your path or decide you need to start fresh, you'll have plenty more forms on hand.

These worksheets were prepared by Barb Kuroff, editorial director of Writer's Digest Books, who uses them successfully at writers conferences and workshops across the country. Although they are designed for fiction writers, nonfiction writers can use them as inspiration to create similar worksheets of their own.

Remember, not every publisher wants the same elements in a submissions package. Some want more; some want less. You should always check each publisher's guidelines before submitting.

Only a strong submissions package will do even the best of manuscripts justice. So don't rush—take all the time you need and only submit when you know you're ready. And good luck!

1. The name of your novel is:

_____.

2. What is your main character's name?

3. Describe your main character. Include physical features, but also briefly identify any background information that is relevant to the actions and motivations of that character in your story. (This will provide information for your character sketch.)

4. What is your main character's goal? What does your main character want to accomplish? (This provides the motivation behind your character's actions.)

5. What thing(s) and/or person(s) stand in the way of your character achieving that goal? (This is the conflict integral to your plot.)

6. Using the answers to the above questions, write a one- to three-sentence description of what your manuscript is about. (This is your "hook" or "pitch.")

1. The title of your novel is:

_____.

2. State the "hook" of your novel (from your "Hook Worksheet"). This hook must contain the core conflict of your novel.

3. Beginning with your main character, write a "character sketch" of each of your main characters. These sketches should concentrate on characters' motivations, especially those that bring them into conflict with one another.

4. Identify your plot highlights. Begin by detailing your beginning and ending scenes and one or two in the middle. These plot points should be only those necessary to make the primary plot hang together and conclude with a logical, even if unexpected, ending.

5. (On another sheet of paper.) Using the above information, outline your novel synopsis, paragraph by paragraph. You may use your own structure, but make sure all the elements of the synopsis are addressed: an opening hook, quick sketches of the main characters, plot high points, the core conflict, and the conclusion.

Dear (agent's name):

I've written a mystery novel, the first of a projected series, that I'd like to submit for your consideration. The enclosed synopsis will outline the basics; let me say here why I believe *Sounding Brass** could succeed in today's market:

(1) The book is in the classic "cozy" tradition, involving pleasant people in an attractive English setting. (2) The protagonist is a sixtyish American woman with whom many mystery readers will be able to identify. (3) The bright, upbeat tone is refreshing for a genre that is growing ever more grim and gritty. (4) The cat is an appealing creature who helps solve the mystery without ever behaving like anything but a cat.

There are no gimmicks, no nonsense, just careful, literate writing and a strongly individual Voice.

Although this is my first book, I've published in national (*Guideposts, Woman's World, Military History*) and local markets. I was a feature writer for over a year for a local newspaper. In addition to the second and third novels of the series, I'm working at present on a small guidebook to London's little museums.

I hope you will agree to read the manuscript of *Sounding Brass*. (Although I am querying several agents at once, I will of course send the manuscript to only one at a time. I realize that no one—including me—has time to waste.)

I look forward to hearing from you.

Sincerely,

Jeanne M. Dams

*title was later changed to *The Body in the Transept*

Dear (agent #2):

The enclosed sample of my mystery novel *Sounding Brass* comes with Michael Seidman's recommendation. He critiqued the first chapter for this year's "Of Dark and Stormy Nights" conference in Chicago and was enthusiastic about it. (I enclose his comments.) Since he won't have time to look at it for a while, and I've already taken an unsuccessful shot at the Malice Domestic contest, I asked him about agents; he named you "one of the few agents I trust."

Sounding Brass is a traditional mystery (which is why I was surprised as well as pleased when Seidman liked it so much). It is my first novel, although I've published shorter stuff. I am at work on the second and third books of the series, and planning another series set in the Midwest. I have, also at Seidman's suggestion, sent the full MS of Sounding Brass to Ruth Cavin at St. Martin's, but I don't expect to hear from her any time soon. I doubt that the slush pile is her first concern. No one else is reading the book.

As a beginner in this peculiar business I am aware that I badly need a literary agent, and hope very much that you will consider representing me and my work. I look forward to your reply.

Cordially,

(Mrs.) Jeanne M. Dams

To: Jeanne Dams
From: Michael Seidman

I enjoyed reading this very much ... I don't think I made a mark on a page. Your voice, your story, your characters ... everything just comes together.

I guess the only question is why it hasn't been published yet. I'd recommend starting the novel on its rounds immediately ... and if nothing happens by October, get in touch with me, because that's when I expect to be looking for more manuscripts.

My first shot would be St. Martin's Malice Domestic contest; this seems far better than anything I've read from it so far.

Editor's Note: Jeanne Dams wrote this cover letter after showing her work to editor and author Michael Seidman, whom she met at a writers conference. Notice in the cover letter how the author successfully references Seidman's comments, which are included here:

SOUNDING BRASS

BY JEANNE M. DAMS

Dorothy Martin is American, sixtyish, recently widowed and living in the small English cathedral and university town of Sherebury. On Christmas Eve, after attending Midnight Mass at the cathedral, she literally stumbles over a body in one of the side chapels.

The body turns out to be that of Canon Billings, the cathedral's librarian, a cold, judgmental man heartily disliked by almost everyone who knew him. He was considered to be an excellent scholar (he was a lecturer at Sherebury University as well) but a poor priest. Although the list of suspects is nearly limitless, because of Billings' unpopularity and because of the thousands of people in the cathedral that night, a few individuals surface as likely. One of these is a university student, Nigel Evans, to whom Dorothy's neighbor Jane has taken a liking. Jane, an old maid with a way with kids, is sure Nigel is innocent, although he worked for the canon and hated him more than most. Dorothy begins nosing around partly to help clear Nigel, but also because the loneliness and depression of her widowed and expatriate state is too much to bear without something to occupy her time.

She makes a new friend, Alan Nesbitt, the Chief Constable of the county. Alan, though unenthusiastic about Dorothy's meddling, is strongly attracted to her (he is a widower), and somewhat grudgingly cooperates. She learns, through gossip and her own observation, that there are at least three excellent suspects besides Nigel: A verger at the cathedral, the cathedral's organist/choirmaster, and an ambitious businessman. The canon represented a threat of one kind or another to all three. Dorothy's favorite is the verger until he also turns up dead, burnt nearly beyond recognition in an arson-caused fire at the late canon's house.

After a conversation with a friend at the British Museum, Dorothy becomes curious about the canon's last research project; he seems to have been close-mouthed about its topic. Dorothy asks everyone; Nigel doesn't know, the Dean of the cathedral thinks it had to do with St. Paul, and George Chambers, Billings' colleague at the university and an old friend of Dorothy and her late husband, says it was about Nero.

Dorothy is distressed after she visits George and catches him in a com-

SOUNDING BRASS continued

promising situation with a coed, because she thinks he might have had reason to kill the censorious canon. When her beloved cat, Emmy, is poisoned in a way that points to George, Dorothy is sure he is the murderer. Emmy recovers, though, and the Chief Constable proves that George's motive is a washout.

When Dorothy finally figures out what the canon was working on, she realizes that George is the villain after all, for academic motives: Billings' research would have ruined George's reputation and chances for advancement. In a slow-motion chase through the shadowy reaches of the medieval cathedral, Dorothy is nearly killed, a priceless ancient document is destroyed, and George dies in a fall to the cathedral floor.

SOUNDING BRASS

BY JEANNE M. DAMS

Dorothy Martin, a sixtyish American, recently widowed, has rented a house in the small English cathedral and university town of Sherebury, as she and her husband had long planned to do. At Christmas time, a rainy, blustery Christmas entirely unlike Dorothy's idea of the way the holiday should be, she is beginning to regret her move. She feels isolated among people who, though friendly, are essentially strangers and "don't speak her language," in more ways than one. Perhaps she was foolish to leave the familiar in her search for a new life.

On Christmas Eve, at midnight Mass in the cathedral, she makes the acquaintance of Alan Nesbitt, a pleasant man who happens to be Chief Constable for the county. When the service ends well after midnight, Nesbitt offers to see Dorothy home, but as they are making their way through a darkened passage she stumbles over a body.

The deceased turns out to be one Jonathan Billings, Canon and Librarian of the cathedral. Billings, a distinguished scholar, was also a cold, judgmental man heartily disliked by almost everyone. Although the death appears to be accidental, the police must still investigate, and since Nesbitt is on the spot and a good friend, the Dean of the cathedral asks him to take charge of matters. By Christmas afternoon the police have established the fact that Billings did not die where he was found, and that the severe wound to his head was caused neither by his fall nor by the heavy altar candlestick found near the body. Verdict: murder.

The TV report of the findings does nothing to cheer Dorothy's Christmas, nor does her tea the next day with George and Alice Chambers, old friends from the days when Dorothy's late husband spent a sabbatical year at Sherebury university. George, under the guise of comforting Dorothy, really wants to gossip about possible murderers, especially young Nigel Evans, whom Dorothy has seen in the cathedral with her best friend and next-door neighbor, Jane Langland. Dorothy, retorting that given Billings' character, almost anyone might have done him in, changes the subject to George's book on an obscure biblical topic, now nearing completion and, according to Alice, destined for great academic distinction.

On the way home from George's, Dorothy, depressed and wet through

SOUNDING BRASS continued

from the penetrating fog, calls on Jane, a redoubtable spinster. There she receives comfort and a warming glass of whiskey, but also learns that Nigel worked for Billings in the Cathedral Library, had a terrible fight with him and was fired, and has a minor criminal record. Jane, who makes a habit of adopting stray dogs and students, is strongly partisan in his favor and convinced of his innocence, but realizes the police will consider him a prime suspect. Dorothy is distressed, while privately thinking that Nigel does, in fact, sound like a possible murderer.

She is not at all reassured by a conversation with Alan Nesbitt, who shows up at her door exuding charm underlain by faint menace. A little skillful conversation extracts her suspicions of Nigel, her interest in the classic English mystery, and her half-formed intent to do some poking around on her own. His warning that murder investigation is a dangerous business, best left to professionals, serves if anything to strengthen her desire to become further involved.

Two important things transpire at church the next day. Dorothy learns from Jeremy Sayers, the quirky, acid-tongued cathedral organist, that there are two other excellent suspects: a verger who has been stealing from the collection (although no one has been able to prove it), and Sayers, himself! Apparently, Billings was about to get the goods on the verger, Robert Wallingford, and Wallingford might have killed to protect himself. And Sayers, who quarreled bitterly with Billings about cathedral music, was in danger of being fired. Dorothy, eager to talk over new developments with Jane, has the wind taken out of her sails when Jane already knows all about cathedral gossip and scandal and doesn't much care because Nigel has been arrested.

Nigel is freed on Monday for lack of solid evidence, and Dorothy, exasperated with the whole situation, keeps a date with friends for shopping, sightseeing, and tea in London. Even in the metropolis, though, she can't get away from the murder. A chance-met acquaintance in the British Museum knew Billings, and hints that there was something mysterious about the piece of research engaging the scholarly cleric at the time of his death.

The continued rain, mist, and general dreariness make Dorothy long, for the tenth time, for some proper Dickensian snow. Even the cat Esmeralda is irritable. On Tuesday Billings' memorial service provides further gloom. Stopping at Jane's before the funeral to cheer herself up, Dorothy meets Nigel for the first time and is charmed, but even more apprehensive. Nigel's temper seems quite hot enough for murder, and he's not talking much about his activities Christmas Eve. After the service Dorothy is captured by Alan (Nesbitt—they're on first-name terms by this time) and taken to tea. She's jollied into a better mood, but can't get Alan to talk about police progress into the investigation. Dinner that night at an inn owned by Dorothy's old friends, the Endicotts, makes matters much worse. Although the Endicotts mention an

SOUNDING BRASS continued

ambitious developer who is delighted Billings is dead, it turns out that the whole Endicott family had good reason to wish the clergyman ill. Not only was he, in his capacity as town councilman, obstructing vital plans for expansion of the inn, but young Inga Endicott is all-but-engaged to Nigel Evans and mightily resented Billings' treatment of him.

A strained conversation with Nigel reveals that he was actually at the cathedral on Christmas Eve, some hours before Midnight Mass. He's sure Billings' body wasn't in the side chapel then, but he did see Inga, apparently coming out of Billings' house in the Cathedral Close. If the two have each been suspecting the other, both are innocent, but are they both telling the truth? Dorothy goes to the cathedral for some answers and learns that Wallingford, the verger, was missing for much of Christmas Eve when he should have been working, and that Sayers, the organist, was at the organ practicing most of the early evening. Good—Dorothy likes Sayers much better than Wallingford, and the case against the verger is getting better and better. She also learns that the Dean's wife placidly accepts the presence of the ghost-monk Dorothy thinks she's seen once or twice in the cathedral.

The next day is New Year's Eve. Before going to a party at Jane's, Dorothy learns from the Dean of the cathedral that Billings' research may have involved the writings of St. Paul, but the canon was very secretive about his work. Her curiosity grows. Could his work have something to do with his murder? At the party an increasingly attentive Alan gives Dorothy the interesting information that George Chambers is a skirt-chaser, but before she can digest what that might mean, the party is interrupted by a fire in the cathedral close just down the street. Canon Billings' house is burning! The investigators find that the fire was set; they also find the body of Wallingford, the verger, in the burned house. He was not the culprit, however, since he was dead before the fire started. There goes Dorothy's favorite suspect. And the rest were, at the time of the fire, either at Jane's party or, in the case of the Endicotts, working in plain view of several dozen people. Dorothy becomes even more eager to know about Billings' research project.

The next day Dorothy drags herself, after very little sleep, to see George. If anyone knows about Billings' work, it will be his colleague at the University. She finds him heading—on New Year's Day—for his office, and with him a very pretty female student. Not just with him, either, but obviously together. Suddenly Dorothy sees a motive for George. What if Billings had threatened to tell Alice, who has the money in the family? She tries to calm down and ask George about the canon's work, but George isn't sure—thinks it had to do with Nero. Billings had just returned from a trip to Corinth, which flourished during Nero's reign. She can make nothing of that, and after a little awkward conversation about the dead plant in the dented pot, she escapes.

A call from her London friends is most welcome. She is invited to join them

SOUNDING BRASS continued

for dinner at a charming country pub, and is able to relax more than she has since the murder. On her return home, however, she finds that someone has tried to murder her beloved cat, Esmeralda, by giving her antifreeze to drink. By the time, hours later, she's sure the cat is going to be all right, she's worked out that it must have been George who did the poisoning. George, who knows little about cars, wouldn't know that there would be no antifreeze in the garage of a Volkswagen Beetle, and would think the poisoning might be taken for an accident. He also knows how devoted Dorothy and Emmy are; Emmy's death would keep Dorothy out of the way for a while. He must have decided she was getting too near the truth when she saw him with the girl. He has to be the murderer!

When she tells Alan and he investigates, however, she is once more out of suspects. It's true enough that George is carrying on with the girl, and makes a habit of it, but Alice has known for years, and puts up with it. There was nothing for Billings to reveal. Dorothy, grimly determined to avenge Emmy, thinks the whole thing through from the beginning, and finally comes up with the truth.

Going to the cathedral to verify her conclusions in the library, she finds George there. George, dressed up like a monk. George, the "ghost" who has been haunting the cathedral lately. He has in his hands the ancient manuscript Billings was working on when he died, a priceless "lost" letter from St. Paul. Its very existence makes George's book—and his academic future—worthless. It is for this that George has killed twice. In a slow-motion chase through the shadowy reaches of the medieval cathedral, Dorothy is nearly made a third victim to George's ambition, the ancient scroll is destroyed, and George dies in a fall to the cathedral floor.

When it's all over and the police have finished with her, Dorothy leaves, alone. She thinks she sees a monkish figure, but is too numb and exhausted to notice anything for sure except that the snow she has longed for is finally falling, pure and cleansing.

CHAPTER NINE

Selling Your Script

Writing for television and film remains the dream of millions. Type in "screenwriter" in any search engine on the Web, and you'll find screen after screen of sites. Books devoted to writing and selling scripts fill bookshelves. How-to articles covering the ins and outs of scriptwriting abound.

But selling a first script also remains one of the most elusive dreams for many writers—virtually the stuff of drama. That's in part because the road to Hollywood is actually many roads. "There's no track," said sitcom writer David Chambers (*The Wonder Years, Frank's Place, Hangin' with Mr. Cooper*). "Everybody has to find his own way. There's a premium on hustling and selling. You're always selling yourself. It's a constant matter of being in sales."

As Jared Rappaport (*Blindness*), who became a screenwriter after studying directing at the American Film Institute, put it, "Everybody absolutely manufactures his own way in."

Write Your Own Calling Card

As obvious as it may seem, the first step to selling your script is writing it. There are plenty of urban legends of screenwriters who make fortunes in Hollywood simply by selling "ideas." The reality is that there is no such thing as a screen*writer* who doesn't *write* scripts.

A script serves as your calling card as a screenwriter. You can have the most impressive résumé in the business with a list of film and television credits as long as your arm, but if you don't have a good script (or the ability to produce a good script in a very, very short period of time) no one is going to hire you as a screenwriter … and no one is going to pay you for an "idea." Ideas, no matter how wonderful they sound to you, are a dime a dozen. If you give the same idea to a dozen writers, you'll get a dozen completely different scripts. What matters in this business is the execution of that idea, the specific character traits, dialogue, and plot turns that make a good (or even great) script. Here's an example: "A sports team made up of players without a shred of athletic talent struggle to overcome far superior opponents. Through perseverance and blind luck, the team transforms from an underdog to a playoff contender." Is this the idea behind *The Bad News Bears, Major League,* or *Necessary Roughness*? The answer: all three.

Every year, hundreds of amateur screenwriters attempt to sue production companies, studios, and networks claiming that someone stole their "idea" for a film or television show. What most people don't know is that most of these cases are thrown out of court before trial because they just aren't true. There are about nine thousand professional screenwriters and tens of thousands of aspiring writers throwing out ideas every year. With those kinds of numbers, similarity of ideas is inevitable. In Hollywood legal terms, it's called "simultaneous creation." We all watch the same television shows, movies, news broadcasts, and plays. We all read the same books, magazines, and newspapers. When multiple people are exposed to the same stimuli, they develop very similar ideas. Your friends and family might think you have an original idea, but there are tens of thousands of other creative souls out there, and at least one of them has had the same idea.

This also explains why you cannot copyright ideas. Copyright does not protect ideas or concepts. Copyright protects you from someone stealing your story, but you need to be able to prove three things in court: (1) You created the story before the other person; (2) the other person had access to your story before they created their version of the story; (3) there are unique elements to your story that have been used in the other person's story.

New scriptwriters worry about having their ideas stolen all the time. Since you cannot copyright your idea and can only copyright the way in which you tell the story, it's best to write a complete script before you hand over the idea. Your script is your key to the front door of Hollywood.

No matter what genre you choose, before trying to sell your script, you must work prodigiously on the writing. Your script should not simply be a good idea sewn together with the same kind of dialogue you've seen on the big and small screen; it should be better. Hollywood is awash in scripts sent in on speculation by would-be writers and from professional writers whose shows have been cancelled and are looking for work. A highly rated television show, for example, may receive two thousand to four thousand such scripts—called spec scripts—every year, excluding several thousand more from agents.

So your spec script must stand out from the rest. It must be polished until each line of dialogue sparkles and each scene progresses both the characters and the plot. Why do you have to work so hard on your script? Because the one thing people in Hollywood agree on is that a good script will find its way in. Your spec script (or scripts) prove to the Hollywood establishment that you know how to tell a story through dialogue, how to format properly, how to write for existing characters or invent entertaining ones of your own, how to make people laugh or cry, how to craft a compelling plot—in short, how to write.

Form and Format

A mark of a serious writer is attention to detail. Paying attention to the way scripts should be written on the page marks you as serious about the craft. But simply studying scripts—analyzing which lines are capitalized, how large the margins are, and whether lines are single- or double-spaced—is also necessary.

When it comes to writing a script, form is function. A properly formatted script allows a trained reader to quickly and accurately gauge its running time, while also making it easy to identify key requirements such as talent, locations, and props. The challenge for writers is that so many different elements (scenes, headings, dialogue, character names, etc.) have separate formatting requirements. Since proper formatting is the first sign that a script has been professionally written, writers have two choices: They can study the rules (there are a number of books to help with this), or they can invest about $200 in one of the latest scriptwriting software programs.

Two of the best books to deal specifically with script formatting are *The Complete Guide to Standard Script Formats* by Hillis Cole & Judith Haag, and *Elements of Style for Screenwriters* by Paul Argentini. Depending on your level of computer savvy, you may or may not have trouble transferring the knowledge into actual settings on your computer. Fortunately, today's scriptwriting software can take care of the mundane details for you, so that you can focus on your craft.

The two most common software products are Final Draft (www.finaldraft.com) and Movie Magic Screenwriter (www.screenplay.com). Each is endorsed by a long list of big names in the entertainment industry. Both function similarly to standard writing programs except that they have extra features to handle the technical details automatically. Character names are indented properly. Smart drag and drop features adjust the formatting when you move text. Other features alert you to formatting errors and inconsistencies. Templates from actual television scripts offer a glimpse into the real world of television scriptwriting. For those writers who would rather focus their attention on crafting great dialogue and plot twists rather than line spacing and capitalization, these script-formatting programs make for an ideal solution.

Since your work style can be as personal as your writing style, the most important factor is your comfort level with a particular software product. Before purchasing either product, download a free trial version and try it yourself.

Finding an Agent

Once you've made your script as good as it can be, finding someone in the business to read it is the next step. Fortunately, there are agents who can help get your scripts into the right hands. Unfortunately, it's often said that getting an agent to represent you is harder than getting your first film produced.

But it's essential, said Richard Walter, professor and chairman of the UCLA Film and Television Writing Program. "Anybody who receives a script direct from an author has got to wonder why this isn't submitted by an agent," he said. "If you want to be a professional, you must treat yourself like a professional—and professionals have professional representation." In short, find yourself an agent.

Of course, there's a paradox here, too. Agents need to read what you've written to decide if they'll represent you. And even though agents are always looking for the next hot property, many say they won't read scripts sent in cold. They might, however, read a query letter. Think of a query letter as "a seduction, a tease, a preview of coming attractions," Walter says. It is usually one page and has a brief description of your idea, a brief summation of your accomplishments and a brief request for the agent to read the script. Don't go into detail about your script in your query, he advises, because it simply makes a "bigger target to shoot at."

Your first step is to find an agent who's willing to read your script. One of the best methods of accomplishing this is to have a friend who is already represented recommend you and your script to his agent (see the section on networking on page 164). If a current client recommends you, the agent is already more interested in you than any of the other unsolicited scripts in his "slush pile." The biggest agencies (Creative Artists Agency, International Creative Management, Inc., and William Morris Agency) won't even accept unsolicited scripts unless you're recommended by one of their current clients. So, find someone to recommend you. It doesn't need to be a family member or best friend—just someone who has an agent. Get her to read your script or listen to your pitch, and then ask her to put in a good word for you.

Another common way to find an agent is to "cold call" or to submit query letters to agents listed in either *Guide to Literary Agents* or the list of agents published by the Writers Guild West. Keep in mind that not all agents are open to new writers, and some agents are very specific about the kind of writers they work with (only television drama writers, only feature film comedy writers, only sitcom writers, etc.). Pay attention and don't call or send queries to agents that won't handle your kind of material. If an agent likes your query, he'll call and either ask for the complete script or ask for a more detailed pitch (see the section on pitching on page 169).

Networking

In the small town of Hollywood, knowing somebody—or knowing somebody who knows somebody—is a big help in breaking into the industry.

Justin Adler's story is as typical as anything ever is in Hollywood. Adler wanted to write scripts, so right after college he got a job as a production assistant, an entry-level job, on *The Larry Sanders Show*. "I got it through family connections, which seems to be the way everything works out here," Adler said. "My uncle's second wife—her first husband's sister's husband was a line producer of *The Larry Sanders Show*."

Between getting coffee for his bosses and answering the phones, Adler kept writing. He also learned by watching staff writers write and rewrite scripts. Eventually, he wrote a spec script and showed it to writers he had met on the job. A couple liked it enough to show it to their own agents. From those contacts, he got calls to meet with agents—and learned that one good script isn't enough. All asked if he had another. "I lied and said I was writing one," he said. "So I frantically went and wrote an *Everybody Loves Raymond* show, a show I had never seen."

After watching tapes of the show again and again, he banged out a script in four days. It was enough to get him an agent with the powerful William Morris Agency. And the agent helped him find a job as a writer on other shows.

The lesson: Use contacts and networks, but keep writing. Even if your first script is a pearl, you'll be expected to write more.

Many people think that if you want to write for Hollywood, you must move to Hollywood. That's because one of the best ways of getting someone to look at your script is to have someone else, already working in the business, recommend it to a friend. Even if that friend isn't involved in actually making the decision about buying it, she may recommend it to others, or she may move up and remember your script.

If you don't live in Hollywood, find a connection to someone who does. Ask your friends if they know anyone in the business. Ask your neighbors. Take a course at a local college from someone who has worked in television or film. Remember, every successful person in Hollywood was a beginner once, and many remember how it feels.

Market the Script on Your Own

If you don't have an agent, and have no contacts in the business, you can still market your script on your own. Before you try, however, take one preparatory step: Register your script with the Writers Guild of America (see the sidebar on page 169 for more on this organization). Registration provides a dated record of the writer's claim to authorship and can be used as evidence in legal disputes about authorship. Note the number the Guild assigns you on the title page. Then, try to get someone to read it. There are, of course, many ways to do that.

If you want to break into television, it's generally not a good idea to write scripts for a series of your own invention. Full-time, experienced, professional writers earn monumental salaries doing just that; why compete with them? Instead, tape several shows of an existing series. Watch them repeatedly. Learn who the characters are, how they would behave in any situation. One writer even advised typing up the script as you watch an episode to help you understand the flow of the dialogue.

Also watch the credits of a show you enjoy, noting the names of the producers. You can write to them, asking them to read your script. While the number of scripts bought from freelancers in television is small, it does happen.

"I've never met a producer who wouldn't kill to get a great script out of the blue sky one morning," J. Michael Straczynski wrote in his *Complete Book of Scriptwriting*. After targeting a show, Straczynski recommends writing polite query letters to producers or story editors (usually people who rewrite scripts and deal with freelancers), explaining your fondness for and familiarity with the show and your desire to send in a spec script.

At any given time, certain shows are hot markets for spec scripts. If you have a friend who knows anyone working in television, you can try to find out which shows "everybody" is writing spec scripts for. Many suggest that it's better to pick a show that you enjoy, that is climbing in the ratings, but that isn't a hit. After all, there are only so many *Everybody Loves Raymond* scripts any one person can stand to read.

Once you write a script, remember another Hollywood paradox: Rarely is a spec script for a show ever bought and produced by that particular show. In fact, many writers advise against even trying to show it to anyone involved with the show. Why? Because the writers of that show know their characters better than anyone else ever could, and rarely can an outsider create a script better than they. One writer suggested that it's rarer still for a producer to admit someone outside his show even could. So, if you want to write for *CSI*, you need to write a script for *NYPD Blue* or another police/investigation drama and submit that as your spec script to the producers of *CSI*.

Then, even if your script is rejected, it may be a good enough calling card to get you invited to pitch other ideas to the producers (see section on pitching on page 169).

To sell a film script, you need to match your script with the appropriate market. The best bet for a beginning writer is a "little" movie, not a big-budget, special-effects-laden extravaganza, said Ronald Tobias, the television and documentary writer and author of *The Insider's Guide to Writing for Screen and Television*. This means you can indulge in little of the sweeping action of a *Saving Private Ryan*, for example, but you can develop an original story line and compelling characters. "A friend of mine just sold a script to Bill Pullman's production company (Big Town Productions/Castle Rock) in which Pullman is slated to star," Tobias said. "Its budget is under $10 million. There's no question that the film wouldn't have made it as far as it has if it had been written as a $30-million to $50-million picture."

Whatever type of movies you enjoy writing, remember to study films and film credits. Note what types of movies a producer, director, or actor typically makes, because you can pitch your script to any of them.

Straczynski recommends listing production companies that might be interested in a script similar to yours, then finding the telephone number for the story department and getting the name of the story editor. Write this person a one-page query letter and hope it will grab his attention.

While many producers will not look at a script unless it is sent by an agent, some of them will. Even if you have an agent, simply waiting for him to sell your script may waste time. Competition is so keen that writers today must be innovative in finding ways to get people to read their scripts. "I once gave a studio head a script by having his endodontist (my friend and a coconspirator) drop it in his lap while he was in the chair," Tobias said. "He thought the approach so novel, he laughed and took it home and read it. Creativity is the key. Find ways around the barricades."

Sending scripts to actors' agents is the worst thing to do, he said, because these agents are "trained to turn people and material away." But it's possible to ask an actor directly to read your script. In his hometown of Bozeman, Montana, for example, Tobias said he can contact at least fifty well-known actors, producers, and directors who pass through the city. Although people believe actors are unapproachable, with the exception of the biggest names, most are receptive if you are friendly, ask politely for help, and defer to their judgment.

Check your local phone book for a film commission, an agency that encourages moviemakers to come to town. Look up the phone numbers of local actors who may be listed in the phone book. They might well be kind enough to read your script, might have contacts in the business, and might send it on to be read by their contacts. Ask.

Another way in is to write. Tobias once had a student who wrote the producer of a television show criticizing the direction the characters had been taking in the show. The result: The show's producer called her, talked with her for two hours, and asked if she would move to Los Angeles to work with him on a new series.

The book *Opening the Doors to Hollywood* recounts how David

Permut, who later became a producer of such movies as *Dragnet* and *Blind Date*, started his career by sending hundreds of letters around Hollywood, asking for "any advice you might have that might further my career." He received hundreds of form letter responses, but also some personal ones. One from writer Sidney Sheldon said, "I can think of nothing that would offer you as much future security, with the possible exception of going over Niagara Falls in a leaky raft. But if you are really interested in pursuing this endeavor, please call me."

UCLA film school chairman Richard Walter said beginners also might try writing flattering letters to other writers or producers. The letters may help you make a friend of someone who knows how hard it is to break in, and who, eventually, might agree to help you.

While many experts caution against sending the full script to anyone unasked, doing so has, paradoxically, worked. When Cynthia Whitcomb, a former columnist for *Writer's Digest*, was starting out, her first scripts accumulated 120 consecutive rejections. Then, she read a *Los Angeles Times* article that said producer Tony Bill, who had produced *The Sting*, was starting a new production company. She got his address from the Producers Guild and dropped off her script—a period piece similar to *The Sting*—cold. He called, told her, among other things, that her script was too expensive, but asked her to work with him on another project. That began a career that has since included the sale of sixty scripts for movies, and television movies and miniseries.

One last paradox to keep in mind: Even if someone in Hollywood adores your script and buys it, chances are it will be rewritten—if not by you, then by others. Film and television are collaborative media, and writers must learn to expect changes to the script. Screenwriter Jim Burnstein once told a reporter that only the title and lead character's first name remained from his first draft of the movie *Renaissance Man*.

Remember, too, however, that the writing is the foundation for all movies and every television comedy or drama ever made. Hollywood will recognize a good script, and the writer who created it will be rewarded.

The Writers Guild of America

The Writers Guild is a union that you must join once you are employed as a scriptwriter, but it's also useful to beginners who have never sold a word.

Actually, there is a Writers Guild East and a Writers Guild West (the larger of the two). They split because in 1954, when they were formed, live television was based primarily in New York and filmed television and films were in Hollywood. Although the guilds' contracts became national by 1981, their governance remained split. Talks to merge the two unions failed in 1998.

The WGA West publishes a monthly magazine, *Written By*, which covers topics of interest to writers, as well as a list of television shows in production, along with contact names and phone numbers.

The WGA West's Web site is full of information, including sections on tools of the trade, interviews with writers about how they got their first breaks, and questions from beginning writers to WGA "mentors." It also includes links to sites and experts who can help writers research stories. In addition, it lists agents who have agreed to abide by the WGA's standards for representing writers, including those who will accept new writers, and more.

The Writers Guilds on both coasts offer another important service to nonmembers: They register written works for radio, theater, television, motion pictures, video cassettes or discs and interactive media. You can register scripts, treatments, synopses, outlines, and written ideas.

Making the Pitch

Even if a producer rejects your script, he still may like your writing style and invite you to pitch more ideas—in person.

It seems paradoxical that someone who is good at writing would be asked to explain his ideas orally. But there's a reason for it: The Writers Guild won't allow writers to be asked to write something without being paid, so you have to tell people your ideas before getting a contract to write them.

Your "pitch" is essentially a short (one to three sentences) description of your script that you can expand upon to add detailed information as you generate interest from an agent or producer. For example, the pitch for *Life as a House* might have started something like this: "A middle-aged man with a failed marriage and a failed career suddenly discovers he has only months to live. He begins a monumental project that draws in his son and ex-wife, and reestablishes ties of love." From that starting point, the writer can provide more information about the story, characters, and plot twists, focusing on whatever elements seem to spark the interest of the agent or producer.

Like most difficult things, pitching gets easier with practice. Practice pitching in front of a mirror, to your friends, to your dog. Be enthusiastic. Remember how much you love your story. Recount the big picture, but expect to be asked questions about details. Above all else, be brief.

Remember to relax. As Heidi Wall, founder of the Flash Forward Institute, a coaching center for the entertainment industry, once told a WGA writer: "Everyone already knows how to pitch. We do it all the time. Whenever you try to convince someone to go to a movie with you, you're pitching."

A pitch can last from a few seconds to maybe as much as fifteen minutes if the producer is interested and keeps asking for more information. Just be sure to go to a pitch meeting armed with several ideas. If the first one doesn't fly, you'll have something to say if the executive's eyes roll back and he and asks, "So what else are you working on?"

Understand the Business

Reading industry publications helps beginning writers procure some marketing savvy: You will learn who makes what types of films—and you won't make the mistake of sending an idea for a musical comedy, for example, to Oliver Stone. Since smaller budget movies are more salable for beginners, when reading industry news you'll learn how much things cost to produce. (The average movie costs about $53 million to make and market, or roughly $530,000 per page of script.) You will learn whether a film studio already is working on a movie that you thought was your very own idea. You will learn which producers make movies or shows similar to your own. Learning about the business of television and film can help you sell your scripts.

Read newspapers, such as *The New York Times* or the *Los Angeles Times*, that offer useful information about film and television production. Peruse trade publications, such as *Variety* or *The Hollywood Reporter*, available in many libraries and also available online. These not only report what types of deals are being made, but they also list movies and shows in production, along with contact information of some key players.

One of the more useful trade publications for writers, however, is *Written By*, the magazine of the Writers Guild of America West. This magazine includes interviews with writers about writing, stories about how writers broke in to the business, and a section listing television shows, with the name and phone number for writers to contact.

Many publications offer addresses and phone numbers of people who may be interested in your script. You can find the address for a writer or his agent from the Writers Guild, for an actor's agent or production company from the Screen Actors Guild, for directors through the Directors Guild of America, and for producers from the Producers Guild of America. The Directors Guild and Writers Guild also publish directories of their members. (See pages 175-176 for contact information for each organization.) *The Hollywood Creative Directory*, published online and three times a year in paper form, also includes detailed staff lists for studios production companies.

Books also can help you target the right market for selling and finding agents. *Opening the Doors to Hollywood*, for example, includes a reference section that lists guilds/unions, libraries, sample contracts, seminars and workshops, trade publications, and writers organizations. *Guide to Literary Agents* lists agencies according to their interests in handling ten categories of movies and of television programs, from animation to variety shows, and also according to subject matter, from action/adventure to westerns/frontier.

Resources for Selling Your Scripts

Use the following books, magazines and trade publications, organizations, seminars and workshops, and Web sites to learn more about scriptwriting and how to sell your script.

Books

Here are some top books on formatting, writing, and selling your script:

Adventures in the Screen Trade: A Personal View of Hollywood & Screenwriting (Warner Books), by William Goldman. This book offers insider advice and instruction on how to be successful in Hollywood.

All You Need to Know About the Movie & TV Business (Simon & Schuster), by Gail Resnik and Scott Trost. This book covers all aspects of the film and television business, including information on business and legal matters.

The Complete Book of Scriptwriting (Writer's Digest Books), by J. Michael Straczynski. This book teaches you how to write and sell your scripts for television, movies, animation, radio, and the theater.

The Complete Guide to Standard Script Formats (CMC Publishing), by Hillis R. Cole and Judith H. Haag. You'll find information on how to properly format your script for submission.

Elements of Style for Screenwriters: The Essential Manual for Writers of Screenplays (Lone Eagle Publishing Company), by Paul Argentini. This step-by-step guide helps you understand industry terminology, formatting guidelines, etc. Also includes information on playwriting.

Four Screenplays: Studies in the American Screenplay (Dell Publishing), by Syd Field. The author looks at why four top films work, including *Dances With Wolves, Thelma and Louise, The Silence of the Lambs,* and *Terminator 2.*

From Script to Screen: The Collaborative Art of Filmmaking (Holt), by Linda Seger and Edward J. Whetmore. This book provides a careful look at the moviemaking process, from the first idea, to the final music score.

Guide to Literary Agents (Writer's Digest Books), edited by Kathryn S. Brogan. This annually updated book includes contact information and submission guidelines for agents.

How to Sell Your Screenplay: The Real Rules of Film & Television (New Chapter Press), by Carl Sautter. This book covers the basics of screenwriting, including information on spec scripts, episodic television, etc.

How to Sell Your Screenplay: A Realistic Guide to Getting a Television or Film Deal (Square One Publishers), by Lydia Wilen and Joan Wilen. This book provides information on screenplay format, sample contracts, how to approach buyers, and more.

How to Write a Selling Screenplay (Bantam Dell), by Christopher Keane. The author takes you step-by-step through the script-writing process, using his own screenplay, *The Crossing*, as a guide.

Making a Good Script Great (Samule French), by Linda Seger. The author uses her expertise as a script consultant, screenwriter, and film critic to provide you with insider knowledge on how to improve your work.

The New Screenwriter Looks at the New Screenwriter (Silman-James Press), by William Froug. This book features interviews with movie and television writers, along with agents.

Opening the Doors to Hollywood: How to Sell Your Idea, Story, Screenplay, Manuscript (Random House), by Carlos de Abreu and Howard J. Smith. This book includes information on how to spot an idea, revision tips, etc.

Screenplay: The Foundations of Screenwriting (Fine Communications), by Syd Field. For beginners and experienced screenwriters, this book covers everything from technique to style.

The Screenwriter's Bible: A Complete Guide to Writing, Formatting, and Selling Your Script (Silman-James Press), by David Trottier. Covering a wide range of scriptwriting issues, this book includes a spec writing guide, a formatting guide, a resource guide, a sales and marketing guide, and much more.

The Screenwriter's Problem Solver: How to Recognize, Identify, & Define Screenwriting Problems (Dell Publishing), by Syd Field. This book looks at twenty different specific problems, each related to plot, character, or structure.

The Screenwriter's Workbook (Dell Publishing), by Syd Field. This "hands-on workshop" will help you refine your skills as a scriptwriter.

Screenwriting Tricks of the Trade (Silman-James Press), by William Froug. The founder of UCLA's film and television writing program, Froug provides you with the encouragement and techniques you need to finish your script.

The Script is Finished, Now What Do I Do? (Sweden Press), by K. Callan. This script-marketing guide provides solid instruction on how to sell your script, including information for playwrights.

Successful Sitcom Writing (St. Martin's Press), by Jurgen Wolff. The author, who wrote episodes of Family Ties and The Love Boat, offers practical advice on how to write a successful sitcom, including tips on character development, subplots, etc.

Writing Screenplays That Sell (HarperPerennial), by Michael Hauge. This step-by-step manual teaches you how to develop your craft from start to finish, and includes a script analysis of *The Karate Kid*.

Magazines and Trade Publications

The publications listed below cover everything from technique to industry news:

Hollywood Creative Directory: www.hcdonline.com. Offers up-to-date contact information for producers, television shows, studio and network executives.

Hollywood Reporter: www.hollywoodreporter.com. A daily trade paper for the entertainment industry, covering film, television, music, and more.

Hollywood Scriptwriter Magazine: www.hollywoodscript-writer.com. Offers articles that give basic information about how to reach your goals in the film industry, and includes advice from experts.

Screenwriter Magazine: www.nyscreenwriter.com. Features interviews with successful screenwriters.

Premiere Magazine: www.premieremag.com. Gives film reviews, stories about celebrities, award information, and more about the film entertainment industry.

Script Magazine: www.scriptmag.com. Offers information and advice to those trying to break into scriptwriting. Includes articles on craft and development, and successful screenwriters.

Variety: www.variety.com. Source for entertainment news and analysis.

Writer's Digest: www.writersdigest.com. Offers basic information about writing and selling scripts.

Organizations

Organizations, such as the ones listed here, can provide you with additional resources for developing your skills as a scriptwriter:

Agent Research and Evaluation, 25 Barrow St., New York, NY 10014. Tel: (212) 924-9942. E-mail: info@agentresearch.com. Web site: www.agentresearch.com. Offers services to help you locate the agent who is right for you.

Association of Authors' Representatives, P.O. Box 237201, Ansonia Station, New York, NY 10003. E-mail: aarinc@mindspring.com. Web site: www.aar-online.org. Agents in this organization must meet professional standards, such as no reading fees.

Directors Guild of America—Los Angeles, 7920 Sunset Blvd., Los Angeles, CA 90046. Tel: (310) 289-2000. Web site: www.dga.org. Offers up-to-date information on the industry and legal rights. Other locations include: Directors Guild of America—New York, 110 W. 57th St., New York, NY 10019. Tel: (212) 581-0370. Web site: www.dga.org. Directors Guild of America—Chicago, 400 N. Michigan Ave., Suite 307,

Chicago, IL 60611. Tel: (312) 664-5050. Web site: www.dga.org.

Produces Guild, 8530 Wilshire Blvd., Suite 450, Beverly Hills, CA 90211. Tel: (310) 358-9020. Web site: www.producersguild.org. offers information on all aspects of producing a motion picture, television show or news media. Has over 1,700 members worldwide.

Screen Actors Guild, East, 360 Madison Ave., 12th Fl., New York, NY 10017. Tel: (212) 944-1030. Web site: www.sag.com. Gives current information on the industry, interviews with high-profile members, and membership gives many other privileges. Another branch is: Screen Actors Guild, West, 5757 Wilshire Blvd., Los Angeles, CA 90036. Tel: (323) 954-1600. Web site: www.sag.com.

Writers Guild of America, East, 555 West 57th Street, Suite 1230, New York, NY 10019. Tel: (212) 767-7800. Web site: www.wgae.org. Offers information and tools for writers and represents writers in motion picture, broadcast, cable and new technologies industries. Another branch is: Writers Guild of America, West, 7000 West Third Street, Los Angeles, CA 90048. Tel: (323) 951-4000. Web site: www.wga.org.

Seminars and Workshops

If you'd like to learn more about scriptwriting, a seminar or workshop may be for you:

Michael Hauge's Screenplay Mastery, P.O. Box 55728, Sherman Oaks, CA 91013. Tel: (800) 477-1947. Web site: www.screenplaymastery.com. For writers and filmmakers trying to get their screenplay produced.

Robert McKee's Story Seminar, P.O. Box 452930, Los Angeles, CA 90045. Tel: (888) 676-2533. Web site: www.mckeestory.com. Three day seminars for screenwriters, television writers, film and television executives, directors, producers, and more.

Linda Seger, 4705 Hagerman Avenue, Cascade, CO 80809. Tel: (719) 684-0405. Web site: www.lindaseger.com. Offers seminars on the art and craft of screenwriting.

Web Sites

The Web sites listed here will keep you up-to-date on the latest industry deals and more:

Done Deal: www.scriptsales.com. A daily news resource for the industry that offers interviews, production company listing, contests, and more.

Drew's Scripts-O-Rama: www.script-o-rama.com. Offers access to free scripts and information about what's new in the industry.

Screenwriters Online: www.screenwriter.com. Offers information from professional screenwriters, expert screenplay analysis, and instruction on the nuts and bolts of screenwriting.

Studio Systems, Inc: www.studiosystemsinc.com. Offers unique and verified information and research for the film and television industries.

WritersNet: www.writers.net. Offers writing resources and news for writers, editors, publishers, and agents.

CHAPTER TEN

Selling to Corporations

The health care industry in America spends more than $1.3 billion a year on printed materials. The auto industry spends nearly as much. Retailers, beverage makers, computer companies, and telecommunications firms spend billions more. In fact, the twenty-five leading industries in the United States spend more than $8 billion a year on printed material, be it brochures, newsletters, catalogs, signage, instruction manuals, press releases, speeches, new home descriptions, or employee handbooks. Words are everywhere we look—and someone has to write them, which gives freelance writers an endless number of markets.

Even the magazine market extends far beyond the well-known titles you typically find at bookstores and newsstands. There are literally tens of thousands of specialty magazines published by corporations, trade groups, and other organizations. The subject matter may be narrow in scope and sometimes technical in nature, but an article that is worth $300 to a consumer magazine could be worth many times that much to the right corporate client.

The trick is to find the right buyer. Fortunately, ~~the~~ the opportunities have never been greater. Corporations of every type are finding that hiring freelancers cuts overhead costs. In addition, they can hire freelancers only when needed instead of hiring an employee who may be idle during slow work periods. Technology now enables freelance writers to interact with any company regardless of location.

Finding Your Own Opportunities

Savvy freelancers keep tabs on the local business scene to find out about new businesses in town or changes in existing businesses, such as new ownership or expansion, that may indicate a need for freelance help. As with any area of business, networking is important when looking for corporate assignments.

Call all writing-related professional organizations in your area and join the active ones. Women in Communications, the Public Relations Society of America, the International Association of Business Communicators, the Society for Technical Communications—many of these national organizations may have branches in your area. Most of them publish directories of their members, often listing the member's place of employment. This gives you an automatic contact—especially if you've involved yourself in the social networking system these organizations encourage.

Take a look at the business community in your area: Who are the ten or twenty biggest employers? Your local business newspaper can give you this information. Keep your eyes and ears open for listings of all kinds: Search them out in business newspapers, papers by the Chamber of Commerce or tourism bureau, and directories of every type. Explore your local library for directories for a variety of fields, often indexed geographically, including the *Encyclopedia of Associations* and the *Directory of Directories*.

To get an idea of just how far you can take this game of "who needs writers?" try this exercise today: Take a conscious look around you at written copy wherever you are—a calendar that has photo captions, signs on the backs of benches or high up on billboards, even your own mail, especially direct mail (also called junk mail). These were all written by someone, somewhere, who presumably collected a nice paycheck for his trouble. Of course, not all of these were written by freelancers, but it's safe to assume that any of them could have been. There are few communications areas left that exclude work-for-hire as a possibility.

It's usually not practical to be a freelance generalist and hire yourself out for any kind of writing. As with most professions, specialization is the key to success. In fact, before you approach any organization you should learn everything you can about its history, culture, products or services, and customer base. Only then can you find your niche and successfully sell yourself as the right person for the job.

Once you've located organizations that might need your help, send a cover letter with a good sales pitch, a short bio, and writing samples to the appropriate person in the communications, public relations, or marketing department. Make sure you send your material to a specific person and that you've spelled her name correctly.

The person to contact at some of the larger companies and organizations may go by any number of titles. She may be a director of publications, corporate communications, or public relations. If the company has a sophisticated operation, it may have borrowed the term *creative services director* from the advertising industry, particularly if it uses both print and audiovisual media. Sometimes the word *marketing* will be in the title; other times that word will lead you into the wrong department altogether. It depends on the kind of company.

The usual methods of networking through individual colleagues as well as professional associations, combined with cold calling, will help you locate the jobs you seek. But whether you are approaching an agency, company, or individual, it's always wise to parlay your previous experience into new opportunities.

When you do find work, be sure to get everything in writing. At the very least, make sure the assignment, deadline, and payment terms are clearly outlined in a letter of agreement. In the business world especially, these kinds of agreements are a sign of professionalism and are appreciated on all sides.

Advertising and PR

One way to sell your writing is to target the kind of company that depends on writers and may frequently use freelance writers: advertising and public relations firms. These are the experts to whom many companies turn for help in developing their various communications-related projects. In fact, if you go to a company on your own to vie for

Job Banks and Agencies

Writers have banded together in many places for mutual aid in finding work. National, regional, and local groups offer help for writers seeking anything from freelance assignments to full-time jobs. Writers should not hesitate to contact these organizations and inquire about their services.

The National Writers Association offers information about freelance market opportunities through its bimonthly newsletter. The National Writers Union has an online listing of opportunities for writers. From more information on these groups, contact:

National Writers Association, 3140 S. Peoria St., #295PMB, Aurora, CO 80014. Tel: (303) 841-0246. Web site: www.nationalwriters.com.

National Writers Union, 113 University Pl. 6th Fl., New York, NY 10003. Tel: (212) 254-0279. E-mail: nwu@nwu.org. Web site: www.nwu.org.

The Editorial Freelancers Association and the American Society of Journalists and Authors provide referral services that offer their members access to job and project leads. For more information on these groups, contact:

Editorial Freelancers Association, 71 W. 23rd St., Suite 1910, New York, NY 10010. Tel: (866) 929-5400. E-mail: info@the-efa.org. Web site: www.the-efa.org.

American Society of Journalists and Authors, 1501 Broadway, Suite 302, New York, NY 10036. Tel: (212) 997-0947. E-mail: execdir@asja.org. Web site: www.asja.org.

Many cities also have for-profit agencies that provide work for freelance writers and editors. The agencies generally screen freelance writers to determine their interests, credentials, and fees. In some instances writers become employees of the agency and receive insurance, retirement, disability, and vacation benefits. Traditional employment agencies and temporary services firms sometimes provide work for freelancers. It's easy enough to look them up in the phonebook and call.

a freelance assignment, you may compete against advertising and PR agencies for an assignment. But for now, let's look at how to get an assignment from such a firm and the advantages of selecting this route.

The biggest advantage to freelancing through an advertising or PR agency is that the agency finds the clients; all you have to do is complete the work. This can be attractive if you tire of freelance hustling, especially if you can become a regular in an agency's stable of freelancers. You may assure yourself a steady source of income, and if it's a quality firm, you enhance your own reputation by association.

If you already have some experience with a specific kind of assignment (you've designed and written brochures in your last job) or you're well grounded in a certain area of expertise (you're a volunteer or a past employee in an organization that caters to senior citizens), sell yourself as an expert in this area.

There are two main reasons public relations firms might hire freelance help. Sometimes expertise is needed, such as in writing about engineering, medicine, accounting, etc. So, it's good to have special knowledge or to develop an expertise. Secondly, because they must produce a large volume of collateral material, firms sometimes find themselves in need of freelance help when the workload gets too heavy. This collateral material can take the form of a postcard, a brochure, or even a direct-mail piece. Sometimes a company will be looking for someone who can shepherd a project from conceptualization to production. Other times they may only need simple copy writing.

Some large—and not so large—organizations may have their own in-house creative department that is in need of occasional—or not so occasional—assistance. Hospitals are especially open to freelance help. Federal cutbacks and outside competition have forced many hospitals to walk a financial tightrope—while producing more written copy. It's no coincidence that hospitals have increased their use of freelancers to supplement or take the place of in-house employees. Many arts organizations are facing a similar situation.

Freelancers with skill in speechwriting are especially in demand. Executives don't hire speechwriters the way a politician does. Someone from the public relations department is usually assigned the job on top of their normal duties. As a freelancer, speechwriting may be something you can do a few times a year, along with numerous other assignments. So if you have a particular knack for speechwriting, serve it up as an area of expertise.

Professional Organizations

Always keep an eye out for local and national organizations that can help you improve your networking opportunities:

American Marketing Association, 311 S. Wacker Dr., Suite 5800, Chicago, IL 60606. Tel: (800) 262-1150. Web site: www.marketingpower.com. Has 38,000 members and provides marketing information through research, case studies and journals that stay on top of emerging trends.

Association for Women in Communications, 780 Ritchie Highway, Suite 28-S, Severna Park, MD 21146. Tel: (410) 544-7442. Web site: www.womcom.org. Promotes advancement of women in communication fields by recognizing excellence, advocating leadership, and positioning members at the forefront of communications.

Public Relations Society of America, 33 Irving Place, New York, NY 10003. Tel: (212) 995-2230. Web site: www.prsa.org. World's largest organization of PR professionals. Offers continuing education, information exchange forums, and more

Other Resources

These publications can help you make the right industry connections:

DM News, 100 Avenue of the Americas, New York, NY 10013. Tel: (212) 925-7300. Web site: www.dmnews.com. This weekly "Newspaper of Record for Direct Marketers," provides information to direct and Internet marketers on trends, news, etc.

Standard Directory of Advertising Agencies (National Register Publishing). Also known as the "Red Book," this resource lists more than 14,000 agencies worldwide along with their area of specialization, annual billings, account rosters, key personnel, and contact information.

Technical Writing

While the goal of creative writing is to entertain and that of advertising writing is to sell, the primary goal of technical writing is the accurate transmission of information. Technical writing, then, can be described as putting complicated information into plain language in a format that is easy to understand. The tone is objective and favors content over style. (This does not mean, however, that you should present the subject in a formal, stunted style.) Above all, technical writing should be concise, complete, clear, and consistent. The best way to achieve all these is to make sure your writing is well organized.

By far the biggest area for technical writers is in the computer industry, though there are a wide variety of possible assignments, including preparation of customer letters, utility bills, owner manuals, insurance benefit packages, and even contracts (some states have "plain language" laws requiring that contracts and insurance policies to be written in simple English). In any technical field, writers who can bridge the gap between engineers who design things and the customers who use them are in high demand.

Technical writers do not necessarily need formal training in the areas they cover. To the contrary, one the greatest talents a technical writer brings to a project is the ability to take a step back from the technical details and see the subject from a different perspective than the engineers, scientists, and experts. Thus, a technical writer becomes familiar with a subject by interviewing experts, reading journals and reports, reviewing drawings, studying specifications, and examining product samples.

Technical writers themselves often shy away from the term *freelance writer*, preferring to be known instead as *independent contractors* or consultants. This probably has a lot to do with the fact that technical writers work mostly with corporations, where the term independent contractor sounds more impressive. It's very important to establish and maintain a high degree of credibility when working with firms.

The number of ways to enter the technical writing field are as varied as the people entering it. If you're cold-calling large companies, you'll want to contact the manager of technical communications or manager of documentation. Local employment agencies may also be of service.

If you lack the experience, build a portfolio by volunteering to write material for a nonprofit organization, or offer to help your colleagues prepare reports and presentations. If you are interested in pursuing this type of work, it is probably a good idea to join the Society for Technical Communications where you can network to gain contacts in the industry. Many businesses hire writers from the STC talent pool.

The National Technical Employment Service is another good source of work. Through its weekly newspaper, *Hot Flash,* it gives job listings for contract employees nationwide. The annual subscription rate also includes a quarterly directory of companies as well as a "shopper index" that publishes summaries of contractors seeking employment in this field.

Professional Organizations

Here's a sampling of the professional associations open to writers:

American Medical Writers, 40 W. Gude Dr., Suite 101, Rockville, MD 20850. Tel: (301) 294-5303. Fax: (301) 294-9006. E-mail: info@amwa.org. Web site: www.amwa.org. Provides educational sources for biomedical writers, and offers networking opportunities.

Council of Science Editors, c/o Drohan Management Group, 12100 Sunset Hills Rd., Suite 130, Reston, VA 20190. Tel: (703) 437-4377. E-mail: CSE@CouncilScienceEditors.org. Web site: www.councilscienceeditors.org. Offers networking opportunities and cutting edge information for those who work in science writing, editing or publishing.

Society for Technical Communications, 901 N. Stuart St., Suite 904, Arlington, VA 22203. Tel: (703) 522-4114. E-mail: stc@stc.org. Web site: www.stc.org. Supports the arts and sciences of technical writing with networking and learning opportunities. Has over 25,000 members and it available to anyone whose work makes technical information available.

Books

The following can help you improve your technical writing skills:

Art of Technical Documentation (Digital Press), by Katherine Haramundanis. This book provides instruction for improving your technical writing, using graphics, editing, etc.

The Complete Guide to Writing and Producing Technical Manuals (John Wiley & Sons), by Leslie M. Haydon. This step-by-step manual takes you through the entire process of putting together a technical manual.

Designing and Writing Online Documentation (John Wiley & Sons), by William Horton. This book provides information on how to write and design screen menus, screen messages, etc.

Elements of Technical Writing (Pearson Higher Education), by Gary Blake and Robert Bly. From grammar and punctuation, to word choice and technical communication specifics, this book has it all.

Good Style: Writing for Science and Technology (Routledge), by John Kirkman. This book provides instruction on putting together a technical report and includes examples.

Science and Technical Writing: A Manual of Style (Routledge), edited by Phillip Rubens. This book includes helpful information on audience analysis, document planning, punctuating scientific jargon, etc.

Copyediting and Proofreading

The real heroes of the writing profession are the copyeditors and proofreaders who labor to make the rest of us look good. If you've ever known someone who excels at copyediting and proofreading, you know that both take real talent. For those who possess the unique ability, copyediting and proofreading can be a good source of additional income.

Copyediting: The writer's direct supervisor or editor usually edits stories for content and organization. The role of the copy editor, then, is to look for additional spelling errors and typos. He may raise questions about conflicting statements and may be charged with smoothing awkward text transitions and ensuring uniform type style. In some cases a copy editor may even rewrite portions of copy to improve the flow of text or to maintain a uniform tone. A copy editor may also be expected to keep an eye out for libel. At newspapers and magazines, it is often the copy editor's job to write headlines and photo captions. Copy editors are also called upon to design pages. This may involve deciding which stories, photos and graphics will run and which will be featured most prominently. (Before beginning any job, freelance editors should determine the level of work expected and base their fees accordingly.)

Proofreading: Proofreaders are charged with looking for typographical and mechanical errors after all other editing is complete. A proofreader may check typeset copy word for word against a manuscript and identify any deviations. They look for misspellings, missing copy, typos, misnumbering, mislabeling, and incorrect cross-references. Proofreaders may also check copy for conformity to type specifications and ensure attractive typography by checking letter or word spacing, margins, and repetitive word breaks.

The extent to which a copy editor or proofreader must verify facts varies widely. Often this is the job of a separate fact checker. A fact checker does not make editorial changes but simply verifies accuracy. One client may request that the fact checker verify all statements, while another client may request the verification of addresses and trademarks only.

Copy editors and proofreaders are in high demand, so if you look hard enough and are willing to start small enough you are likely to find work. Smaller papers frequently need help. The pay may not be great, but jobs like that can build a résumé and provide an extra source of income. Keep in mind that there is plenty of copyediting and proofreading work at places other than publications. So don't overlook nonprofit organizations and big companies—any place that publishes anything.

To get any work you will almost certainly have to pass a test. To do this, study the stylebook for your chosen field or publication (most likely the *Associated Press Stylebook, The Chicago Manual of Style,* or

MLA Stylebook). Also memorize a list of most commonly misspelled words. You'll most likely out-test most of the competition.

Correspondence and Online Courses

If you want to improve your copyediting and/or proofreading skills, there are plenty of correspondence and online courses available:

American Press Institute, 11690 Sunrise Valley Dr., Reston, VA 20191. Tel: (703) 620-3611. E-mail: info@americanpressinstitute.org. Web: www.americanpressinstitute.org. Offers a week long seminars that focus on new technology in the field, and they each feature plenty of group discussions and individual attention.

Editcetera, 2034 Blake St., Suite 5, Berkeley, CA 94704. Tel: (510) 849-1110. E-mail: info@editcetera.com. Web: www.editcetera.com. Offers courses in developmental editing, copyediting, proofreading, and more either at Berkeley or via mail correspondence.

Graduate School, USDA, Capital Gallery Building, 600 Maryland Ave., SW, Suite 280, Washington, DC 20024. Tel: (888) 744-GRAD. E-mail: CustomerServiceCenter@grad.usda.gov. Web site: grad.usda.gov. Offers a wide variety of career-related continuing education for professionals throughout the country at various different times.

The New School Online University, 68 Fifth Ave., New York, NY 10011. Tel: (212) 229-5880. Web site: www.dialnsa.edu. Once registered, offers coursework, information, class discussions, and research links all online.

University of California Extension, UC Berkeley Extension Online, 2000 Center St., Suite 400, Berkeley, CA 94704. Tel: (510) 642-4124. E-mail: askus@ucxonline.berkeley.edu. Web site: learn.berkeley.edu. Offers a variety of interactive courses online for professionals.

University of Minnesota, 150 Wesbrook Hall, 77 Pleasant St. SE, Minneapolis, MN 55455. Tel: (800) 234-6564. E-mail: indstudy@umn.edu. Web site: www.idl.umn.edu. Offers accredited courses in a variety of subjects. Offers extended courses so students can work at their own pace for up to nine months.

Indexing

The indexes in the back of most nonfiction books are another source of income for freelance wordsmiths. While the index is sometimes the responsibility of the book's author, few actually do it themselves. Freelance indexers hired by the author or publisher usually do the work.

To do the job, an indexer will typically receive a set of page proofs, which are exact images of how pages will appear in the book, complete with page numbers. The indexer reads these proofs and compiles a list of subject headings, subheads, and the location of each key reference. Upon completing a rough draft of the index, the indexer then edits it, organizes it, and proofreads it.

Since indexing is one of the last steps in completing a book, indexers frequently work under intense pressure and time constraints. Indexing cannot be started until final page proofs are available. By that time the printer wants to get the job on the press and the publisher is clamoring for a finished product. As a result, skilled indexers must possess more than good language skills, attention to detail, patience, and an analytical mind—they must also be able to work well under pressure.

The indexing features of good word processing programs can help you handle the page numbering and sorting that is necessary for indexing. Special software also is available to help with editing, sorting, and formatting. But the bulk of the work must still be done manually.

Any college with an information science or library science program is likely to offer indexing courses. But before you invest in any training, research the field thoroughly to make sure you have what it takes.

Probably the best way to break into the business is to send résumés with cover letters to publishers. You can find their addresses in *Literary Marketplace*, *Writer's Market*, and *Books in Print*. It is hard to get established in the indexing business, but once you do get work—and do it well—it is easier to get jobs through word of mouth and a little networking.

Professional Groups

Joining a professional indexing organization may help improve your indexing skills and provide you with excellent networking opportunities:

American Society of Indexers, 10200 W. 44th Ave., Suite 304, Wheat Ridge, CO 80033. Tel: (303) 463-2887. E-mail: info@ asindexing.org. Web site: www.asindexing.org. Only professional organization in U.S. devoted to advancement of indexing.

Indexing and Abstracting Society of Canada, P.O. Box 664, Station P, Toronto, ON M5S 2Y4, Canada. Web site: www.index-ingsociety.ca. Encourages production and use, improves techniques, and provides communication between indexers in U.S. and Canada.

National Federation of Abstracting and Information Services, 1518 Walnut St., Suite 307, Philadelphia, PA 19102-3403. Tel: (215) 893-1561. E-mail: NFAIS@nfais.org. Web site: www.nfais.org. Serves groups that aggregate, organize, and facilitate access to information. Addresses common interests through education and advocacy.

Books

Want to learn more? Listed below are books to help you learn more about indexing:

The Art of Indexing (John Wiley & Sons), by Larry S. Bonura. Each step of the indexing process is covered in this book, as well as tips for online indexing and a style guide.

Indexes: A Chapter From the Chicago Manual of Style (University of Chicago Press). This brief guide offers solutions to common indexing problems, includes several examples, etc.

Indexing Books (University of Chicago Press), by Nancy C. Mulvany. Written by a professional indexer, this book covers the indexing process from start to finish.

Indexing From A to Z (H.W. Wilson), by Hans H. Wellisch. You'll find information on how to compile a standard index, as well as information on indexing periodicals.

Courses and Training

To learn more about indexing, or to enroll in a course or training session, try contacting one of the following places:

EEI Communications, 66 Canal Center Plaza, Suite 200, Alexandria, VA 22314. Tel: (703) 683-0683. E-mail: info@eeicommunications.com. Web site: www.eeicommunications.com. Offers online courses in indexing in a two-part series.

Graduate School, USDA, Capital Gallery Building, 600 Maryland Ave., SW, Suite 280, Washington, D.C. 20024. Tel: (888) 744-GRAD. E-mail: CustomerServiceCenter@grad.usda.gov. Web site: http://grad.usda.gov. Offers a wide variety of career-related continuing education for professionals throughout the country at various different times.

St. John's University, Library and Information Science Division, 8000 Utopia Parkway, Jamaica, NY 11439. Tel: (718) 990-6200. E-mail: velluccs@stjohns.edu. Web site: www.stjohns.edu. Offers courses in library sciences, as well as specific courses in indexing and abstracting.

Ghostwriting

When a book is ghostwritten, the person whose name appears on the book as primary author has done little or none of the actual writing. He is merely a source of information—providing content, background information, and, hopefully, credibility. Typically this person is a celebrity or someone well respected in his field of expertise. While he has the experience and the name recognition that can make for a best-selling book, he lacks professional writing credentials. As a result, the so-called author relies on a more experienced writer—a ghostwriter—to put his ideas into book form.

The ghostwriter gathers information for the book by interviewing the author and will often conduct her own research and interview several other sources as well for background material. While each collaboration is different, the author usually will review the manuscript and possibly even edit it for content. For their part, ghostwriters may be credited as a co-author or get no visible credit at all. (Their motivation is often a five- or six-figure check and the opportunity to get even more lucrative work either as authors or as ghostwriters.)

The arrangement that a ghostwriter walks into is inherently more complex than the typical relationship between a writer and publisher (which is complex enough). It's easy for misunderstandings to arise between the so-called author and publisher, with the ghostwriter being caught in the middle. In one sense, the ghostwriter is a translator—taking what the author has to offer and trying to deliver what the publisher expects. The best way to diffuse some of this conflict is to clearly map out in writing what each party expects from the arrangement. When all is said and done there may still be misunderstandings, but at least the ghostwriter can justify what he has done.

There are a number of ways to break into ghostwriting. One is to seek out a rising star, either in sports, entertainment, business, or politics. Publishers are often in search of new talent and new celebrities. Armed with a collaboration agreement and the right amount of talent, you can sell your services to a publisher.

As you gain experience and become specialized in a certain subject area, you will find it easier to sell your talents to publishers who are looking for ghostwriters in that field of expertise. Along the way you can build your résumé by collaborating on magazine articles with celebrities or experts in your chosen field of specialization. Magazines do not knowingly accept ghostwritten articles, but they would accept, for instance, an article on the modern history of baseball, "as told to" John Doe.

Very often, successful executives or entrepreneurs are looking for writers who can help them self-publish a book of their own. The finished books are then distributed through their businesses to clients, coworkers, and relatives. This is a great way to get work and hone your talents, and possibly even make a name for yourself.

Selling Your Work Online

W hen the first edition of this book was published in 2000, the Internet was much of a plaything, its full utility yet to be understood. Today, it is hard to imagine how anyone ever got anything accomplished without it—and that's particularly true for writers.

The Internet is at once a tool for communication and research, and writers are expected to use e-mail to query and submit articles to publications. It's also becoming essential for writers to have their own Web site to showcase their work and expertise. What is unclear, however, is when the Internet will become a viable market for writers.

While advertising dollars spent in online markets have been slow to increase since the technology sector declined in 2001, the industry is reviving, and interest in online information among consumers has only increased. Trends indicate that more online publications will begin charging for their content to become healthy enough to pay freelancers. At present, however, the number of profitable online markets is few, and those that do remain are often extensions of print publications that repurpose their materials for online use. So you have to look harder than maybe you did several years ago to find well-paying gigs.

Finding Markets and Other Online Opportunities

The process of selling your work online doesn't dramatically differ from selling to paper-and-ink publications. As any successful freelancer knows, to make the sale, you must find a market that matches the story you want to write—whose audience and style you understand and appreciate. Also, never forget that you should be paid for your work, online or off. Even if the pay is low, if you retain your rights to your work, you can resell it to other markets to make it pay again and again.

Some basic places to start your online market search include:

- **Print publications**. Most traditional magazines have online counterparts that publish original content. *Popular Mechanics*, *Christian Camp & Conference Journal*, and *Wine Spectator* are just three examples of print magazines that feature original content on their respective Web sites. To find out if a print magazine you like publishes original online contact, check its writers guidelines.

- **Electronic publications**. These online-only publications may not pay as much as print publications, but they can provide you with invaluable experience. For example, *American Woman Road & Travel*, a biweekly online magazine that covers automotive and travel topics for women, buys thirty articles per year. *Simple Joy*, a monthly online publication focusing on home and relationship articles, buys more than a hundred articles each year. To find other online-only publications, search the Internet or consult an online directory like WritersMarket.com that allows you to narrow your search to online-exclusive publications.

- **E-newsletters**. Many electronic newsletters accept content from freelancers. Check with the editors of some of your favorite newsletters and see if they hire freelancers. If so, send a professional query outlining your idea.

- **Corporate Web sites**. Securing a corporate assignment may depend on your contacts, which can be invaluable in uncovering well-paying online markets. Still, the ease of finding things on the Web may make it easy for an you to find an employer.

- **Start a Web log.** Sometimes writers overlook one of the major advantages of the Internet: instant free publicity. On a blog, writers can post commentary on news, invite comments, interact with their readers, annotate links to sites, and post their own writing. To a potential employer, your blog shows the stuff you're made of and can lead to paying assignments.

- **Bookmark and frequently visit sites that align with your interests.** More often that you think, small or privately owned sites need help maintaining, editing, and updating content—and they'll put a call on their site asking for help. For a monthly retainer, freelancers might be paid to load the site with content in the public domain (not copyrighted), lead digital discussions, and keep readers abreast of new developments.

- **Subscribe to chat groups and listservs in your area of interest.** The wonderfully serendipitous nature of the Internet means that if you just follow your interests, you may find opportunities.

Books for Finding Online Markets

Having trouble finding the right online markets? These books may help:

Novel & Short Story Writer's Market (Writer's Digest Books), edited by Anne Bowling. This annually updated book lists thousands of fiction publishers, and includes a special section featuring online-only publications.

Writer's Market Deluxe Edition (Writer's Digest Books), edited by Kathryn S. Brogan and Robert Lee Brewer. This special edition of Writer's Market provides access to the book's continually updated online database that allows you to search for online-only publications and print publications that publish online-exclusive content on their Web sites.

The Writer's Online Marketplace (Writer's Digest Books), by Debbie Ridpath Ohi. Whether you're trying to sell your fiction, nonfiction, reviews, interviews, or poetry, this book can point you in the right direction.

Writing.com: Creative Internet Strategies to Advance Your Writing Career (Allworth Press), by Moira Anderson Allen. The revised edition features information on researching, communicating, and publishing online.

Sending E-Queries

Online sites expect to be queried via e-mail, but be sure to check the publisher's Web site, or check with a reputable site for freelancers, such as WritersMarket.com. To make sure your ideas survive filtering soft-

---

No Excuses—You Need a Home Page

The Internet should be your primary avenue for self-promotion. It costs very little (or nothing) to maintain your own Web site that displays your talents for all to see. Of course, just because you build it doesn't mean they will come, but employers do sometimes find writers because a search engine turns up the writer's Web site. At www.geercom.com, David Geer provides his writing specialties, writing samples, résumé, kudos, clients, and more. "Not having a good site detracts from your overall image as a writer. You're giving an incomplete presentation, which someone who really cares about their work would never do," Geer said.

If you're not sure how to create your own Web page, there are numerous books available to get you started:

The Complete Idiot's Guide to Creating a Web Page (Alpha Books), by Paul McFedries. This easy-to-follow book covers al the basics of creating your own Web page.

Create Your First Web Page in a Weekend (Premier Press), by Steve Callihan. This book includes a CD-ROM with tools to create a Web page.

Easy Web Page Creation (Microsoft Press), by Mary Millhollon, with Jeff Castrina. This book offers "nontechnical" instruction for creating your first Web site or page.

Make Your Site SELL! (SiteSell, Inc.) by Ken Envoy. This e-book includes information on setting up your own Web site to promote yourself and your work.

(Source: Writer's Market Deluxe Edition at www.writersmarket.com)

ware, put the query in the body of the e-mail message, not as an attachment. Many times, querying via e-mail seems less formal than typing and mailing a letter, but you shouldn't approach it with any less care. Editors are quickly turned off by flippant queries that clearly weren't given much thought—a real temptation when using e-mail. So follow the same rules as you would for a paper query, and keep your professional demeanor front and center.

If you need to send clips with an e-mail query, you can approach it in several ways: (1) Direct the editor to your Web site, where materials are available for viewing or downloading; (2) offer to send the materials as a PDF attachment in an e-mail; or (3) fax your documents if they cannot be sent or viewed electronically.

For more on query letters, see chapter six. There's also a sample e-query at the end of this chapter that may help you write your own.

Writing for the Web

Once you land a Web assignment, it's time to start writing. As you begin, keep in mind that people read copy differently on the Web. They read more slowly, they scan, their eyes bounce around the screen. As a result, you must adjust your writing style to suit.

- **Brevity.** Keep your writing focused and brief. The Internet provides readers with a lot of options. If you drone on too long, they may be tempted to click away. Brevity also helps in condensing download times, since long text files can cause lengthy delays.
- **White space.** Remember that white space relieves tired eyeballs. So break longer sentences into shorter sentences, and break stories into chunks, with catchy subheads.
- **Interactivity.** The Internet allows readers to interact with content by providing places where readers can post their opinions on a subject, take instant surveys, and participate in real-time chats.
- **Additional elements.** Internet stories can take full advantage of the latest technology by adding audio and video options into articles, and including hyperlinks to related stories or additional references.

Books on Writing for the Web

Here are some books to help you hone your Web writing skills:

Developing Online Content: The Principles of Writing and Editing for the Web (John Wiley & Sons), by Irene Hammerich and Claire Harrison. This resource includes information on writing, organizing, and delivering quality Web content.

Hot Text: Web Writing That Works (New Riders), by Jonathan Price and Lisa Price. This book provides information on writing for database-driven sites, creating FAQs, blogs, newsletters, etc.

The Web Content Style Guide (Prentice-Hall), by Gerry McGovern, Rob Norton, and Catherine O'Dowd. This nontechnical book includes information on writing, editing, and designing effective Web content.

The Web Writer's Guide (Focal Press), by Darlene Maciuba-Koppel. Featuring checklists, worksheets, and other tools, this book provides writers of all levels with the tools needed to create online content.

Writing for the Web (Self Counsel Press), by Crawford Kilian. The author stresses three principles of Web text (orientation, information, and action) as he teaches you how to write effectively online.

E-Books Abound

People have predicted for years that the books of the future will all be electronic. The electronic books that exist now are searchable. They can be interactive. There's no delivery charge. They can be downloaded anywhere in the world. You can read them on your computer screen, personal digital assistant, or e-book reader, or you can print them out. Their text can be enlarged for the visually impaired, or text-to-speech software can read them aloud to blind people. And they're generally less expensive than print versions.

But e-books have failed to capture the public imagination. One problem is that the e-book industry has yet to develop a dominant format or reader, not to mention the fact that the readers themselves—

clunky and unattractive—leave much to be desired. The technology will have to improve enough so that you can envision yourself using such a reader in bed or in your easy chair. However, there is hope: A new technology, electronic reusable paper, is on the horizon. This "paper" would have similar properties to conventional paper (such as flexibility), but it would have the ability to store and display images—like a computer monitor—thousands of times.

Until that time comes, however, many mainstream publishers and booksellers are shying away from the e-book industry. Nearly every New York publisher that launched a special e-book line has since ended its program, at least for now. Barnes & Noble's Web store, BN.com, stopped selling e-books because of slower than expected sales. Yet there is a market, even if it is a small one. In September 2003, the trade group Open E-Book Forum conducted a survey on e-book sales and production. Among its findings were that in the first half of 2003, the total number of e-books sold by retailers was 660,991 (a 40 percent increase from the year before) and another 620,266 (a 60 percent increase) were sold by publishers. While those percentage increases appear impressive, sales of e-books still lag far behind sales of paper books. As noted in chapter one, about 1.6 billion books were sold in 2001, a figure that increases to as many as 2.4 billion books if professional, text, and other types of books are included

Alternative and self-publishers have been quicker to embrace the e-book phenomenon. Angela Hoy, co-owner of Writer's Weekly.com and Booklocker.com, an online company that publishes e-books, says the company is profitable and has shown "consistent growth" since its inception, despite the recent economic downturn. Sales of fiction e-books have been relatively slow, compared to nonfiction, probably because while readers don't mind downloading nonfiction to read on their computers, they aren't as eager to do that with a novel.

Writers who are thinking of signing with an e-book publisher should carefully read any contract before signing it, or hire a lawyer to do so. The Authors Guild has criticized some e-book publishers for acquiring every possible right, including "any means of delivering digital content, regardless of whether those means have yet been invented." Make sure the contract spells out how often you'll be paid—quarterly being desirable, although some e-book publishers even pay writers monthly.

Because of the uncertainty of in e-book publishing, Hoy advises authors to not sell their rights to an e-book publishing house, noting that her company does not buy its authors' copyrights. Writers, however, shouldn't think it's easy to get an e-book published (with the exception of vanity publishers). BookLocker's acceptance rate hovers around 5 percent to 10 percent, Hoy notes. Larger publishing houses may simply convert a paper book into e-book form, so the chances of getting published remain the same.

Whether an e-book author earns a profit on his work primarily depends on timing and marketing, as with traditional book publishing. It's incumbent upon an e-book author to market his own words. At WritersWeekly.com, readers can subscribe to Hoy's free e-magazine about freelancing writing, which is also a marketing vehicle for her work. "Our sales always spike on Wednesdays, when each issue comes out. Nonfiction writers should create e-zines that target their book's audience. Fiction authors should turn portions of their novels into serials. Fiction authors of multiple titles should publish e-zines for their fans to not only stay in touch, but to also continue to sell books to their readers. (Doing so) provides readers with a regular reminder that you have books for sale."

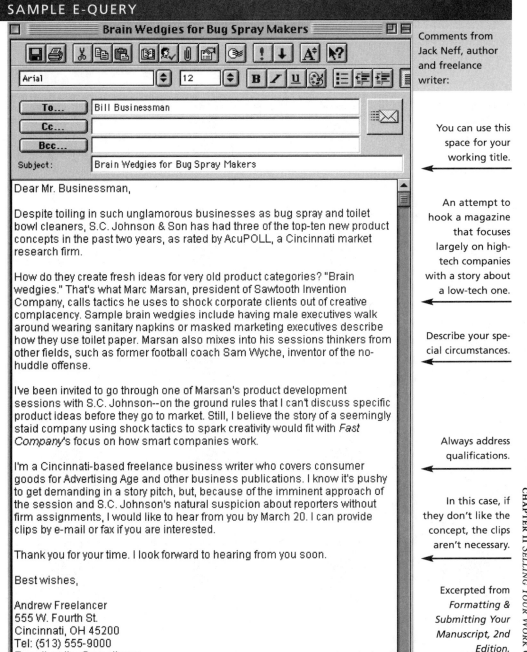

Brain Wedgies for Bug Spray Makers

Arial   12   **B** *I* <u>U</u>

To... Bill Businessman

Cc...

Bcc...

Subject: Brain Wedgies for Bug Spray Makers

Dear Mr. Businessman,

Despite toiling in such unglamorous businesses as bug spray and toilet bowl cleaners, S.C. Johnson & Son has had three of the top-ten new product concepts in the past two years, as rated by AcuPOLL, a Cincinnati market research firm.

How do they create fresh ideas for very old product categories? "Brain wedgies." That's what Marc Marsan, president of Sawtooth Invention Company, calls tactics he uses to shock corporate clients out of creative complacency. Sample brain wedgies include having male executives walk around wearing sanitary napkins or masked marketing executives describe how they use toilet paper. Marsan also mixes into his sessions thinkers from other fields, such as former football coach Sam Wyche, inventor of the no-huddle offense.

I've been invited to go through one of Marsan's product development sessions with S.C. Johnson--on the ground rules that I can't discuss specific product ideas before they go to market. Still, I believe the story of a seemingly staid company using shock tactics to spark creativity would fit with *Fast Company*'s focus on how smart companies work.

I'm a Cincinnati-based freelance business writer who covers consumer goods for Advertising Age and other business publications. I know it's pushy to get demanding in a story pitch, but, because of the imminent approach of the session and S.C. Johnson's natural suspicion about reporters without firm assignments, I would like to hear from you by March 20. I can provide clips by e-mail or fax if you are interested.

Thank you for your time. I look forward to hearing from you soon.

Best wishes,

Andrew Freelancer
555 W. Fourth St.
Cincinnati, OH 45200
Tel: (513) 555-9000
E-mail: writer@email.com

Comments from Jack Neff, author and freelance writer:

You can use this space for your working title.

An attempt to hook a magazine that focuses largely on high-tech companies with a story about a low-tech one.

Describe your special circumstances.

Always address qualifications.

In this case, if they don't like the concept, the clips aren't necessary.

Excerpted from *Formatting & Submitting Your Manuscript, 2nd Edition.*

CHAPTER 11 SELLING YOUR WORK ONLINE

PART FOUR

Protecting & Developing Your Work

CHAPTER TWELVE

Protecting Your Writing

History offers few greater mismatches than that of publisher and writer. On one side you'll find one of the world's largest and most profitable industries with armies of lawyers at its disposal. On the other is one of the world's most competitive, low-paying, and unprotected professions. Many writers live in large part by trusting editors and publishers they've never met without anything prudent souls would consider security.

Clearly the best security you can have as a writer is a written contract. For books, contracts are the norm. But understanding the contract's implications can be difficult. For articles, contracts are somewhat less common. Of course a contract is only as good as your ability to enforce it. If the language is vague, or the cost of a lawsuit far outweighs the benefits, the contract becomes fairly useless. And if drafted the wrong way, a contract can become more like a chain than a bond.

As a writer, you probably can't afford to level the playing field by having a lawyer on retainer. But you can learn the important legal issues. This chapter describes contracts and laws that apply to writers to help you avoid some of the common and more costly mistakes.

Your Rights

Understanding what rights you're selling to a publisher is important. The term *selling* may not even be a good word. In most cases it is more like you are leasing your work to a publisher. Here, then, is an overview of the options you have when offering your work to a publisher.

- **First Serial Rights.** Rights that the writer offers a newspaper or magazine to publish the manuscript for the first time in any periodical. All other rights remain with the writer. Sometimes the qualifier "North American" is added to these rights to specify a geographical limitation to the license.

  When content is excerpted from a book scheduled to be published, and it appears in a magazine or newspaper prior to book publication, this is also called first serial rights.

- **One-Time Rights.** Nonexclusive rights (rights that can be licensed to more than one market) purchased by a periodical to publish the work once (also known as simultaneous rights). That is, there is nothing to stop the author from selling the work to other publications at the same time.

- **Second Serial (Reprint) Rights.** Nonexclusive rights given to a newspaper or magazine to publish a manuscript after it has already appeared in another newspaper or magazine.

- **All Rights.** This is exactly what it sounds like. All rights mean that an author is selling every right they have to a work. If you license all rights to your work, you forfeit the right to ever use the work again. If you think you may want to use the work again, you should avoid submitting to such markets.

- **Electronic Rights.** Rights that cover a broad range of electronic media, from online magazines and databases to CD-ROM magazine anthologies and interactive games. The contract should specify if—and when—electronic rights are included. The presumption is that unspecified rights remain with the writer.

- **Subsidiary Rights.** Rights, other than book publication rights, that should be covered in a book contract. These may include various serial rights; movie, television, audiotape, and other electronic rights; translation rights, etc. The contract should specify who controls the rights (author or publisher) and what percentage of sales from licensing of these rights goes to the author.

- **Dramatic, Television, and Motion Picture Rights.** Rights for use of material on the stage, in television, or in the movies. Often a one-year option to buy such rights is offered (generally for 10 percent of the total price). The party interested in the rights then tries to sell the idea to other people—actors, directors, studios, or television networks. Some properties are optioned numerous times, but most fail to become full productions. In those cases, the writer can sell the rights again and again.

Rights are nearly always negotiable. If you feel uncomfortable with a publisher's proposal, ask if he would consider other terms. If you do sign away all rights to a piece of work, you are normally only selling the rights to a particular group of words set in a particular order. In many cases you can take the same information, rewrite it from a different angle, and resell it.

In the absence of any written agreement, in most cases the copyright law assumes that an author is only giving a publisher one-time rights. The key exception is a work-for-hire arrangement. In these cases the work becomes the property of the publisher. Generally something is considered a work for hire if it is produced by an employee, such as a staff writer. In some cases freelancers are also subjected to work-for-hire arrangements. But most in most instances freelancers and independent contractors own the rights to their creative work unless stipulated otherwise in writing.

Electronic Rights

With the proliferation of books and magazines on the Internet, electronic rights have become a controversial issue between writers and publishers. In one high-profile case (Tasini vs. New York Times) the federal courts initially sided with publishers, allowing them to reproduce articles in electronic form without owing the authors additional compensation. The court ruled that putting articles into electronic databases and onto CDs fell under the "collective works" provision of the Copyright Act. The Supreme Court ultimately reversed that ruling in 2001, deciding that newspaper and magazine publishers had infringed on freelancers' copyrights by republishing their work in online databases.

Given the current state of technology, is putting an article in a database that much different than storing a magazine on microfiche? On the other hand, some publications are developing pages on the Internet that hold the potential of becoming quite profitable. Tracking user "hits" on particular articles is relatively easy, and some writers want a share of those profits.

As technology—and its use—continues to evolve, these issues are far from settled. In the wake of the Tasini vs. New York Times ruling, some publications are demanding that freelancers sign away all rights to their work. Depending on the situation, writers of both books and articles may want to make electronic rights a point of negotiation.

Nearly all print publications these days seek some control over electronic rights. When all is said and done, your primary goal is to retain as much control of your material as possible, so that you can profit from its use in the future. Following, then, are some additional terms relating to electronic rights that you will likely see in contracts, and some words of advice for dealing with these issues.

- **First Electronic Rights.** These rights give the publication the first shot at using your material while allowing you afterward to sell reprints in any medium.
- **One-Time Electronic Rights**. This grants publishers the nonexclusive right to use material once in an electronic publication. You can grant this right to more than one publication at a time.
- **Nonexclusive Electronic Rights.** Publications are likely to ask for such rights in perpetuity, or indefinitely. Because the language is nonexclusive, you can still resell or reuse your material electronically at any time. The downside is that the original publication can also resell your work without compensating you.
- **Exclusive Electronic Rights.** If a publisher asks for any type of exclusive rights, it should only be for a reasonable period of time (usually three to six months). Afterward, you are then free to resell or reuse your own material.

- **Archival Rights.** Many print and electronic mediums expect to archive material online indefinitely. Make sure this request is nonexclusive, so that your are free to resell or reuse your own material.
- **First Worldwide Electronic Rights.** Since the Internet does not stop at any border, first North American serial rights has little meaning in the online world. Many publications are therefore using the first worldwide clause as a result. As always, try to avoid signing away exclusive rights indefinitely.

Magazine Contracts

Contracts and negotiations for periodicals are relatively simple. In some cases there will be no contract at all, just an editor giving you the go-ahead to write an article. Yet whenever possible you should try to get some kind of written agreement, even if it's just an informal assignment letter from the editor. If you get nothing in writing, try sending your own letter confirming the assignment. If nothing else it may clear up costly misunderstandings.

If you are presented with a contract or letter of agreement, it should cover the key issues listed below. In cases where there is no written agreement, you should at least talk through these key issues so you are clear on what the publication expects of you:

- What rights are you granting to the publisher? First rights (as defined earlier in this chapter) are a good starting point.
- How and when will you be paid? The best option is to be paid on acceptance, since publication will often occur months later.
- What kill fee will the publisher pay if the finished article is rejected? And under what circumstances is a kill fee normally paid?
- What expenses will the publisher cover?
- Is the publisher responsible for defending you against a libel suit?
- Will you have the right to approve the final version of your work? Most publications retain the right to edit for space and style. This can mean almost anything. But generally if you

write professionally and follow the style of the publication, you won't experience much revision.

- Are you expected to provide additional materials such as sidebars, photographs, or illustrations? If so, the agreement should spell out whether you will be paid separately for them.
- Will you receive complimentary copies of the publication in which your work appears? You should be given at least a couple copies of the publication.
- What is the deadline for the completion of the work? This should be spelled out clearly.

When you are presented with a contract, remember that many points can be negotiable. If you're new to the game you may have less of a chance to negotiate. But as you gain more publishing credits, along with a solid reputation, you will also gain more leverage.

Book Contracts

Regardless of your excitement about getting a book deal, take a long, hard look at how you're treated under the terms of the contract. Better yet, consider getting a lawyer or agent who can. After all, you will have to live with the terms of the contract for years to come.

Book contracts fall within a fairly standard format. But you have every right to negotiate the individual terms. There are no "right" ways to handle the various issues in a book contract. You should simply hold out for the best overall deal you can. Some points are more important to the publisher than others, just as some points are more important to you. Try to hold firm on the issues of most importance to you, while "giving in" on other points that are more important to the publisher.

The following are some contract issues that may come up:

- When is the advance to be paid? If payable in two or three stages (as is the norm), what are these stages? If some stages are delayed for reasons beyond your control, is there a time limit to prevent foot-dragging by the publisher?

- Are royalties based on a percentage of the list price or the publisher's net? In the latter case, getting a fair accounting becomes harder. Most writers organizations recommend royalties be based on list prices. Also, is there a provision for an audit of the publisher's records in accounting for royalties due you?
- Does the contract provide a time frame in which the manuscript is considered to be accepted even if the publisher does not expressly indicate it?
- Do you have the right to review the edited manuscript? If so, how long is the review period? Does the contract specify a time frame in which you must complete any revisions? If so, is it enough time?
- If an accepted manuscript is never published, does the contract become void, allowing you to sell it elsewhere? If so, do you retain the money paid in advance?
- Is there an arbitration clause that allows for peaceful resolution of disputes? If arbitration of contract disputes is called for, the arbitration should be in accordance with the American Arbitration Association's (www.adr.org) rules. Also, does the contract state the place for the arbitration? It should be a locale equally convenient to both parties.
- If the book is to be indexed, who is responsible for hiring and paying the indexer? Who is responsible for the cost of providing photographs and illustrations? If you are responsible for such costs, are they to be withheld from the advance or royalties? This is in the writer's best interest.
- Do you have veto power over the title of the book and the cover design?
- Does the contract provide for free copies to be furnished to you? Are you allowed to purchase additional copies at a discount?
- Does the contract specify a dollar amount for publisher's promotional expense? Does it obligate you to make promotional appearances without being paid for your time and expense?
- Does the contract give the publisher any options on your future work? Unless the publisher wants to pay you for this option, you should probably reject it.

- Does the contract have a "noncompete" clause prohibiting you from writing, editing, or publishing another competing book without written permission of the publisher? Some clauses are so vaguely worded that they seemingly would give the publisher control over virtually anything else you produce. If you must have such a clause, make sure it's narrowly worded.
- Do publication rights revert to you when the book goes out of print? Do you have the right of consent to any sales of subsidiary rights, such as motion picture, book club, or anthology rights? Is there a provision for full subsidiary rights to revert to you should the publisher fail to exercise such rights in a specified time? Many writers mistakenly hand over potentially lucrative rights to publishers who have no interest or expertise in exercising such deals.
- Does the publisher promise to pay for legal expenses arising from any libel action in connection with the book? If so, do you have the right to choose your own lawyer? If you are partly responsible for any of the legal costs, does the publisher agree not to settle any claim without your consent? Finally, can the publisher freeze royalty payments after a suit is filed? If so, what are the provisions for the resumption of payments following a settlement?

Agents and Attorneys

Whenever you are faced with a lucrative contract or complex negotiations you should consider the services of a literary agent or attorney. This is the norm. Four of five books sold to publishers are sold through agents. Many book publishers and film producers will not even deal directly with writers when its comes to contract issues and negotiations.

Of course the money in question must be substantial for the services of an agent or attorney to be worthwhile. Most agents want a 15 percent share of your proceeds. Attorneys charge $150 or more an hour, and most negotiations will consume at least several hours of expensive legal service. Accordingly, it is not in your best interest (nor theirs) for an agent or attorney to get involved unless several thousand dollars are at stake.

In some cases, agents and attorneys are well worth the cost and can increase your net income. Here's how:

1. Good agents and attorneys know more about contracts and negotiations than most writers can ever learn. And by keeping you out of the direct negotiations, they enable you to preserve your working relationship with publishers and editors.

2. Professional representation by an agent or attorney shows a publisher that someone with credibility thinks your work is worthwhile. It means more when someone else does your boasting for you—especially when it's an agent or attorney who understands the publishing world.

3. Most important of all, agents and attorneys relieve much of the work and stress involved in building a successful career. This allows you to be more productive as a writer.

While both can be equally beneficial, there are major differences in what agents and attorneys can do for you. Attorneys only come into play once you have a contract to negotiate. Agents are often necessary early in the process to help you find a publisher. An agent's role can be that of salesman and business consultant. Some will even work with you to develop your talent.

One of the best ways to find an agent or literary attorney is to talk with satisfied customers—other writers. You can also find leads in *Writer's Market* and *Guide to Literary Agents* or through some of the resources given at the end of the chapter.

While an agent can be a great benefit in negotiating contracts on your behalf, consider carefully the terms of the agreement you sign with an agent. Agents customarily make at least nominal contact with all the appropriate publishers. How vigorously and competently they handle those contacts is another issue. If the writer, entirely through his own efforts, later lands a deal with one of those publishers, the agent could still be entitled to a cut, depending on how your relationship is structured.

Contracts with agents should spell out the agent's responsibilities clearly and prevent agents from claiming a share of income from projects they didn't procure. That's one reason to negotiate short-term agent contracts rather than long-term relationships.

Beware of an agent who charges a fee to review a manuscript. The fees don't obligate the agent to make any other effort on your behalf and can end up costing you several hundred dollars.

Copyright

The basic rules of copyright are easy to understand. All works created after 1977 are protected for the length of the author's life and another fifty years thereafter. After that the work falls into the public domain and anyone can use it without permission. (Any work created in 1977 or earlier can be copyrighted for up to seventy-five years from the time of its first publication or its registration with the copyright office.)

Obtaining a copyright for your work is truly effortless. The way the law is structured today, copyright is assumed the moment your words hit the paper or the computer screen. Technically, you need not even place a copyright notice on your work. There are, however, additional benefits to registering your work with the copyright office:

- Adding a copyright notice allows you to defeat claims of "innocent infringement."
- You must register your work with the copyright office before you can file suit against someone who steals your work. If you wait to register your work until after the theft takes place, you may not recover attorney fees or some damages from the defendant.

To register a copyright, request the proper form from the Register of Copyrights at the Library of Congress, then Follow these steps:

Step 1: Request and complete the proper form, either Form TX for books, manuscripts, online work, and poetry, or Form PA for scripts and dramatic works.

Step 2: Into an envelope, put your:

- Completed application form
- $30 payment (current rate) to "Register of Copyrights"
- Nonreturnable copy or copies of the material to be registered

Step 3: Send the package to the Library of Congress Copyright Office at the address below.

For more information about copyrights, contact the Library of Congress, Copyright Office, 101 Independence Ave., SE, Washington, D.C. 20559-6000. Tel: (202) 707-3000. Web site: www.copyright.gov.

The Copyright Office Web site makes available all copyright registration forms and informational circulars, plus other announcements and general copyright information. The Web site also provides a means of searching copyright registrations and recorded documents from 1978 forward.

You can also use the Forms and Publications Hotline [(202) 707-9100)] to request application forms or informational circulars. The Fax-on-Demand service [(202) 707-2600] allows you to use any Touch-Tone phone to order up to three circulars and/or announcements via fax. (Application forms are not available via fax.)

Of course, not even a registered copyright can protect your most valued assets—your ideas. In reality, most articles are written on the basis of an idea proposal, a query, which protects you from starting a piece without being paid. But since you can't copyright an idea, you must trust the editors who read your queries. Fortunately, the vast majority of editors are trustworthy. They have to be. An editor with a reputation for stealing other people's ideas won't last long in the business. (Sometimes what appears to be piracy is simply the result of a project being already in the works when your query arrives. An editor, however, should inform you of this when rejecting your query.)

The American Society of Journalists and Authors defines a story idea as a "subject combined with an approach." It says a writer shall have a proprietary right to an idea suggested to an editor and have first shot at developing it. Any editor with integrity will respect this ethical standard.

Fair Use

Aside from protecting their work, the copyright issue of most concern to writers is the doctrine of fair use. It is this principle that allows you to quote briefly from someone else's work. It's important to note, however, that the rules of fair use have never been clearly defined by the courts, nor have they been spelled out in law. Fair use can only be judged in the context in which it occurs. If you are unsure of the limits, obtain permission before quoting from any copyrighted material.

To get permission to quote from copyrighted material, you must submit a request to the copyright owner, which usually means contacting the publisher. In a brief letter explain exactly what you want to quote, and note when and where it was first published. Be sure to include information about how you will use the material and the name of the publication in which it will appear. In most cases you will be granted permission, on the condition that you credit the original source. In some cases you may have to pay a fee, which can range from a few dollars to a few thousand dollars. You must decide whether the material is worth the cost involved.

Libel

You are guilty of libel if you publish a false statement that is damaging to another living person's reputation. The false statement can be unintentional and still be ruled libelous in court, which is why the law requires writers to take every reasonable step to check for accuracy. While it is up to the plaintiff to prove falsehood, it is up to you to prove that you made every reasonable effort to be accurate.

Few writers would knowingly publish falsehoods. Yet the pitfalls for writers are numerous. You can accurately print what you have been told and still commit libel—if the person giving you the information was wrong in his facts. Many writers get in trouble simply by failing to check minor facts, which is why you must double-check and triple-check information—even when you believe it is correct.

Misspell someone's name while writing about a crime and you can implicate an innocent person in wrongdoing. That's libel. You can be held just as libelous if you falsely state someone has died. The "lucky living" have won such cases on claims of undue hardship and emotional distress. Errors in something as innocent as a high school sports story have even resulted in libel suits. While such instances are rare, the important point is that nearly any form of writing can put you at risk of libel.

The only way to be safe is to always be 100 percent certain of your facts. An *Associated Press Stylebook and Libel Guide* is an excellent source of information on libel and how to protect yourself.

Freelance writers have some special issues of concern with libel. First, keep in mind that you aren't necessarily going to be defended by the publisher if your work prompts a libel suit. If the publisher alone is sued and loses, it could come after you for damages.

To protect yourself from groundless suits, it's good to have tapes of your interviews. Bear in mind, however, that taping phone conversations is illegal in some states unless the other party is aware he is being taped.

Not all libel suits may stem from anything you did. Bad editing can cause errors that result in a suit. The best protection is to see a proof of the edited version, including headlines and photo captions. For your own protection keep a hard copy of manuscripts you send to a publisher.

Resources for Contract and Legal Advice

The organizations listed below can help you protect your rights and your work, so that you can have a successful writing career.

Organizations for Legal Advice

The writers groups below offer legal advice and contract help for writers. Contact them or check their Web sites to find out what specific legal services they offer:

Authors Guild, 31 E. 28th St., 10th Floor, New York, NY 10016. Tel: (212) 563-5904. Fax: (212) 564-5363. E-mail: staff@authorsguild.org. Web site: www.authorsguild.org. Offers legal advice regarding contracts and also can step in and help resolve legal issues and disputes, or help writers find an attorney.

National Writers Union, 113 University Pl., 6th Floor, New York, NY 10003. Tel: (212) 254-0279. Fax: (212) 254-0673. E-mail: nwu@nwu.org. Web site: www.nwu.org. Offers contract advice and guidance on dealing with grievances and what to do if they occur. Also advocate for rights of freelancers and writers.

Volunteer Lawyers for the Arts, 1 E. 53rd St., 6th Floor, New York, NY 10022. Tel: (212) 319-2787. E-mail: jtominar@vlany.org. Web site: www.vlany.org. Provides pro bono services, education, and advocacy for the New York arts community.

Organizations for Locating Literary Agents and Attorneys

The organizations below offer listings and reports on various literary agents and attorneys. Some are free of charge, but some require a fee. Check their Web sites to find out what services they offer:

Writers Guild of America, East, 555 W. 57th St., Suite 1230, New York, NY 10019. Tel: (212) 767-7800. Web site: www.wgae.org. . Offers information and tools for writers and represents writers in motion picture, broadcast, cable and new technologies industries. Another branch is Writers Guild of America, West, 7000 W. Third St., Los Angeles, CA 90048. Tel: (800) 548-4532. Web site: www.wga.org.

Association of Authors' Representatives, P.O. Box 237201, Ansonia Station, New York, NY 10003. E-mail: aarinc@mindspring.com. Web site: www.aar-online.org. Agents in this organization must meet professional standards, such as no reading fees.

Agent Research and Evaluation, 25 Barrow St., New York NY 10014. Tel: (212) 924-9942. E-mail: info@agentresearch.com. Web site: www.agentresearch.com. Offers services to help you locate the agent who is right for you.

CHAPTER THIRTEEN

Promoting Your Work and Yourself

One of the most important but least considered aspects of being a successful writer is self-promotion. Take some advice from writer Victoria Secunda, who learned a lesson about promoting early in her book career: "Publishing is more than writing a book. It also about doing all the things that can feed your book, and that includes public speaking, the thought of which make writers take to their beds."

Although antianxiety medicine may be required before a going to a speaking engagement, self-promotion is still something writers should work at tirelessly. Like Secunda, you should spend nearly as much time on promotion as on writing and research. You know your book better than anyone, which means you can promote it better than anyone. Ideally, authors should work together with publicists to find promotional strategies that work. But you must do some research in order present viable ideas to publicists. You have to know what your options are and what is feasible for both you and your publisher in relation to your particular book.

Sometimes you must do backbreaking research in order to do this effectively. Secunda compiled long lists of names, addresses, and phone numbers of publications and groups she thought might be interested in her work and gave them to her publicist. For her book on father-daughter relationships, for example, she went to the library and looked up men's groups that could be sent a news release. Realizing that her title, *When Madness Comes Home*, is hardly light reading for the beach, she got involved with the National Alliance for the Mentally Ill, a group that supports families of people with mental illness. She spoke at the association's national convention and at several local chapters around the country, offering herself as a spokeswoman for the organization on local radio and television shows.

These opportunities did not present themselves to Secunda. She had to make them happen. The same is true for any author. When you create an opportunity for yourself, be aware that it is your responsibility to make sure it is successful. For example, while some news organizations have reporters who specialize on particular beats, it's more likely that reporters won't know much about you, your book, or even the topic. So help them do their jobs. Secunda once appeared on a radio show that didn't expect her until the next day. Although they weren't prepared, she was. She handed them a list of questions to ask about her book, and the next thing she knew, the hour was up.

Who Else But You?

Promotion doesn't start the minute the presses stop; many authors plan their promotional efforts when their books are still in the proposal stage. Success as a writer often depends upon speeches, book signings, newsletters, television appearances, radio interviews, Web sites, visits to groups, and campuses, and more. Who else knows your book better? Who else is as dedicated to its success? Who else can talk about it as ardently?

In fact, even though you may have a wonderfully written nonfiction book, oftentimes the good writing isn't all that is needed to make it a success. How much you are willing to talk about your book is essential because many publishers are not able to give each book the promotional attention it needs to make it a success. That is up to you, the writer. If you have a book with a wide national audience, the promotion plan is equally, if not more important than the actual contents of the book. Even well-known authors go on the road, give talks, and do interviews to promote their works. Self-promotion is even recognized by writers as a technique as much a part of writing success as knowing the difference between active and passive voice.

Speak Up

While public speaking is frightening to most writers, it is important to take advantage of any opportunity that allows you to speak about your work to an audience. Not only should you be willing to speak when asked, but you should also seek out speaking opportunities. Speaking gives you the chance to create excitement about your work in a personal way. You are forming a memorable relationship with the audience if you are prepared and enthusiastic. Getting to hear about an author and his work firsthand will prompt many people in an audience to be interested in your work. They will also be likely to tell someone else about it. If you can walk away with even just a handful of people interested in your book, you have created more potential sales than would have otherwise occurred.

To talk up your work, it can be helpful to think of an interesting angle or angles that will appeal to a broader audience than simply people who are interested in its topic. Find a way to hook people who may not know much about your topic. Be creative and confident, and you may attract more listeners than you would have ever guessed.

If public speaking gives you the tremors, enroll in a speech class at a local college for instruction, practice, and feedback. Toastmasters International (www.toastmasters.org) offers a good Web site for help in making speeches. You can contact Toastmasters by writing to P.O. Box 9052, Mission Viejo, CA 92688, by calling (949) 858-8255, or by sending an e-mail to tmembers@toastmasters.org.

You also can call your local bookstores and offer to do a talk and a book signing. But be imaginative about other groups to address. *The Encyclopedia of Associations*, available at libraries, is a compendium of organizations around the world. It can help you find audiences. If you write about nursing, for example, you can find dozens of nursing associations, each of which may have newsletters for members and meetings where you may be permitted to give a presentation. Look up your topic in the *Yellow Pages* to find local businesses, churches, and groups that may agree to let you promote your work to their members.

Use visual aids. Whitney Otto created a slide show to promote *The*

Passion Dream Book, a novel that explores the relationship between art and the lives of artists. The slides also helped her add originality to her tour and broaden it to include libraries and art schools. Visuals are a great way to make your presentation more interesting and engaging, and even more importantly, more memorable.

Go Visit

Remember, part of your job as a writer is also to be a publicist. One way to publicize and promote is to make a point of visiting local bookstores to meet the staff and talk about your book. If bookstore staff know you, they're more likely to put your book in the window. They also may be more likely to recommend your book to customers interested in your topic because your book will stand out in their minds above the others.

Jeanne M. Dams used the *Deadly Directory*, which she calls an indispensable reference for mystery writers, to find mystery bookstores. She visited every store within driving distance to supplement the book tour arranged by her publisher. "Even when I drew very few people, I established a personal relationship with the bookseller," Dams said. "That really matters because mystery bookstores hand sell their books." Today, even the chain stores call her.

If you are aggressive in your promotion efforts, your publisher may be willing to put more time and money into you as well. Victoria Secunda's publisher believed her to be promotable because of her success on television and radio shows. So for her book *When You and Your Mother Can't Be Friends*, the publisher wanted to send her on a ten-city tour. Secunda, with the support of her husband, decided to add five more cities to the tour. Although they had to pay for the additional cities, she said, "It was worth every cent and gave me phenomenal experience." And after that book, the publisher sent her on fifteen-city tours.

If your publisher doesn't spring for book tours, don't be afraid to plan your own. Some writers have combined book tours with family vacations, hauling the kids and sometimes even the dog along as they traverse the country.

Libraries and bookstores often welcome visiting authors who wish to speak or give readings. To find those outside your telephone book's area, try these sources:

American Booksellers Association allows you to search for members by state and zip code at BookWeb.org (www.bookweb.org).

American Book Trade Directory (R.R. Bowker) lists contact information for more than thirty thousand booksellers in the United States and Canada, arranged geographically.

American Library Directory (R.R. Bowker) lists more than thirty-six thousand libraries throughout the United States and Canada, arranged geographically, with names of department heads.

Directory of Special Libraries and Information Centers (Gale) includes more than twenty-two thousand places that house special collections.

Once you plan your tour, send a news release to media outlets in every city you'll visit, then follow up with a phone call before you arrive. This will help ensure that you get some media coverage and publicity.

Use the Media

If your publisher doesn't do it for you, you should also write a news release and send it to your media and to any other publication or electronic news organization you want to visit. If you've written a speech, it should be easy to adapt into a news release, focusing on whatever major aspect of your work is most useful to a general audience.

You should send your release to the editor of the appropriate department at a newspaper, and also to the book editor if the newspaper employs one. For example, releases about books on management should go to the business editor; those on relationships go to the features editor. Send your release to the producer of television shows.

A radio "tour" allows you to promote your book without leaving your kitchen. But you may be doing interviews in early morning hours as local news broadcasts are starting earlier and late at night to meet deadline cycles of stations in a different time zone.

To let radio and television shows know you're available, you can take out an ad in *Radio-TV Interview Report* (www.rtir.com), a publication made up completely of ads. It is published three times a month and circulates to more than four thousand radio and television producers looking for people to interview. Contact Bradley Communications Corp. at 135 E. Plumstead Ave., P.O. Box 1206, Lansdowne, PA 19050-8206, by calling (610) 259-0707, or by sending an e-mail to Circ@rtir.com.

Directories such as *Bradley's Guide to the Top National TV Talk Shows, Talk Shows and Hosts on Radio,* or *Talk Show Selects* also are helpful in finding hosts on radio and television. Television demands different skills than radio or print interviews, because your appearance is critical. If you're going to be on a television show and can't afford a media coach, try role-playing an interview and then watching a tape of it. Are any of your mannerisms distracting? Are your answers clear? Can you speak in sound bites of thirty seconds or so? Is your voice expressive? Are you entertaining? And, despite all those questions, do you seem relaxed?

Television can be an intimidating medium, so it's best to start small, with your local cable station. Your chances of scheduling a television interview will be better with a local station, and it won't be as overwhelming. These stations aren't as hectic and will be able to make you feel more comfortable about your experience. They may be more encouraging because they know you are a beginner. Knowing that the audience for these stations is smaller should also help to calm some of your public speaking fears.

If you are still intimidated and can afford it, consider hiring a media coach. They can help you learn how to do and practice doing interviews. Don't feel like this is necessary though, because as long as you are passionate about your topic, even if you aren't perfect, you will still be successful.

Check out the resource section at the end of the chapter for a list of books in the library that contain contact information for the media. And don't forget to send a release to wire services, such as the *Associated Press,* which transmit copy to newspapers and broadcast stations around the globe.

At the end of the chapter there is a list of some of the major publications that review books. But don't neglect your local print publications; a book sold in Dayton, Ohio, earns as much profit as a book sold in New York City. Call each publication for the name of the appropriate editor to review your genre or your topic, and send either galley copies (photocopies of the book's pages before it's published) or the books as early as you can—as soon as four months prior to publication.

Utilizing News Releases

A news release should be a page or two at most, double-spaced. At the top of the release, include a phone number where you can be reached, days and evenings.

The release's goal is to tell people not only what your work is about, but more importantly, why they should care. What's in it for them? It should lead with the most intriguing point of your book or the most useful aspect of your findings. Write it in third person, and include a few strong quotes from yourself.

Make it read like a news story you'd see in your paper, complete with a headline—smaller, overworked news staffs sometimes simply reprint releases. Larger news organizations may call you for an interview, using your release as a starting point for their own reporting. Either way, you win. But the better your presentation and writing are, the better chance you have of getting your release printed.

It's a good idea to prepare a list of talking points, questions that a reporter can ask that will highlight important parts of your book, because many reporters must fit author interviews between covering fires, reporting on car wrecks, and sitting through school board meetings. Assume they don't have time to read your book. If you go in person for an interview, bring a copy of your talking points, just in case they've misplaced the one you sent. You have to take on the responsibility of preparing not only for yourself but also for them.

Before you mail your releases, verify the names and addresses of editors and producers by phone. This will ensure that your release will reach the correct person and won't have to be rerouted, saving precious time. If you don't want to mail your own release, you can pay the PR Newswire to distribute releases electronically to print and broadcast news organizations across the country. Contact PR Newswire at: 810 Seventh Ave., 35th Floor, New York, NY 10019. Tel: (212) 596-1500 or (800) 832-5522 (toll free). E-mail: public_relations@prnewswire.com. Web site: www.prnewswire.com.

Write

Another way to promote your work involves writing. You are already a writer, so this avenue should appeal to you. One way to drum up interest in your work is to start a newsletter. You could do your own, or team up with other writers you know who are looking to promote their work as well.

Jeanne Dams and three other mystery writers, Barbara D'Amato, Hugh Holton, and Mark Zubro, started a newsletter to promote their books. They started their mailing list by asking their publishers to slip a postcard for a subscription into their books. They mail their newsletter to anyone who responds to the post card and also to anyone else they think might be interested. Into it goes an article by each author, mystery quizzes, even recipes for foods mentioned in their books. Most importantly, the newsletter always includes a list of the authors' appearances and their books in print. It can be a time-consuming and expensive promotional tool, but if you team up with other authors, you can split the costs and still reap the rewards.

In addition to mailing print newsletters, consider doing an e-mail newsletter. The cost for this could be significantly less. If you have a Web site (which you should), you can add a link asking people to subscribe to your free e-mail newsletter. Include information about your work, appearances, and anything else that might interest people who enjoy your work or the topics you write about.

Network

Everyone was a beginner once, and many successful authors remember how difficult it was to become established. These authors are often a tremendous resource to beginners. The book you're reading now wouldn't exist without the generosity of writers, agents, and editors who took time to share their expertise.

Joining a writers association and attending writers conferences can help you learn how to write and sell your work, but more importantly, these networks help you meet people who may be able to help you.

And whom you also may be able to help. You must be sincerely willing to help others and unafraid to ask for help yourself. You never know what someone else is willing to do for you until you ask. (See chapter fifteen for help in finding a community of writers.)

Writers groups also can help their members promote their work. C.J. Songer, author of the Meg Gillis crime novel series, used a list published by Sisters In Crime, a group for mystery writers, to reach independent bookstores. Through the group, she also bought a discounted ad in *Publishers Weekly*. "Although it was a fair amount of money, *Bait* was my first-ever book and it was a treat to myself," Songer said. Because she had taken that ad, she also earned a discount on a promotional page for her book on the *Publishers Weekly* Web site at BookWire.com. "It was very gratifying to be able to go online and see my own book, plus it was accessible then for family and friends (and acquaintances) all across the country," she said.

Get Linked

The Internet is a vast shopping mall, virtually as interactive as a real mall. Authors can capitalize on that fact. Create a Web site that offers brief reviews of your books, copies of the books for sale at discounts, and your e-mail address for readers. Add links to other Web sites that will be of interest to anyone interested in your work. If you write about science, for example, include links to scientific Web sites.

John Kremer, author of *1001 Ways to Market Your Books*, offers an electronic and paper newsletter with promotional tips for authors (to subscribe, visit www.bookmarket.com/newsletters.html). In one of those newsletters, Kremer mentioned that he noticed a listing for his book had no reviews at Amazon.com other than the one he provided. So, he offered a free copy of a book to anyone who wrote the best review. And he suggested that other authors do the same for their books.

Think of your Web site as a storefront. Once it's built, you'll need to invite people to come in and browse. But first, you need to let readers know it's open for business. You can submit your site's URL directly to major search engines and directories by following onscreen directions.

The online sites for Amazon and Barnes & Noble allow authors to submit information about their books, and, important for small presses, provide a distribution network for those books. Writers Write (www.writerswrite.com) includes information on promotions and markets. Writer's Write also offers book promotion services for a fee. Author L.L. Thrasher shares some useful tips at her "Practical Book Promotion for Writers" page (www.teleport.com/~baty/promo.html). Para Publishing (www.parapublishing.com) is full of promotional tips, particularly aimed at self-publishers, and it also sells mailing lists. The Gebbie Press also has some solid advice on promotional strategies (www.gebbieinc.com/article.htm).

Hundreds of other promotional tactics, ranging from buying mailing lists of potential customers to creating refrigerator magnets, can help you sell your work. While many beginning writers simply want to write, many successful writers know that if you want readers, you'll have to promote yourself. You may even end up enjoying it. Contact with other people who are interested in you and promoting your work can be very exciting and encouraging.

Promotional costs for early books may not pay off in increased book sales. But you must take the long-term view, and consider how promotion now will benefit you down the road. You may have to make some initial sacrifices to be successful in the end.

Resources for Promoting Your Work

The directories, magazines, and books listed below can provide you with the information you need to successful promote yourself.

Directories

Some of the directories listed below may be difficult to find, so be sure to check your local library:

The Adweek Directory (Adweek Directories). Lists about 9,000 contacts in top markets in radio, broadcast and cable television, daily newspapers, and magazines.

Bacon's Newspaper/Magazine Directory (Bacon's Publishing).

The multiple volumes list nearly 15,000 trade and consumer magazines, and daily and weekly publications.

Bacon's Radio/TV/Cable Directory (Bacon's Publishing). The multiple volumes include more than 10,000 radio and television stations, including college, public television, and cable stations.

Broadcasting & Cable Yearbook (R.R. Bowker). Lists all television and radio stations in the United States, its territories, and Canada, with names of contact people.

Burrelles Media Directory (Burrelles). Lists 60,000 print and electronic media outlets in North America, with names of key contacts.

Editor & Publisher International Yearbook (Editor & Publisher). Lists newspapers in the United States and Canada, with names of department chiefs.

Gale Directory of Publications & Broadcast Media (Gale). Contains more than 50,000 entries, including listings for radio stations, television stations, and cable companies. Each entry provides addresses and phone numbers.

Literary Marketplace (R.R. Bowker) Includes lists of contacts and addresses for book reviews, direct mail specialists, lecture agents, and public relations services. It is well worth the trip to the library.

Ulrich's International Periodicals Directory (R.R. Bowker). A huge listing of more than 240,000 periodicals and newspapers worldwide.

Magazines

Below, are major publications that review books. See their Web sites for specific submission guidelines:

The Booklist, American Library Association, 50 E. Huron St., Chicago, IL 60611. Tel: (800) 545-2433. E-mail: library@ala.org. Web site: www.ala.org. Reviews books in all categories; galleys must be submitted fifteen weeks prior to publication.

Chicago Tribune Books, 435 N. Michigan Ave., Room 400, Chicago, IL 60611-4022. Tel: (312) 222-3232. E-mail: publiceditor@tribune.com. Web site: www.tribune.com. Contact the publication or check the Web site for more information on the reviewing process.

Kirkus Reviews, 770 Broadway, New York, NY 10003. Tel: (866) 890-8541. E-mail: Kirkusrev@Kirkusreviews.com. Web site: http://Kirkusreviews.com. Reviews books in their publication that comes out twenty-four times annually; submit galleys two to three months prior to publication.

Library Journal, 360 Park Ave. S., New York, NY 10010. Tel: (646) 746-6819. E-mail: ljquery@reedbusiness.com. Web site: www.libraryjournal.com. Reviews all books except textbooks, children's books, technical books or books in a foreign language (unless it is a bilingual book). Submit galleys three to four months prior to publication.

Los Angeles Times Book Review, 202 W. 1st St., Los Angeles, CA 90012. Tel: (213) 237-5000. E-mail: bookreview@latimes.com. Web site: www.latimes.com. Reviews books in a separate Sunday section; submit galleys three months prior to publication.

Midwest Book Review, 278 Orchard Dr., Oregon, WI 53575. Tel: (608) 835-7937. E-mail: mwbookrevw@aol.com. Web site: www.midwestbookreview.com. Reviews books in several monthly publications for library systems in California, Wisconsin, and the Upper Midwest.

New York Review of Books, 1755 Broadway, 5th Floor, New York, NY 10019. Tel: (212) 757-8070. Web site: www.nybooks.com. Accepts books for reviews in all categories and will contact you if your book is chosen for review.

New York Times Book Review, 229 W. 43rd St., New York, NY 10036. Tel: (212) 556-1234. E-mail: the-arts@nytimes.com. Web site: www.nytimes.com. Accepts books for review in all categories; children's books are submitted to a different editor.

Publishers Weekly, 360 Park Ave. S., New York, NY 10010. Tel: (646) 746-6758. E-mail: pwreviewstatus@reedbusiness.com. Web site: www.publishersweekly.com. Reviews adult and children's books in every issue; submit galleys three months prior to publication.

USA Today, 7950 Jones Branch Dr., McLean, VA 22108. Web site: www.usatoday.com. Contact the publication or check the Web site for more information on the reviewing process.

Wall Street Journal, 200 Liberty St., New York, NY 10281. Tel: (212) 416-2500. Web site: www.wsj.com. Contact the publication or check the Web site for more information on the reviewing process.

Washington Post Book World, 1150 15th St. NW, Washington, DC 20071. Tel: (202) 334-6000. Web site: www.washingtonpost.com. Contact the publication or check the Web site for more information on the reviewing process.

Books

Check your local library for the following books that can help you reach more people with your work:

1001 Ways to Market Your Books, for Authors and Publishers (Open Horizons), by John Kremer. Offers practical tips and ideas for promoting books and cites real examples that have worked for other writers.

An Author's Guide to Children's Book Promotion (Two Lives Publishing), by Susan Salzman Raab. Shows authors and illustrators how to get their books looked at by teachers, librarians, booksellers, and reviewers. Includes a resource directory with children's book sources and trade and educational publications.

Book Promotion for the Shameless: 101 Marketing Tips That Really Work (Spilled Candy Publications), by Lorna Tedder. Gives book promotion and marketing techniques for penny-pinching authors and includes a section specifically on Internet marketing.

Guerrilla Marketing for Authors: 100 Weapons to Help You Sell Your Work (Writer's Digest Books), by Jay Conrad Levinson, Rick Frishman, and Michael Larsen. Shows writers hundreds of low-cost ways to market their books, before and after they are published.

Jump Start Your Book Sales: A Money-Making Guide for Authors, Independent Publishers and Small Presses (Communication Creativity), by Marilyn and Tom Ross. Teaches you how to get free publicity and capitalize on it. Contains resource lists, forms, checklists, and samples to help you get started.

The Publicity Handbook, New Edition: The Inside Scoop from More than 100 Journalists and PR Pros on How to Get Great Publicity Coverage (McGraw-Hill), by David R. Yale. Offers guidelines for working with journalists to create valuable publicity and includes a step-by-step publicity plan.

Publish to Win: Smart Strategies to Sell More Books (Rhodes & Easton), by Jerrold R. Jenkins and Anne M. Stanton. Helps you evaluate the marketability of your book before you write it. Gives advice for the market, and has thorough information on nontraditional markets.

CHAPTER FOURTEEN

Your Writing Business

Each year thousands of writers fail in their dream of becoming freelancers. Sadly, many fail not because they couldn't write well enough, but because they never mastered the business side of the profession.

While just as important to success, the business side of freelancing is a lot less appealing. So it's easy to shove business matters into the bottom drawer, where they slowly kindle into a blaze of uncollected bills and overdue taxes. If you take the right approach, however, the details of business need not consume much of your hard work and talent. A few hours a week keeping your business matters well organized and up-to-date is all it really takes.

This chapter focuses on what you need to know to keep the business side of freelancing from overwhelming you—so that your success as a writer is unfettered by the mundane details of business and taxes.

Finances for Writers

Setting up a simple budget is not only essential for business, it can make your life easier as well. For our purposes we'll assume you are a full-time freelancer, or are about to become one. If this is not the case, you may still benefit from having a more complete understanding of the business side of the trade.

As with any budget, what you're trying to create is only a rough representation of what's likely to happen. As you go through the steps keep in mind that it will get easier each year. Once you are established as a freelancer you'll have the previous year's income and expenses as a basis for planning. You'll also have a regular base of clients to make your income more predictable.

The best way to start the budgeting process is to estimate your costs. Monthly overhead (what you must pay whether you work or not) should be the first category. This includes any payments on your computer or other equipment, office rent, publications, answering service, and an estimate of auto expenses.

After figuring overhead, take a look at your household budget and calculate the minimum amount you'll need for living expenses. Include your rent, mortgage, car payment, other consumer debt, groceries, and the like. Then, subtract from this amount any take-home pay from your spouse, or other sources of steady income.

Financial planners recommend freelancers have two to six months of overhead and living expenses available when they start their business. Even if you start with as much work as you can handle, you should still count on two to three months for the checks to appear in your mailbox. One survey by the Editorial Freelancers Association found that freelancers waited anywhere from a week to a year to get paid, with one or two months being typical.

Ideally, your capital reserve will be your savings account. Realistically, the start-up costs for a freelance writing business are small enough that most can get by without borrowing. If you need to borrow money, it makes sense to apply for a separate credit card for business use. (It can still be in your name.) Any interest paid for business purposes is tax deductible, and it's a lot easier to maintain your books with a separate business account. If your card has a grace period, and you pay your balance every month, your card works like a rolling line of credit with no interest cost whatsoever.

If you have a good credit record or other assets, such as sufficient home equity, you may have other loan options. To get a bank loan, you may need to develop a business plan. (You should develop one anyway.) Such a plan should include:

- A description of your business, including your background and why your services are unique.
- An analysis of the market, including the characteristics of the publications or clients that will use your services.
- Your marketing or sales plan.
- An outline of your finances, which will include a balance sheet, cashflow statement, and break-even analysis.

If you're turned down for a loan—a distinct possibility—you may be eligible for a government-guaranteed loan through the Small Business Administration. Even if the SBA doesn't give you a loan, it can give you something that may be more valuable. The Service Corps Of Retired Executives (SCORE) is an SBA service that offers free advice to small businesses. The retired executives who volunteer their time can help steer you through a business plan.

Planning Income

The overhead calculation you did earlier is important in figuring how much you should charge for your services. To calculate an hourly rate, figure the amount you hope to earn. That may be what you used to make at your old job or what you dream of making at your new one. Then, add in your annual overhead expenses. Divide that figure by the number of billable hours you expect to work in a year. (Count on spending a quarter of your time marketing your services, maintaining your records, and reading professional publications.)

Most magazines and clients won't pay by the hour but by the word, inch or article. You can, however, analyze how long an assignment will take and multiply that by your hourly rate. Remember to consider expenses, too. Try to estimate your costs for phone charges, mileage, and other expenses. Add these to the fee you negotiate.

Always keep in mind what the market will bear when making your calculations. Check with other freelance writers in your area to find out what they charge. Don't charge more than you can get, but don't underestimate yourself either. Lowball pricing may get you a few jobs. But it will hurt your image with clients and editors, and often, your self-esteem.

(For more information on setting your prices, see Appendix A.)

Records and Accounts

Nobody becomes a freelance writer to do bookkeeping. But freelancers quickly find it becomes an important part of their jobs. Again, it need not be cumbersome. Ideally, record keeping should take no more than two hours each week.

Your record keeping system can be as simple as a daily log of income and expenses. If you're more comfortable keeping records on your personal computer, your local computer store should have a wide array of software that can do the job.

Financial planners recommend that you set up a separate checking account for your business. This will keep you from tapping your business funds for personal needs. And it will provide clearer documentation of your income and business expenses.

You also need some kind of documentation for each business transaction. That can be a canceled check or cash receipt. You should write the business purpose on the receipt or check. Your system for saving receipts can be something as simple as a shoebox.

Since you'll probably deduct auto expenses on your tax form, you'll need a mileage log to substantiate them. The log must show the date of each trip, the beginning and ending mileage, and the business purpose.

The IRS strongly recommends you keep expense records for as long as the period of limitations for audits. In most cases, that's three years from the date the return was filed or two years from when the tax was paid, whichever is later.

Keep income records for six years after each tax return is filed. That's the IRS period for going after unreported income.

You'll need records for the cost of your home or improvements for as long as you own the home if you take the home-office deduction. Also, you must keep records of items for which you claim depreciation, such as cars, for as long as you depreciate them, plus the three years after you file your return.

Though costly and time-consuming, audits are relatively rare. The IRS audits fewer than 1 percent of tax returns each year. Among businesses and the self-employed the chances are about 4 percent. Even if you're audited you won't necessarily owe money. About a fifth of those audited don't owe any additional taxes, and some even get refunds.

Tracking Income

Expenses are only half of what you'll be tracking. You'll also need to record income as you receive it and keep pay stubs that document your earnings. Each source that pays you more than $500 a year must report your earnings to the IRS and send you a 1099 form showing the amount. Income records are important for comparing to the amounts reported on each 1099.

If you've been bartering with other businesses (receiving goods or services rather than cash) the law requires you to report the fair market dollar value.

Cash Flow

That first big check for your writing will be a thrill. But don't rush out and spend it. There's going to be a lean period. With the right strategy you can minimize the ups and downs.

The best way to avoid cash-flow problems is to continually work on developing new clients. That means sending out queries or contacting potential clients even when you're busy. Try to set aside a couple days each month for such marketing.

Additionally, never rely too much on any one source of income. Developing a few key accounts, preferably large and reliable enough to cover your overhead and basic living expenses, is important. But don't become complacent. Nothing lasts forever, so don't let any single account become more than a third of your business.

Dealing with the choppy seas of cash flow requires discipline. Using your budget, establish a maximum amount that you will spend in any month. Keeping your earnings in a business account separate from your personal savings or checking account is one good way to keep from spending it all.

You should also meticulously track what your clients owe you. Record who owes you money, how much, and when it's due. As best as possible, arrange payment on your terms. Remember, book authors are not the only ones who get paid some money in advance. You may be able to get some money up front for copywriting or even expense money from magazines.

For article writers, publications that pay on acceptance are obviously more desirable than those that pay on publication. If you're getting paid on publication, you could wait months for your article to be published, and at least a month after that to get paid. If paid on acceptance, you should get paid within a month of your final rewrite.

Fast action is the key to good cash flow. To maximize your income:

- Incorporate billing into your weekly schedule.
- Tabulate your phone or other expenses as soon as the bill comes due.
- Bill as soon as payment is due.
- Don't let a new, unproven account run up huge tabs before you get paid. In most cases, you won't know how good a publisher's or client's payment practices are until they owe you money.

Getting Paid

Waiting for checks is one of the most nerve-racking parts of being a writer. Let's face it: As writers we rely heavily on the creative side of our brain. Business and finances are not something most of us enjoy dealing with. So we like to think that our creative efforts will always be rewarded fairly. Yet even when our rights are carefully spelled out in a contract, there's no guarantee that payment will arrive when it's due.

For sure, one skill that writers acquire is patience. But we needn't be too patient. No matter how bad the publisher's cash flow, it's usually better than ours. So when the wait gets too long, here are some steps you can take:

1. If payment is thirty days past due, call and/or write immediately. You need not be confrontational. Simply send a late notice, or call to check on the status of payment or to make sure your

invoice wasn't lost. If you call, be sure to get a commitment from the editor or accounting office on when the payment will be sent.

2. If payment isn't in your mailbox by the time promised, call and talk to the person in charge of payment. Be polite but firm. If you're told the check is on its way, get specifics about when it was mailed or when it will be mailed. This is a good time to let them know you won't be able to send any more work until payment is received. Your leverage increases greatly if you're working on another assignment that's needed soon.

3. If payment isn't forthcoming after the second time you call or write, and the money you are owed warrants it, send a final notice informing the publisher that you will have to turn the account over for collection or legal action if payment isn't received by a specified date. Take that "further action" promptly if the deadline passes. It could be a letter from a lawyer, or you may want to hire a collection agency.

    If the amount in question does not warrant hiring an attorney or collection agency, you may be able to get help from certain writers organizations if you are a member. Some writers organizations will send letters on behalf of members who have not been paid for published work. A letter from a third party is an attention-getter that will sometimes disgorge a check from many slow payers.

4. If your payment dispute is with a book publisher, the expense of a lawsuit may be justified. In other instances small claims court can be a solution. Filing fees are nominal and lawyers aren't required. Best of all, novices are tolerated.

    Although you save considerable money with small claims court, you should expect to invest some time, which for a writer is often the same as money. You'll have to wait in line to get papers to file, and wait in line again to file them. In front of you will be lots of people who are just as unfamiliar with the process.

Later, you may have to spend the better part of a day in court waiting for your case to come up. This can also work to your advantage. Faced with the prospect of wasting a day in court, the editor may become your staunchest advocate before the accounting department.

Small claims court won't handle every situation. Depending on the state, the court will have a claim limit of $1,000 to $5,000. Also, you may not be able to sue an out-of-state publisher in your local court. And winning your suit is no guarantee you'll be paid. You may need to follow up by filing a claim against the publisher's assets. And if the bank is out of state, you may not succeed.

5. If all else fails and there's little hope of seeing the money owed you, you can get some sense of satisfaction (and save others from a similar problem) by alerting your fellow writers about the problem publisher. Several organizations will note nonpayments in their newsletters. You can spread the word rapidly through online forums and bulletin boards frequented by writers. The threat of such disclosure can even work in your favor.

    If you learned about the publication in a directory, inform the directory's staff of your problem. They may also write on your behalf, or at least consider deleting the publication from the next edition of their directory.

Credit-Checking Tips

The following points are not scientific methods but they are certainly prudent steps that can save you from being cheated:

- Look at several copies of a publication before you do any work. Editorial quality is often a sign of business integrity. If a publication cheats its readers, what makes you think it won't short-change its writers? Some danger signs are headlines that promise what articles don't deliver, and articles that are misleading, over-hyped, and under researched.
- Try to contact some of the publication's current writers to find out about the publication's payment practices.

- Compare the amount of advertising to the same period a year earlier. If the ad pages are slipping seriously, this could be a sign of a failing publication that will have trouble paying its bills.

Should I Incorporate?

Generally, when professionals form corporations, only the assets of the corporation are liable for seizure by creditors or potential litigants as opposed to the assets of the individual. Libel is one of the largest litigation traps a writer faces. But because libel may be considered a personal statement, a court could still make your personal assets part of a settlement, even if you are incorporated.

Whether to incorporate is a complex question best handled by an accountant or lawyer who knows your situation. Should you opt for incorporation, the state office that oversees corporations, such as the secretary of state, will send you information detailing the steps you need to take.

For further information contact:

Service Corps of Retired Executives (SCORE), SCORE Association, 409 3rd St., SW, 6th Floor, Washington, DC 20024. Tel: (800) 634-0245. Web site: www.score.org.

Volunteer Lawyers for The Arts, 1 E. 53rd St., 6th Floor, New York, NY 10022-4201. Tel: (212) 319-2787, ext. 1. Web site: www.vlany.org.

Saving For the Future

While you may be able to write in your retirement years, you still will need some other savings if you hope to maintain your standard of living. For many people, this means investing in an Individual Retirement Account (IRA).

The formulas for setting up a plan can be pretty complicated, so it's a good idea to get help from a financial planner or accountant in the early stages. The following points can give you a general overview.

An IRA is a personal savings plan that provides income tax advantages to individuals saving money for retirement. Most people who invest in a traditional IRA can claim an income tax deduction for the year in which the funds are contributed into the account. These contributions, as well as any gains, accumulate tax-free until you withdraw the money. You can therefore accumulate greater earnings each year that the funds remain in the account.

Withdrawals are subject to income tax, generally in the year in which you receive them. Since the goal of a traditional IRA is to provide retirement income, the government assesses tax penalty of 10 percent if you withdraw money from an IRA prior to age 59 ½, unless certain exceptions apply.

A Roth IRA is a newer type sheltered account that is growing in popularity. It has a tax structure different from any other IRA in that contributions are post-tax. Since you have already paid taxes on the money that you place into a Roth IRA, your earnings are tax free. Since withdrawals are not reportable income, they won't affect your adjusted gross income during retirement.

The Roth IRA has one potential downside in that you pay taxes while working rather than when retired, when your tax rate is likely to be lower. So the Roth IRA loses one of the advantages of the traditional IRA. The Roth IRA can still offer advantages over traditional IRAs because it provides tax-free growth.

As with traditional IRAs, you can open a Roth account through a stockbroker or other provider of investment accounts. As with all IRAs, there are restrictions on your eligibility. You can stay up-to-date on the rules with IRS Publication 590.

Health Insurance

Health insurance will be one of the biggest expenses you'll face as a free-lancer. If you're leaving a job with health benefits, federal law requires employers to continue your coverage for up to eighteen months (at your expense.) Beyond that you can choose from other group plans or individual coverage. Whatever route you choose, expect it to cost no less than $2,000 a year and as much as several thousand dollars.

Many business or writers organizations offer group health insurance. Some even offer choices, including major medical plans with a range of deductibles and health maintenance organizations

(HMOs). But membership in one of these organizations may not guarantee you'll be accepted for coverage.

You should check with the organization or its insurance carrier for details of the plan. Most are perfectly acceptable. But some organizations provide only a fixed amount of coverage based on the number of days in the hospital and cover no expenses for physician treatment outside a hospital.

Depending on your state, an individual plan may leave you vulnerable to cancellation or steep rate increases should you develop a lengthy illness. Also, most independent coverage will have a waiting period of several months.

A less costly approach is to opt for an individual plan with relatively high deductibles and co-payments. It will still do what insurance is supposed to do, which is to keep you from getting wiped out by a huge medical bill. If you ask, most hospitals and doctors will let you pay off what you owe over time.

One of the best cheap-insurance options, if you can find it, is an HMO that will offer you a high deductible in exchange for low premiums. This way your deductible may still be cheaper than the rates charged to those people who have traditional coverage.

Other Insurance

Going in business for yourself should not mean forgoing disability insurance. To the contrary, you should seek out a plan that covers the highest possible percentage of income for as long as possible. No insurance company will underwrite a policy that pays 100 percent of your income, because that would provide no incentive for you to go back to work. But policies may go as high as 80 percent and last as long as ten years or to age sixty-five.

Many writers organizations offer group disability coverage. The groups may also offer relatively inexpensive group life insurance that can cover such items as your mortgage. But it's important to look at disability plans closely. Some plans cover only a fixed period, so you'd be out of luck and money in the event of long-term disability.

If you work from home, you should also check with your home or renter's insurance carrier to make sure your business equipment is covered. Professional liability is another coverage to consider. Your largest liability exposure is for libel. If your work seems likely to involve you in libel litigation somewhere down the road, you may want to take out a separate policy through a group like the National Writers Union.

Some national groups for writers and small businesses that offer insurance to their members include:

Editorial Freelancers Association, 71 W. 23rd St., Suite 1910, New York, NY 10010-4102. Tel: (212) 929-5400. E-mail: info@the-efa.org. Web site: www.the-efa.org.

National Association for the Self-Employed, P.O. Box 612067, DFW Airport, Dallas, TX 75261-2067. Tel: (800) 232-6273. Web site: www.nase.org.

National Small Business United, 1156 15th St., NW, Suite 1100, Washington, D.C. 20005. Tel: (202) 293-8830.

National Writers Union, 113 University Pl., 6th Fl., New York, NY 10003. Tel: (212) 254-0279. E-mail: nwu@nwu.org. Web site: www.nwu.org.

Small Business Service Bureau, P.O. Box 15014, 554 Main Street, Worcester, MA 016015-0014. Tel: (800) 343-0939. E-mail: membership@sbsb.com. Web site: www.sbsb.com.

Tax Issues

Becoming a freelancer means saying goodbye to the days you spent thirty minutes filling out your annual taxes. As soon as you make any money freelancing, you'll have to fill out the long form 1040 and Schedule C for business profit or loss. If you plan to deduct car or equipment expenses, you'll have another even more complex form to fill out.

You can hire someone to do your taxes and keep your books. But you'll still be responsible for keeping receipts and records. The best strategy is to spend a little time learning the tax rules and adopt a simple system of keeping records. Even if you do hire an accountant or tax preparer, keeping good records will save time and fees.

Estimated Taxes

Freelancers don't have any tax withheld from their income. Like any self-employed person, they are liable for paying estimated taxes quarterly. You can use IRS form 1040-ES to calculate and make your estimated payments.

If you can't estimate this year's income accurately, you will usually be safe from penalties if you base your quarterly taxes on what you owed the prior year. Your state and city may also require you to withhold taxes. To be safe, you should put aside at least 33 percent of your net earnings to cover your federal, state, and local taxes. It is better to be prepared than to be surprised.

Auto Expenses

If you work from home, you can deduct mileage from home and back to any interview, trips to the library for research, or travel for any business function. This is true even if you don't qualify for the home office deduction. If you work from an office outside the home, however, you can't deduct mileage for commuting to the office.

You can calculate auto expenses using the standard mileage rate or the actual-cost method. To use the standard mileage rate, multiply your the mileage driven by the current mileage rate (37.5 cents in 2004). The rate frequently changes, but is stated each year in the instructions that come with Schedule C, the IRS form for reporting business income and expenses. Using the standard mileage rate is the easiest method in terms of record keeping.

As the name implies, the actual-cost method measures what it really costs you to operate your car. For this method you'll have to keep receipts for all automobile expenses, including gas, maintenance and repairs, insurance, taxes, loan interest, and depreciation of the car's cost.

If you use the car for both business and personal reasons, calculate the percentage of business miles each year and deduct that percentage of your costs. There are limits to how much of your car's value you may write off each year. For details you'll need a current copy of IRS publication 917.

Home-Office Expenses

Qualifying for the home-office deduction means jumping through regulatory hoops and increasing your risk of an audit. But the tax savings can be worth it. You may be able to deduct a percentage of your mortgage interest or rent, utilities, and upkeep for your home each year.

To qualify for the deduction you must use an area of your home regularly and exclusively for business. Occasional or incidental use of your home office won't cut it, even if you don't use the space for anything else.

"Exclusive use" means just that—no games on your personal computer, no personal calls from the phone in your office. No relatives rolling out sleeping bags there on the weekend. Some furnishings are banned in a home office, like televisions and sofas. The IRS sees them as signs of personal use. Although it is best to have an entire room set aside for a home office, a portion of a room set aside exclusively for business also satisfies the Internal Revenue Code.

The most accurate way to calculate the business portion of your home is to divide the square feet of the work area by the total square feet of your home. Expenses you can deduct include the business percentage of:

- Mortgage interest.
- Utilities and services, such as electricity, heat, trash removal, and cleaning services.
- Depreciation of the value of your house.
- Home security systems.
- Repairs, maintenance, and permanent improvement costs for your house.
- All costs of repairs, painting, or modifications of your home office. (Repairs you can write off the first year. Permanent improvements are considered capital expenditures and subject to depreciation over several years.)

One other word of caution—you can't use home office expenses to put you in the red. They can't be used to help create a tax loss.

Before you take any home-office deductions, figure out what the tax savings will be. If the savings are minor, you may not want to bother.

What you lose in taxes, you may gain in peace of mind because you'll be saving yourself extra work. You can get more information from IRS Publication 587.

Other Expenses

The IRS applies the "ordinary" and "necessary" rules in judging the validity of a business expense. This means the expenses should be ordinary for your profession and necessary for carrying out your business.

Office equipment is a necessary—and often major—expense for freelance writers. Computers, desks, chairs, shelves, filing cabinets, and other office furnishings are deductible expenses if you use them in your business. These can be deducted even if you don't opt for the home-office deduction. IRS publication 534 provides more details on how to depreciate business property.

Among the largest costs for freelancers are phone expenses. The IRS prohibits deductions for your personal phone line, even if you use it for business. But you can still deduct the cost of long-distance business calls, even if they're from a personal line. You can also deduct the cost of a second line or other services used exclusively for business, such as a distinctive ring or voice mail.

If you entertain sources or clients you can deduct 50 percent of that expense. You must keep a log of the date, location, person entertained, and business purpose of the entertainment for every item you deduct. If you travel in connection with your writing you can deduct the cost of transportation, lodging, and meals.

Other deductible expenses include the cost of:
- Dues to professional organizations
- Newspapers, magazines, and journals used for your business
- Research, copying services, and online databases
- Office supplies
- Postage for business use
- Cleaning supplies for your office
- Legal, accounting, and other professional services
- Business licenses

If publishers or clients reimburse you for some of your expenses, remember to keep records of those payments and either report them as income or subtract them from the expenses you report.

Self-Employment Tax

Besides ordinary income tax, freelancers must pay a self-employment tax for Social Security and Medicare. Employees pay social security tax too, but the self-employed pay roughly twice as much (about 15 percent), because they're expected to cover both the "employee" half and the "employer" portion. When you look at your tax bill, you'll find that's one of the strongest motivations for taking every deduction you're allowed.

Keep in mind that the more you cut your self-employment tax, the lower your Social Security check will be once you retire. That said, you'll still likely do better if you take some of your tax savings and put them in a tax-exempt retirement account.

Schedule C Pointers

Schedule C is a catchall form for all businesses, so much of it can be meaningless and mysterious for a freelancer. Here are a few things to remember if you fill out the form yourself:

- You'll probably be checking the "cash" box for accounting method. That just means you record income when you get the check and expenses when you pay them. Few freelancers will use the more complicated methods.
- Check the "does not apply" box for method used to value closing inventory. You don't have any. Unpublished manuscripts don't count.
- Under the income section, such items as returns and allowances and cost of goods sold probably will not apply to you.
- In the expenses section, you can't write off any bad debts (unless you use the more sophisticated accrual accounting method).
- The office expense category is a catchall that includes office supplies, postage, etc.
- You only fill out the pension and profit-sharing portion if you

have employees participating in a plan. Your own plan contribution, if any, is reported on form 1040.

- The tax and license expenses that you can deduct include real estate and personal property taxes on business assets, and employer Social Security and federal unemployment taxes.
- Long-distance charges fall in the utilities line. Since long-distance calls can be a big expense it may be wise to itemize your utility expenses on a separate sheet and attach it.
- A big total in the "other expenses" column can make the IRS very suspicious. Break these items down as much as you can in the space provided.
- Ignore the "cost of goods sold" section because you're not a retailer or manufacturer.
- Your principal business or professional activity code will most likely be 711510 (the category for independent artists, writers, and performers) unless you work in advertising or related services (541800), the publishing industry (511000), or Internet publishing (516110).

Professional Help

As you've figured out by now, business tax forms are a lot more complicated than ordinary tax forms. So you may want professional help. If so, your options include tax preparation services and accountants. You may also get tax preparer training offered by H&R block or other services, which can save you money and even allow you to start a sideline preparing taxes.

If you're incorporated or face particularly complex business issues, you may need help from a certified public accountant. Small or medium-size CPA firms are most likely to be familiar with issues that concern you. Franchise tax services provide a consistent, mass-produced product. They're the cheapest option. But they may be less familiar with some of the unusual situations of freelancers.

Year-End Tax Strategies

The end of the year presents some opportunities to minimize your taxes:

- Bill late in December so checks won't arrive (and the taxes won't be due) until the new year.
- Buy equipment you're planning to use next year before December 31, so you can take advantage of depreciation or deduction this year.
- Load up on office supplies and other essentials you'll need for the coming year before January 1.
- Pay for next year's subscription and professional dues in December.

Publications and Assistance

Many IRS publications and help guides are available at public libraries. You also may order them by calling 800-TAX-FORM [(800) 829-3676]. Be aware, however, that the IRS's publications will only detail how the IRS interprets the law. They may not explain all the deductions for which you qualify.

You also can get free help from the IRS in preparing returns. Look under "telephone assistance—federal tax information" in the index of your tax form. The IRS phone numbers in your phone book can give you more information about free help available in your area. Also check out the IRS Web site at www.irs.gov.

Other resources, like *Writer's Pocket Tax Guide*, by attorney Darlene A. Cypser, may prove helpful. Available in a CD-ROM format, the annually updated resource covers federal tax rules for freelance writers in the United States.

CHAPTER FIFTEEN

Finding a Writing Community

W riting is a solitary pursuit, but that doesn't mean you have to go it alone. Thousands of organizations exist to assist you in fulfilling your dreams of publication. This chapter explores a variety of places you can turn to for insight, ideas, and advice.

Writers organizations offer a range of support for writers from writing advice to insurance options. There are also critique groups where writers can get together to get feedback on their work and give feedback to others. A colony is just another way writers can break out of their creative and physical confines to find a new sense of community among other writers. Writers conferences, university programs, and correspondence schools are three other options. If your goal is to pick up skills from top professionals or expand your contacts in the business, conferences are probably the best investment of your time. University programs and correspondence schools require a long-term commitment, but are especially useful if you are just getting stared in the business of writing. Which of these you choose depends on where you are in your career and what your needs are at the time.

Organizations for Writers

Some writers need a group for support or for critiquing their work. Others want advice on selling their writing, finding a job, or applying for a grant. Thankfully, thousands of writers organizations exist to offer help in these areas and in a variety of other ways. Some are small groups of writers who meet weekly over coffee to read each other's work. There are also nationwide organizations, with up to several thousand members, that offer a broad range of services, including health insurance.

Some groups, especially national organizations, have stringent guidelines for membership. Local and regional groups usually are more open to new members and are less expensive to join. They generally emphasize feedback and interaction between members. Other organizations, such as the Authors Guild, work on the business side of writing. Still others, such as the American Medical Writers Association, serve a special niche of writers.

Your involvement with a professional organization depends a great deal on your specific needs. Whatever route you choose, you won't have to spend a lot of money to join. You'll typically pay one hundred to two hundred dollars for a yearly membership to a large group, while many local groups are free.

Joining a Writers Organization

Before you join a writers organization you should compare your needs and goals to those of the group. Consider the following information:

1. **What are the benefits?** If you are a full-time freelance writer and need medical benefits, you'll want to look for an organization large enough to offer them. Visit a meeting before you join to determine whether you'll benefit from the group's programs, or talk to a few writers in the organization to determine what they like best.

2. **Are your goals compatible?** Some groups are organized solely to exchange business and marketing information. Others focus more on critiquing. You must look at the group as an extension of your interests to justify the time away from the keyboard.

3. **What size is the group?** For some people, the most beneficial group is one that's small and allows them to participate in each session. Others value the resources of a large group. Some feel the best of both worlds is available through a local chapter of a large organization.

4. **What's the experience level?** If you're experienced and the majority of members are not, you eventually may feel as though you are wasting time. If, on the other hand, the members are very experienced, they may be unwilling to help you develop in a specific area. Many organizations have membership surveys that state the average experience level.

5. **What's the cost?** If you're paying for a high-service organization but are not using the services, you might want to consider a less expensive, local group.

To locate a writers group, see the state by state listing included in the resources section at the end of this chapter.

Critique Groups

Critique groups are a great way for writers who are ready to share their work with others and receive feedback. Critique groups also can help motivate you to create deadlines for yourself so that you have something to show at your next meeting. No two critique groups are alike. Each varies depending on the personalities and experience of its members. If you think you are interested in joining a critique group, there are a few ways to go about doing it and a few things you need to remember.

Starting a Critique Group

One option is to create your own group. If you know other writers who might be interested in joining a group this might be a good way to get constructive criticism about your work. When forming

Power in Numbers

Two of the largest organizations for writers are the Editorial Freelancers Association (EFA), with more than 1,500 members, and the National Writers Union (NWU), with more than 7,000 members. Their services are also among the most comprehensive. One of the chief differences between these two national groups is that the NWU has a couple dozen local and regional offices across the United States, whereas the EFA offers its services from a central office in New York. Let's take a closer look at each:

Editorial Freelancers Association: The EFA is a national nonprofit organization open to any full- or part-time freelancer. Full membership costs $95 per year. (New York-area residents pay $115 because they can take advantage of local events.) In addition to freelance writers, EFA membership is open to desktop publishers, editors, indexers, proofreaders, researchers, and translators, among others.

Membership benefits include accounting and legal services, a group directory, education programs, events, health insurance, a job list, a bimonthly newsletter, and so on. For additional information, contact the group at 71 West 23rd Street, Suite 1910, New York, NY 10010. Tel: (866) 929-5400. E-mail: info@the-efa.org. Web site: www.the-efa.org.

National Writers Union: NWU is a labor union that represents freelance writers in all genres and formats. Membership is open to all qualified writers who have published a book, a play, three articles, five poems, a short story, or an equal amount of similar work for a company, government, or institution. You are also eligible for membership if you have written an equal amount of unpublished material and are actively seeking to publish your work. Full membership costs $160 or more per year, depending on your writing income. NWU is open to professional writers of any kind.

Membership benefits include: contract advice, grievance resolution, health insurance, media rates database, networking opportunities, and a résumé bank. For additional information, contact the group at 113 University Place, 6th Floor, New York, NY 10003. Tel: (212) 254-0279. E-mail: nwu@nwu.org. Web site: www.nwu.org.

your group, remember to do the following things if you want your group to be successful:

- **Determine your goals.** If everyone's not on the same page, this isn't going to be a useful experience. Is the common goal working on query letters? Trying to improve the members' novel-writing craft? Serving as a cheerleading or support network? Your group will be all these things and more at one time or another. But the members must agree on the key purpose.

- **Limit the size.** It's best if you keep the group to somewhere between six and a dozen members. Much smaller and you run the risk of quickly losing freshness; much bigger, and there won't be an opportunity for healthy interaction.

- **Set a meeting place and time upon which everyone agrees.** You can rotate among each others' homes, meet at someone's workplace, or get together at the local coffeehouse. The starting time should work for everyone—it's aggravating to wait for someone who's consistently fifteen minutes late, or to lose feedback from someone who always has to leave early. Set a regular meeting schedule (preferably twice a month; certainly no less frequently than once a month).

- **Set ground rules and follow them.** This doesn't have to be a dictatorship but an effective critique group has to have some order. What will the standard agenda be? Will all members share work at each meeting? Will manuscript copies be distributed prior to each meeting? Who's responsible for copying and/or distributing the manuscripts? Does the work being shared have to be new? Are outside guests welcomed? (We suggest not.) What happens when a member doesn't show up or has nothing new to read for two or three sessions?

- **Determine the form for critique.** We all want to know how to make our writing better, and that's what most of us want from a critique group. Agree that when members don't like something about another's work, they will offer solutions: "The first page seems to run a bit long. How would it read if you eliminated paragraphs one through three and started with the fourth paragraph?"

is much more helpful—even if the advice ultimately is not followed—than "I thought it was boring."

Locating a Critique Group

If starting your own group is not something you are interested in, you may be able to join an existing group. Check with local community centers, libraries, bookstores, colleges, or universities to see if there are any critique groups near you. When choosing your group, keep these things in mind:

- **Just as in setting up a group, be sure that members share your goals.** Do their ground rules and usual agenda mesh with what you hope to achieve? If not, keep looking at bulletin boards at area bookstores, libraries, or local colleges and universities until you find a group more to your liking—or start putting up your own notices to start a group.
- **Ask about the experience level/publication record of the members.** It's fun to be a bunch of newbies together, but you won't necessarily learn very much. If you're looking for a new social circle, this group may be for you. If you are serious about reaching your writing goals, then find a group with at least one member who has achieved your goal (finishing a novel, finding an agent, getting a magazine article published) in the past year. While you don't want to be in a critique group with five National Book Award finalists if you're still on the first chapter of your first novel, it's better for you if the others in your group are a bit more advanced than you are. That way, you can learn from them.

If there aren't any critique groups close to you, or you don't know enough writers nearby to make starting a group feasible, a final option could be to join an online critique group. Online critique groups give you the opportunity to have your work critiqued by other members of the group without having to accommodate to each other's schedules. It also allows for a more diverse group because you are not confined by proximity, which means more diverse opinions. Online groups can also offer support and assistance in all aspects of your writing from grammar to overall structure, and they can provide you with links and newsletters about writing. It may seem that online groups would be impersonal, but in fact, you may find that you can become just as close to your online critiquers as you would with people in the same room.

If online groups are something you are interested in, explore these groups to see if they meet your needs. If not, there are others out there. Search until you find one that's good for you:

The Writer's BBS: http://writersbbs.com. Offers more than fifty active forums for writers of all types and genres.

My Writer Buddy: www.writerbuddy.com. Is a community and reference center for writers of all levels and interests.

WriteCraft Writers Resource Center: www.writecraftweb.com. Offers constructive criticism to help writers learn the nuts and bolts of the craft.

Writer's Digest.com: www.writersdigest.com/forum. Offers expert critiques monthly and also posts work so others can critique as well.

Is a Writers Colony Right for You?

Writers colonies (sometimes called retreats) offer a wonderful change of pace—providing an opportunity to get the most out of your creative powers in a short span of time. The ways in which colonies are set up to do this can be as varied as a writer's imagination.

Some allow you to work virtually uninterrupted. Others provide space for quiet work but also encourage participants to interact and learn from each other during breaks, or through critiques, readings, and workshops. Some even bring together creative people from different disciplines—painters, writers, musicians—believing you can learn more about your own art by talking with others about theirs. At some retreats the interaction takes place randomly throughout the day as different people gather together informally.

Most colonies require that you submit an application, including samples of your work and a description of how you will utilize your time. All of this is reviewed by a selection committee, whose goal is to make sure applicants are serious about their work. To get accepted you must demonstrate how you will use your time to begin or complete a project.

Few, if any, colonies enforce a regimented schedule or keep tabs on your progress. Writers respond to this freedom differently. Some overwork and burn out in a short period of time. More commonly, writers need several days to adjust their newfound freedom before they can develop a routine for their work.

Some colonies select writers with substantial professional credentials. Others cater to emerging talent. Still others try to foster a mix of better-known and lesser-known talent. Some colonies are highly competitive—receiving dozens of applications for every position they have open. One way to improve your chances is to consider going in the off-season when there are fewer applicants.

A typical stay at a colony lasts from a couple of weeks to several months. The cost of colonies is generally inexpensive, with most charging a small application fee and a weekly cost around $75 to $200 per week. (Keep in mind that the costs can vary greatly from retreat to retreat depending on travel, food, and lodging expenses, and the availability of scholarships and grants.) The majority of colonies stress that payment is voluntary and no qualified applicant will be turned away simply because she cannot pay. Many require that you bring along whatever equipment you plan to use.

Before you select a writers colony, consider the following information:

- Most colonies schedule visits six months in advance, so make sure you assemble your writing samples and apply at least eight months before you would like to attend.
- Look for a colony that fits your lifestyle. Some writers thrive in a rural atmosphere; others find the peace and quiet uninspiring. Some writers like to cook their own meals at their convenience. Others prefer to have their meals prepared for them. Compare all aspects of the colony before applying.

- Some colonies offer weekend programs, but the majority of them want you to stay two weeks to two months. Since most writers work more quickly at a colony, plan your work ahead of time, even if the colony doesn't require it. If possible, talk to other writers who've been to colonies to find out how they used the experience.

Locating Writers Colonies

Several sources offer information on writers colonies, including the *Guide to Writers Conferences* published by Shaw Guides. As a service to its members, The Authors Guild compiles a list of colonies. *Poets & Writers* magazine frequently carries advertisements and notices of colonies. The Alliance of Artists' Communities is another good source. To reach any of these organizations use the information below. You may also want to check with your state arts council.

Alliance of Artists Communities, 255 South Main Street, Providence, RI 02903. Tel: (401) 351-4320. E-mail: aac@artist-communities.org, Web site: www.artistcommunities.org. Provides networking services, conferences, workshops, newsletters, directories, advocacy, and more.

Novel & Short Story Writer's Market, Writer's Digest Books, 4700 E. Galbraith Road, Cincinnati, OH 45236. Tel: (513) 531-2690. E-mail: anne.bowling@fwpubs.com. Web site: www.writersdigest.com. Contains listings for writing conferences, writing programs, and writers organizations.

Poets & Writers, 72 Spring Street, Suite 301, New York, NY 10012. Tel: (212) 226-3586. Web site: www.pw.org. Has links to over 125 writing conferences and residencies.

Shaw Guides, P.O. Box 231295, Ansonia Station, New York, NY 10023. Tel: (212) 799-6464. E-mail: info@shawguides.com. Web site: www.shawguides.com or www.writersdigest.com. Offers a search through over 1200 conferences and has a specific link for residencies and retreats.

Getting the Most Out of Writers Conferences

Whether you are just starting in the business or are already a professional writer, attending writers conferences can be very beneficial. Beginners can learn a lot about the creative and the business sides of writing. Established writers can gain added insights into all aspects of the trade.

Writers—whether beginners or seasoned—have many different goals when they attend a conference. Some want to explore a new writing area or learn from a particular instructor. Others are interested in making contacts with writers, editors, and agents. Still others like the inspiration of spending time with fellow writers.

If you are thinking of attending a writers conference, consider the following points:

- Your chances of individual meetings or instruction are greater at a small conference, but smaller conferences are less likely to attract prominent speakers. Instead of focusing on the total number attending, ask about the number in each session. If the number is thirty or less, you'll have more opportunities to ask questions and discuss your work with the instructor.

- Money is a key consideration for almost any writer. But don't choose a conference solely on the basis of cost. Attending a conference is an investment in your future success. The least expensive option may not be the best for you. A one- or two-day workshop can cost up to $200. Conferences that last up to a week can cost $800 or more, which usually includes the cost of lodging and some meals. One way to work a conference into your budget is to combine it with a vacation.

- The caliber of the conference faculty is usually the most important criteria when evaluating a conference. Look for writers who have credentials in the particular area they will be teaching.

- Some conferences offer individual consultations with instructors, editors, or agents for an additional fee. Such personal feedback must be arranged ahead of time. If you are paying for an appointment you have every right to know what to expect from the meeting. Don't go in expecting to find an editor who will want to publish your work or an agent who will want to represent you. Such overnight success stories are few and far between.

- Most conferences attract writers of a variety of skill levels and are geared accordingly. Check the program for clues as to which sessions are geared toward beginners or professionals. You should avoid sessions that seem too far below or above your level of experience.

- A conference's format can make a big difference. The best conferences are set up to provide interaction between the attendees and the instructors/speakers, rather than just lectures. Also look for panel discussions where writers, editors, and agents offer their opinions on subjects of interest to you.

Locating Writers Conferences

One of the most comprehensive and readily available lists is sponsored by Shaw Guides and found on the *Writer's Digest* Web site (www.writersdigest.com). Thanks to information supplied by Shaw Guides, you can browse more than 5,300 conferences and workshops by location, date, and subject matter. You can even identify conferences by the authors, agents, and publishers attending.

Choosing a College Program That Suits Your Needs

For some people a college environment is a great way to develop their skills and immerse themselves in the writer's world. Yet attending a college or university writing program is expensive and requires a large commitment of time. So if you're already earning a decent living as a writer, or if you have a full-time job and can still find the time to pursue a writing career, a degree may not be a wise investment of time or money. Agents have been known to scout the well-known programs for talent, but there are other ways to attract attention that cost far less than a degree.

There may be other reasons to enroll in classes, however, including the opportunity to study with a writer whom you admire or the chance to develop specific skills. Universities also support more experimental writing and have literary magazines that will publish student's work.

Consider the following guidelines in making your decision:

- Programs are almost as varied as the number of schools. Some schools offer small programs where students receive individual attention. Others offer larger programs with prestigious faculties. Some are conducted in a traditional classroom setup. Others take a workshop approach in which you bring in work to be critiqued by the teacher and fellow students. You can tell a lot about a program by the type of degree it confers. A master's degree usually requires more reading while a master of fine arts requires more writing. Try talking to past graduates to decide which approach is best for you.

- Besides the program itself, inquire about the caliber of the visiting writers, the faculty, and the literary publications affiliated with the program. The community surrounding a program can be just as important to your creative development.

- Reading the program's literary publications and the works of its faculty is a great way to evaluate the program. It can also help you select the best submissions from your own writing. (A sample poetry submission will have ten to twenty poems, and a fiction or nonfiction sample typically includes three pieces.)

- If cost is a major consideration, be sure to check out financial aid options at different schools as well as the availability of teaching assistantships. In addition to the cost of instruction, be sure to compare the cost of living in various areas. And since you're going to be there a while, choose a place where you feel comfortable.

- Weigh the benefits of several programs and be flexible in your choice of institutions. It's not unusual for more renowned programs to receive hundreds of applications for only a few dozen openings.

Locating Writing Programs

The best source for locating a writing program is *The AWP Official Guide to Writing Programs* published by Associated Writing Programs at George Mason University. The guide has information on more than two hundred programs in North America both at the undergraduate and graduate level. For more information, contact Associated Writing Programs, Tallwood House, Mailstop 1E3, George Mason University, Fairfax, VA 22030. Tel: (703) 993-4301. E-mail: awp@gmu.edu. Web site: www.awpwriter.org.

Picking the Best Correspondence School

A correspondence course is a good choice if you lack easy access to a college, or if your schedule prevents you from attending classes. Most home study courses can be finished in less than a year, and most offer one-on-one instruction with the same teacher for the length of the course. But choose your course wisely. You cannot always adapt the course to your needs if you require specialized instruction.

Correspondence programs also allow you to work at your own pace, but only up to a point. If you have difficulty meeting deadlines, a correspondence course is not for you. Most courses have a deadline and getting an extension usually costs extra.

Evaluate correspondence courses with the following points in mind:

- Some courses offer a range of topics that cover everything from newswriting to fiction. Others focus on a single subjects such as poetry or short story writing. Be sure to pick a course that suits your specific goals.
- The costs of correspondence courses can vary from a few hundred dollars to a few thousand dollars. Compare different courses against each other because the most costly do not always offer what is best for you. Ask what payment plans are available. Look for a course that allows you to return the materials for a refund if you are not initially satisfied.
- Any reputable school will share information about the caliber of

its instructors. Look for instructors who not only know the subject but have recent sales in their chosen genre. Of course feedback from the instructor can make or break your learning experience, so it's important to get a good match. Look for a school that is willing to assign you to another instructor if things don't work out.

- Inquire about the level of feedback that you can expect from your instructor. Ideally you will want frequent detailed critiques of your work—not just overall evaluations.

Locating Correspondence Programs

For listings of correspondence programs check *Peterson's Guide to Distance Learning Programs* (Petersons Guides). Also check with your local university to see if it offers correspondence or independent study courses. Groups such as the National Writers Association also offer correspondence instruction.

Resources for Locating Writers Organizations

As you know, there are writers organizations small and large in towns all across the country. Here's a list of some of the organizations found in the United States and Canada.

Organizations in the United States

Organizations exist on state and national levels. Below, you'll find a list of organizations listed by state. In some states, there is more than one chapter for an organization; you should contact the one most convenient for you. National headquarters for groups are indicated, as well. For additional information, such as membership fees, size, group benefits, etc., contact the individual organizations. For additional information about writers groups and organizations, consult *Literary Market Place*. State arts councils sometimes have lists of writers groups, as well. And talk to other writers; they may have helpful suggestions and contact information for groups in your area.

Alabama

Alabama Writers' Conclave, 637 Cary Dr., Auburn, AL 36830-2503, (334) 821-2036, www.alabamawritersconclave.org.

Alabama Writer's Forum, 201 Monroe St., Montgomery, AL 36130, (334) 242-4076, www.writersforum.org.

National League of American Pen Women, 2305 Queensview Rd., Birmingham, AL 35226, (205) 822-0182, www.americanpen-women.org.

National League of American Pen Women, 107 Maximillion Dr., Madison, AL 35758, (256) 430-0667, www.americanpenwo men.org.

National League of American Pen Women, 733 E. Westmoreland Dr., Mobile, AL 36609-0162, (251) 343-0958, www.americanpen women.org.

Alaska

Alaska State Writing Consortium, 1108 F St., Juneau, AK 99801, (907) 465-8643, http://pec.jun.alaska.edu:1608 0/aswc.

Fairbanks Arts Association, P.O. Box 72786, Fairbanks, AK 99707, www.ptialaska.net/~akttt/faasc.html.

Sisters in Crime, P.O. Box 100382, Anchorage, AK 99510, (907) 566-7500, www.sistersincrime.org.

Arizona

Arizona Authors' Association, P.O. Box 87857, Phoenix, AZ 85080, (602) 769-2066, www.azauthors.com.

National League of American Pen Women, 3122 E. Oraibi Dr., Phoenix, AZ 85050, (602) 493-8688, www.americanpenwo men.org.

National League of American Pen Women, P.O. Box 30879, Tucson, AZ 85751, (520) 749-8968, www.americanpenwo men.org.

Society of Southwestern Authors, P.O. Box 30355, Tucson, AZ 85751, (520) 546-9382, www.azstarnet.com/nonprofit/ssa.

Arkansas

Arkansas Literary Society, P.O. Box 174, Little Rock, AR 72203, www.arkansaswords.org.

National League of American Pen Women, 12 Flathead Dr., Cherokee Village, AR 72529, (870) 257-3837, www.american penwomen.org.

Ozark Poets & Writers Collective, P.O. Box 3717, Fayetteville, AR 72702, www.uark.edu/ALADDIN/opwc.

California

Alpine Writers Guild, 1878 Rancho Jorie, Alpine, CA 91901, (619) 445-5537.

Asian American Journalists Association, 1182 Market St., Suite 320, San Francisco, CA 94102, (415) 346-2051, www.aaja.org.

Beyond Baroque, P.O. Box 2727, 681 Venice Blvd., Venice, CA 90291, (310) 822-3006, http://artscenecal.com/BeyondBaro que.html.

California Writers' Club, P.O. Box 606, Alamo, CA 94507, www.cal writers.org.

Feminist Writer's Guild, 881 Coachman Pl., Clayton, CA 94517.

Horror Writers of America, National Headquarters, P.O. Box 50577, Palo Alto, CA 94303, www.horror.org.

Independent Writers of Southern California, P.O. Box 34279, Los Angeles, CA 90034, (877) 79-WRITE, www.iwosc.org.

Mystery Writers of America, Northern California Chapter, 650 Castro St., #120-252, Mountain View, CA 94041, (650) 961-3849, www.mwanorcal.org.

Mystery Writers of America, Southern California Chapter, P.O. Box 27051, Los Angeles, CA 90027, www.socalmwa.com.

PEN Center USA West, 672 S. Lafayette Park Pl., #42, Los Angeles, CA 90057, (213) 365-8500, www.pen-usa-west.org.

Playwrights Foundation, 131 10th St, 3rd Floor, San Francisco, CA 94103, www.playwrightsfoundation.org.

Plaza de la Raza, 3540 N. Mission Rd., Los Angeles, CA 90031, (323) 223-2475, www.plazadelaraza.org/Redone/Plaza.html.

Poets & Writers Inc., 2035 Westwood Blvd., Suite 211, Los Angeles, CA 90025, (310) 481-7195, www.pw.org.

Sacramento Poetry Center, 1631 K St., Sacramento, CA 95814, (916) 441-7395, www.sacramentopoetrycenter.org.

San Diego Writers/Editors Guild, P.O. Box 881931, San Diego, CA 92168, (858) 576-3800, http://sdwritersguild.org.

Small Press Traffic Literary Center, 2215-R Market St., #447, San Francisco, CA 94114, (415) 285-8394.

Small Press Writers and Artists, 13 Southwood Dr., Woodland, CA 95695.

Society of Children's Book Writers & Illustrators, National Headquarters, 8271 Beverly Blvd., Los Angeles, CA 90048, (323) 782-1010, www.scbwi.org.

Songwriters Guild of America, 6430 Sunset Blvd., Suite 705, Hollywood, CA 90028, (323) 462-1108, www.songwriters.org.

Writer's Center of California, 18 E. Blithedale, #31, Mill Valley, CA 94941, (415) 381-1825.

Writers Connection, P.O. Box 24770, San Jose, CA 95154, (408) 445-3600.

Writers Guild of America, 700 W. Third St., Los Angeles, CA 90048, (323) 951-4000, www.wga.org.

The Writing Center, 416 3rd Ave., San Diego, CA 92101, (619) 230-0670.

Colorado

Boulder Writers Alliance, P.O. Box 18342, Boulder, CO 80308, www.bwa.org.

Christian Writers Guild, P.O. Box 88196, Black Forest, CO 80908, (866) 495-5177.

Mystery Writers of America, Rocky Mountain Chapter, 806 Pope Dr., Erie, CO 80516, (303) 665-3992, www.mystery-tales.com.

National League of American Pen Women, 8321 S. Ammons St., Littleton, CO 80128, (303) 979-2463, www.americanpenwo men.org.

National Writers Club, 1450 South Havana, Suite 620, Aurora, CO 80012, (303) 751-7844.

Rocky Mountain Fiction Writers, P.O. Box 260244, Denver, CO 80226, (303) 331-2608, www.rmfw.org.

Women Writing the West, 8547 East Arapahoe Rd., Greenwood Village, CO 80112, (303) 773-8349, www.womenwritingth ewest.org

Connecticut

Connecticut Chapter of Romance Writers of America, 19 Bethlehem Rd., Woodbury, CT 06798, www.geocities.com/ Athens/Forum/1766.

National League of American Pen Women, 150 Butternut Ln., Stamford, CT 06903, (203) 329-0774, www.americanpen women.org.

National League of American Pen Women, 56 Meadow Rd., Trumbull, CT 06611, (203) 268-7165, www.americanpen women.org.

National League of American Pen Women, 108 Butternut Hollow Rd., Greenwich, CT 06830, (203) 869-4228, www.americanpen women.org.

National League of American Pen Women, Writers-In-Exile Center, American Branch, 42 Deby Ave., Orange, CT 06477, (203) 397-1479.

Writers Pending, 912 Stonington Rd., Pawcatuck, CT 06379.

Delaware

Newark Arts Alliance, P.O. Box 1085, Newark, DE 19715, (302) 266-7266, www.newarkartsalliance.org.

District of Columbia

Education Writers Association, 2122 P St. NW, Suite 201, Washington, DC 20037, (202) 452-9830, www.ewa.org.

National League of American Pen Women, National Headquarters, 1300 17th St., NW Washington, DC 20036,

(202) 785-1997, www.americanpenwomen.org.

National Association of Black Journalists, 8701A Adelphi Rd., Adelphi, MD 20783, (301) 445-7100, www.nabj.org.

Newspaper Guild, 501 Third St., NW, Suite 250, Washington, DC 20001, (202)434-7177, www.newsguild.org.

Washington Independent Writers Group, 220 Woodward Bldg., 773 15th St. NW, Washington, DC 20005, (202) 347-4973.

Word Works, P.O. Box 42164, Washington, DC 20015, www.word worksdc.com.

Florida

Florida Freelance Writer's Association, P.O. Box A, North Stratford, NH 03590, (603) 922-8338, www.ffwamembers.com.

International Society of Dramatists, P.O. Box 1310, Miami, FL 33153.

Mystery Writers of America, Florida Chapter, 6056 NW 56th Dr., Coral Springs, FL 33067, www.mwa-florida.org.

Small Press Writers and Artists, 167 Fox Glen Ct., Ormond Beach, FL 32174.

Tallahassee Writers' Association, P.O. Box 38328, Tallahassee, FL 32315, (850) 539-6397, www.tfn.net/Writer_Association.

Tampa Writers Alliance, 10028 Strafford Oak Ct., #706, Tampa, FL 33642, (813) 908-3095, www.tampawriters.org.

West Florida Literary Federation, 400 South Jefferson St., Suite 212, Pensacola, FL 32502, (850) 435-0942, www.westfloridaliter aryfed.com.

Georgia

Atlanta Writer's Roundtable, P.O. Box 671123, Marietta, GA 30066.

Atlanta Writing Resource Center, 750 Kalb St. SE, Suite 104, Atlanta, GA 30312, (404) 622-4152.

Georgia Writers Association, 1266 West Paces Ferry Rd., Suite 217, Atlanta, GA 30327, (678) 407-0703, www.georgiawriters.org.

National League of American Pen Women, 2479 Big Creek Terrace, Stone Mountain, GA 30087, (770) 469-1264, www.americanpen women.org.

National League of American Pen Women, 3650 Denewood Ct., Columbus, GA 31909, (706) 563-3674, www.americanpen women.org.

Southeastern Writers Association, P.O. Box 20161, St. Simons Island, GA 31522, www.southeasternwriters.com.

Hawaii

National League of American Pen Women, 94-261 Keaolani St., Mililani, HI 96789, (808) 627-1079, www.americanpenwomen.org.

Pacific Writers Connection, c/o Native Books, 1050 Ala Moana Blvd., Bay A-8, Honolulu, HI 96814, (808) 596-8885, www.paci ficwriters.org

Idaho

Idaho Writers League, P.O. Box 1113, Hayden, ID 83835, www.ida-howritersleague.com.

Log Cabin Literary Center, 801 S. Capitol Blvd., Suite 100, Boise, ID 83707, (208) 331-8000, www.logcablit.org.

Illinois

Chicago Alliance for Playwrights, 1225 W. Belmont, Chicago, IL 60657, (773) 929-7367, www.chicagoallianceforplayw rights.org.

Chicago Literary Club, P.O. Box 350, Kenilworth, IL 60043, (312) 435-1040, www.chilit.org.

Chicago Women in Publishing, P.O. Box 268107, Chicago, IL 60626, (312) 641-6311, www.cwip.org.

DestinAsian, 5945 N. Lakewood, Suite 2, Chicago, IL 60660, (312) 275-7101.

Guild Complex, 1532 N. Milwaukee, Suite 210, Chicago, IL 60622, (773) 227-6117, www.guildcomplex.com.

Independent Writers of Chicago, 5465 W. Grand Ave., Suite 100, Gurnee, IL 60031, (847) 855-6670, www.iwoc.org.

National League of American Pen Women, 1004 Matthew Dr., O'Fallon, IL 62269, (618) 632-1881, www.americanpenwo men.org.

National League of American Pen Women, 2601 47th St., Moline, IL 61265, www.americanpenwomen.org.

National League of American Pen Women, 2901 Ireland Grove Rd., Bloomington, IL 61704, (309) 663-2741, www.american pen women.org.

Poetry Center of Chicago, 37 S. Wabash Ave., Room 301, Chicago, IL 60603, (312) 899-1229, www.poetrycenter.org.

Society of Midland Authors, P.O. Box 10419, Chicago, IL 60610, (773) 506-7578, www.midlandauthors.com.

Indiana

Central Indiana Writers Association, 328 E. Southern, Indianapolis, IN 46225, www.geocities.com/centralindi anawritersassociation.

National League of American Pen Women, 1545 Trace Ln., Indianapolis, IN 46260, (317) 872-7401, www.americanpen women.org.

National League of American Pen Women, 4516 N. Tillotson, Muncie, IN 47304, (765) 289-6059, www.americanpen women.org.

Mystery Writers of America, Midwest Chapter, P.O. Box 6804, South Bend, IN 46660, www.mwamidwest.org.

The Writers' Center of Indiana, P.O. Box 30407, Indianapolis, IN 46230, (317) 255-0710, www.indianawriters.org.

Iowa

Iowa Poetry Association, 1911 Spencer St., Grinnell, IA 50112, www.iowapoetry.com.

National League of American Pen Women, 782 Westside Dr., Iowa City, IA 52246, (319) 341-7166, www.americanpen women.org.

Kansas

National League of American Pen Women, 361 S. Woodchuck, Wichita, KS 67209, (316) 721-4720, www.americanpen women.org.

Novelists Inc., P.O. Box 1166, Mission, KS 66222, www.ninc.com.

Partners in Crime, 18100 Berryhill Dr., Stillwell, KS 66085.

Sisters in Crime, 15240 SW Queen's Lace Rd., Rose Hill, KS 67133, (316) 218-1405, www.sistersincrime.org.

Kentucky

Kentucky State Poetry Society, 2315 S. Wilson Rd., Radcliff, KY 40160, (270) 351-3268, http://windpub.com/ksps/news.htm.

National League of American Pen Women, 494 Lea View Ave., Campbellsburg, KY 40011, (502) 532-7055, www.americanpen women.org.

Sisters In Crime, 10405 Timberwood Cir., Louisville, KY 40223, (502) 245-6170, www.sistersincrime.org.

Louisiana

Arts Council of Greater Baton Rouge, 427 Laurel St., Baton Rouge, LA 70801, (225) 344-8558, www.artsbr.org.

Louisiana Poetry Society, 2217 Edenborn Ave., #203, Metairie, LA 70001, (504) 834-4417, http://community-2.webtv.net/mcmkel ly/NewOrleansPoetry.

Maine

Deer Isle Writers' Workshops, P.O. Box 100, Deer Isle, ME 04627, (207) 348-2791.

Maine Writers & Publishers Alliance, 1326 Washington St., Bath, ME 04530, (207) 386-1400, www.mainewriters.org.

Maryland

American Medical Writers Association, National Headquarters, 40 W. Gude Dr., Suite 101, Rockville, MD 20850, (301) 294-5303, www.amwa.org.

Baltimore Writers' Alliance, P.O. Box 410, Riderwood, MD 21139, www.baltimorewriters.org.

National League of American Pen Women, 9472 Quail Run Rd., Denton, MD 21629, www.americanpenwomen.org.

Science Fiction and Fantasy Writers of America, P.O. Box 877, Chestertown, MD 21620, www.sfwa.org.

Writer's Center, 4508 Walsh St., Bethesda, MD 20815, (301) 654-8664, www.writer.org.

Massachusetts

Amherst Writers & Artists, P.O. Box 1076, Amherst, MA 01004, (413) 253-3307, www.amherstwriters.com.

Massachusetts State Poetry Society, 64 Harrison Ave., Lynn, MA 01905.

Mystery Writers of America, New England Chapter, 286 Washington St., Marblehead, MA 01945, (617) 491-2660, www.mysterywriters.org.

National League of American Pen Women, 66 Willow Rd., Sudbury, MA 01776, (978) 443-2165, www.americanpen women.org.

National League of American Pen Women, 579 Buck Island Rd., #147, West Yarmouth, MA 02673, (508) 775-4811, www.ameri canpenwomen.org.

National League of American Pen Women, 3 Julio St., Chelmsford, MA 01824, (978) 256-7243, www.americanpenwomen.org.

National League of American Pen Women, 27 Walnut St., Upton, MA 01568, (508) 529-6005, www.americanpen women.org.

New England Poetry Club, 137 W. Newton St., Boston, MA 02118, (781) 643-0029, www.nepoetryclub.org.

Sisters in Crime, 4 Braeburn Rd., Chelmsford, MA 01824, (978) 256-2933, www.sistersincrime.org.

Michigan

Arts and Humanities Program, YMCA of Metropolitan Detroit,

10900 Harper Ave., Detroit, MI 48213, (313) 267-5300,
www.ymca-artsdetroit.org.

Poetry Society of Michigan, 8242 Stubb Hwy., Eaton Rapids,
MI 48827.

Minnesota

Duluth Depot, 506 W. Michigan St., Duluth, MN 55802, (218)
727-8025, www.duluthdepot.org

The Loft Literary Center, Suite 200, Open Book, 1011
Washington Ave. S., Minneapolis, MN 55415, (612) 215-
2575, www.loft.org.

Minneapolis Writers Workshop, P.O. Box 24356, Minneapolis,
MN 55424, www.minneapoliswriters.com.

National League of American Pen Women, 7114 Pontiac Cir.,
Chanhassen, MN 55317, (952) 470-5969, www.americanp
enwomen.org.

Playwrights' Center, 2301 Franklin Ave., Minneapolis, MN
55406, (612) 332-7481, www.pwcenter.org.

Missouri

Investigative Reporters and Editors, 138 Neff Annex, Missouri
School of Journalism, Columbia, MO 65211, (573) 882-2042,
www.ire.org.

Missouri Writers' Guild, 16 Rio Vista Dr., St. Charles, MO
63303, http://mwg.missouri.org.

National League of American Pen Women, 6143 Tennessee Ave.,
St. Louis, MO 63111, (314) 752-5210, www.americanp
enwomen.org.

Private Eye Writers of America, 4342-H Forest Deville Dr., St.
Louis, MO 63129.

St. Louis Writers Guild, P.O. Box 771765, St. Louis, MO 63177,
(314) 542-9888, www.geocities.com/soho/exhibit/7176.

Writers Place, 3607 Pennsylvania, Kansas City, MO 64111, (816)
753-1090, www.writersplace.org.

Montana

Authors of the Flathead, P.O. Box 7711, Kalispell, MT 59904, (406) 755-7272.

Hellgate Writers, Inc., 2210 N. Higgins, P.O. Box 7131, Missoula, MT 59807, (406) 721-3620.

Outdoor Writers Association of America, 121 Hickory St, Suite 1, Missoula, MT 59801, (406) 728-7434, www.owaa.org.

Nebraska

National League of American Pen Women, 212 Bellevue Blvd., Bellevue, NE 68005, (402) 293-1818, www.americanpen women.org.

Nebraska State Poetry Society, P.O. Box 431, Stanton, NE 68779.

Nevada

Cactus Rose Chapter, Romance Writers of America, P.O. Box 230063, Las Vegas, NV 89123, http://cactusroserwa.ho me.att.net.

Nevada Poetry Society, P.O. Box 7014, Reno, NV 89510.

New Hampshire

Cassell Network of Writers, P.O. Box A, North Stratford, NH 03590, (603) 922-8338, www.writers-editors.com.

New Hampshire Writers' Project, P.O. Box 2693, Concord, NH 03302, (603) 226-6649, www.nhwritersproject.org.

New Jersey

Delaware Valley Poets, P.O. Box 6203, Lawrenceville, NJ 08648, www.delawarevalleypoets.com.

Mendham Poets, 10 Hilltop Rd., Mendham, NJ 07945.

Songwriters Guild of America, National Headquarters, 1500 Harbor Blvd., Weehawken, NJ 07086, (201) 867-7603, www.songwriters.org.

Walt Whitman Center, 409 Hickman Hall, 89 George St., New Brunswick, NJ 08901, (732) 932-6861, http://wwc.rutgers.edu.

New Mexico

National League of American Pen Women, 4717 Larkspur Ct., El Paso, TX 79924, (915) 755-6395, www.americanpenwomen.org.

National League of American Pen Women, HC 32 Box 8157, Truth or Consequences, NM 87901, www.americanpenwomen.org.

Southwest Writers Workshop, 8200 Mountain Rd. NE, Ste. 106, Albuquerque, NM 87110, (505) 265-9485, www.southwestwriters.com.

New York

Academy of American Poets, 588 Broadway, Suite 604, New York, NY 10012, (212) 274-0343, www.poets.org.

American Society of Journalists and Authors, 1501 Broadway, Suite 302, New York, NY 10036, (212) 997-0947, www.asja.org.

American Society of Magazine Editors, 810 Seventh Ave., 24th Floor, New York, NY 10019, www.magazine.org.

Asian American Writers' Workshop, 16 W. 32nd St., Suite 10A, New York, NY 10001, (212) 494-0061, www.aaww.org.

Authors Guild, 31 E. 28th St., 10th Floor, New York, NY 10016, (212) 563-5904, www.authorsguild.org.

Bronx Writer's Center, 2521 Glebe Ave., Bronx, NY 10461, (718) 409-1265, www.bronxarts.org.

Dramatists Guild of America, 1501 Broadway, Suite 701, New York, NY 10036, (212) 398-9366, www.dramaguild.com.

Hudson Valley Writers' Center, 300 Riverside Dr., Sleepy Hollow, NY 10591, (914) 332-5953, www.writerscenter.org.

International Women's Writing Guild, P.O. Box 810, Gracie Station, New York, NY 10028, (212) 737-7536, www.iwwg.com.

Just Buffalo, 2495 Main St., Suite 436, Buffalo, NY 14214, (716) 832-5400, www.justbuffalo.org.

Mystery Writers of America, 17 E. 47th St., 6th Floor, New York, NY 10017, (212) 888-8171, www.mwa-ny.org.

Mystery Writers of America, New York Chapter, 17 E. 47th St., 6th Floor, New York, NY 10017, (212) 888-8171, www.mysterywriters.org.

New Dramatists, 424 W. Forty-fourth St., New York, NY 10036, (212) 757-6960, www.newdramatists.org.

New York State Writers Institute, New Library, LE 320, University at Albany, SUNY, Albany, NY 12222, (518) 442-5620, www.albany.edu/writers-inst.

PEN American Center, National Headquarters, 568 Broadway, 4th Floor, New York, NY 10012, (212) 334-1660, www.pen.org.

Poetry Project at St. Mark's, 131 E. 10th St., New York, NY 10003, www.poetryproject.com.

Poet's House, 72 Spring St., New York, NY 10012, (212) 431-7920, www.poetshouse.org.

Poetry Society of America, 15 Gramercy Park, New York, NY 10003, (212) 254-9628, www.poetrysociety.org.

Poets & Writers Inc., 72 Spring St., Suite 301, New York, NY 10012, (212) 226-3586, www.pw.org.

Small Press Center, 20 W. Forty-fourth St., New York, NY 10036, www.smallpress.org.

Songwriters Guild of America, 1560 Broadway, Suite 1306, New York, NY 10036, (212) 768-7902, www.songwriters.org.

Writers Alliance, 12 Skylark Ln., Stony Brook, NY 11790, (516) 751-7080.

Writers & Books, 740 University Ave., Rochester, NY 14607, (585) 473-2590, www.wab.org.

Writers Guild of America–East, 555 W. Fifty-seventh St., Suite 1230, New York, NY 10019, (212) 767-7800, www.wgae.org.

Writers' Center at Chautauqua, P.O. Box 28, Chautauqua, NY 14722, (800) 836-ARTS, www.geocities.com/Athens/Parthenon/2516.

North Carolina

Murder We Write—Triad Chapter, Sisters in Crime, P.O. Box 2118, Kernersville, NC 27285.

North Carolina Writers' Network, P.O. Box 954, Carrboro, NC 27510, (919) 967-9540, www.ncwriters.org.

Society of American Travel Writers, 1500 Sunday Dr., Suite 102, Raleigh, NC 27607, (919) 861-5586, www.satw.org.

Tarheel Gumshoes, 16424 Beech Hill Dr., Huntersville, NC 28078, (704) 896-5784.

Writers' Workshop, 387 Beaucatcher Rd., Asheville, NC 28805, (828) 254-8111, www.writer.org/asheville.

Ohio

Association for Applied Poetry, Pudding House Publications, 81 Shadymere Ln., Columbus, OH 43213.

Cincinnati Writer's Project, P.O. Box 29920, Cincinnati, OH 45229, www.cincinnatiwriters.com.

Ohio Poetry Association, 129 Columbus Rd., Fredricktown, OH 43019, www.geocities.com/theohiopoetryassociation.

Poets' and Writers' League of Greater Cleveland, 12200 Fairhill Rd., Townhouse 3-A, Cleveland, OH 44120, (216) 421-0403.

Thurber House, 77 Jefferson Ave., Columbus, OH 43215, (614) 464-1032, www.thurberhouse.org.

Oklahoma

National League of American Pen Women, P.O. Box 6505, Norman, OK 73070, (405) 325-7266, www.americanpenwomen.org.

National League of American Pen Women, 1529 Craford Ct., Oklahoma City, OK 73159, (405) 691-5799, www.americanpenwomen.org.

Oklahoma Writers' Federation, Rt. 1 Box 6160, Chandler, OK 74834, www.owfi.org.

Poetry Society of Oklahoma, P.O. Box 331, Crowder, OK 74430.

Oregon

American Crime Writers League, 18645 SW Farmington Rd., #255, Aloha, OR 97007, www.acwl.org.

Lane Literary Guild, P.O. Box 11035, Eugene, OR 97440, www.laneliteraryguild.org.

Literary Arts, 219 NW 12th, Suite 201, Portland, OR 97209, (503) 227-2583, www.literary-arts.org.

Mountain Writers Center, 3624 SE Milwaukie Ave., Portland, OR 97202, (503) 236-4854, www.mountainwriters.org.

National League of American Pen Women, 15690 SW Oakhill, Tigard, OR 97224, (503) 968-8865, www.americanpen women.org.

Northwest Playwrights Guild, 318 SW Palatine Hill Rd., Portland, OR 97219, (503) 452-4778, www.nwpg.org.

Oregon State Poetry Association, 27023 Lower Smith Rd., Reedsport, OR 97647, www.oregonpoets.org.

Willamette Writers, 9045 SW Barbur Blvd., Suite 5A, Portland, OR 97219, (503) 452-1592, www.willamettewriters.com.

Pennsylvania

American Poetry Center, 1204 Walnut St., Philadelphia, PA 19107.

Greater Lehigh Valley Writers Group, P.O. Box 96, Nazareth, PA 18064, (610) 746-4163, www.glvwg.org.

Lehigh Valley Writer's Guild, 9943 Kenrick St., Bethlehem, PA 18017.

National League of American Pen Women, 101 Glendale Rd., Exton, PA 19341, (610) 363-1127, www.americanpen women.org.

National League of American Pen Women, 1952 Wyntre Brook N., York, PA 17403, (717) 741-1377, www.americanpen women.org.

Society of Environmental Journalists, P.O. Box 2492, Jenkintown, PA 19046, (215) 884-8174, www.sej.org.

Rhode Island

Community Writers Association, P.O. Box 312, Providence, RI 02901, (401) 846-9884.

South Carolina

Christian Writers Fellowship, 1624 Jefferson Davis Rd., Clinton, SC

29325, (864) 697-6035, www.cwfi-online.org.

Mystery Writers of America, Southeast Chapter, P.O. Box 4251 CRS, Rock Hill, SC 29732, www.semwa.com.

South Carolina Writers Workshop, P.O. Box 7104, Columbia, SC 29202, (803) 794-0832, www.scwriters.com.

South Dakota

Black Hills Writers Group, 1015 N. Seventh St., Rapid City, SD 57701, (605) 341-3224.

South Dakota State Poetry Society, 4600 E. 26th St., #30, Sioux Falls, SD 57110.

Tennessee

Knoxville Writers' Guild, P.O. Box 10326, Knoxville, TN 37939, www.knoxvillewritersguild.org.

National League of American Pen Women, 338 N. Rowlett, Collierville, TN 38017, (901) 853-0626, www.americanpe nwomen.org.

National League of American Pen Women, 114 Burrus Ave., Hendersonville, TN 37075, (615) 824-1563, www.americanpe nwomen.org.

Songwriters Guild of America, 1222 16th Ave. S., Suite #25, Nashville, TN 37212, (615) 329-1782, www.songwriters.org.

Tennessee Mountain Writers, P.O. Box 5435, Oak Ridge, TN 37831, (865) 671-6046, www.tmwi.org.

Tennessee Writers Alliance, P.O. Box 120396, Nashville, TN 37212, (615) 292-3830, www.tn-writers.org.

Western Writers of America, 1012 Fair St., Franklin, TN 37064, www.westernwriters.org.

Texas

Alamo Writers Unlimited, Bethany Congregational Church, 500 Pilgrim Dr., San Antonio, TX 78240, http://lonestar.texas.net/~mikerod/AWU/windex.html.

American Crime Writers League, 219 Tuxedo, San Antonio, TX

78209, www.acwl.org.

Austin Society of Children's Book Writers and Illustrators, 2014 Lakeline Oaks Dr., Cedar Park, TX 78613, www.austinscbwi.com.

Dallas Screenwriters Association, 10455 N. Central Expwy, #109, PMB 295, Dallas, TX 75231, (214) 922-7829, www.dallasscreen writers.com.

Golden Triangle Writers Guild, 4245 Calder, Beaumont, TX 77706, (409) 898-4894.

Houston Poetry Fest, P.O. Box 22595, Houston, TX 77227, (713) 521-3519, www.houstonpoetryfest.org.

Houston Society of Children's Book Writers and Illustrators, 3111 E. Hickory Park, Sugar Land, TX 77479, www.scbwi-hous ton.org.

Inprint Inc., 1524 Sul Ross, Houston, TX 77006, (713) 521-2026, www.inprint-inc.org.

Mystery Writers of America, Southwest Chapter, (713) 797-8464, www.mwasw.org.

National League of American Pen Women, 3701 Grasmere Dr., Carrollton, TX 75007, (972) 492-4443, www.americanpe nwomen.org.

National League of American Pen Women, 6412 Country Day Trail, Fort Worth, TX 76132, (817) 731-2677, www.americanpe nwomen.org.

North Central/Northeast Chapter, Society of Children's Book Writers and Illustrators, Wesley House, 3216 West Park Row, Arlington, TX 76013, (817) 465-3068, www.janpeck.com/txscb wi.htm.

North Texas Romance Writers of America, P.O. Box 1921, Burleson, TX 76097, www.ntrwa.com.

Poets of Tarrant County, First Methodist Church, 800 W. Fifth, Fort Worth, TX 76102, http://texaspoet.homestead.com/PTC.html.

Poetry Society of Texas, 7059 Spring Valley Rd., Dallas, TX 75254, http://members.tripod.com/psttx/pst7.htm.

Writers' League of Texas, 1501 W. Fifth St., Suite E2, Austin, TX 78703, (512) 499-8914, www.writersleague.org.

Utah

National League of American Pen Women, 145 Eccles Ave., Ogden, UT 84404, (801) 393-5089, www.americanpen-women.org.

Writers at Work, P.O. Box 540370, N. Salt Lake, UT 84054, (801) 292-9285, www.writersatwork.org.

Virginia

American Society of Newspaper Editors, 11690 B Sunrise Valley Dr., Reston, VA 20191, (703) 453-1122, www.asne.org.

American Translators Association, 225 Reinekers Ln., Suite 590, Alexandria, VA 22314, (703) 683-6100, www.atanet.org.

Charlottesville Writing Center, 405 Third St. NE, Charlottesville, VA 22902, (434) 293-3702, www.cvillewrites.org.

Mid-Atlantic Society of Children's Book Writers and Illustrators, 2073 Bingham Court, Reston, VA 20191, www.scbwi-midatlantic.org.

National Federation of Press Women, P.O. Box 5556, Arlington, VA 22205, (800) 780-2715, www.nfpw.org.

Vermont

League of Vermont Writers, P.O. Box 172, Underhill, VT 05490, www.together.net/~trzepacz/lvw.

National League of American Pen Women, 8 Daisy Ln., Bridport, VT 05734, (802) 758-2366, www.americanpen women.org.

Washington

National League of American Pen Women, P.O. Box 2238, Ocean Shores, WA 98569, www.americanpenwomen.org.

Northwest Playwrights Guild, P.O. Box 95259, Seattle, WA

98145, www.nwpg.org/wa.

Pacific Northwest Writers, P.O. Box 2016, Edmonds, WA 98020, (425) 673-2665, www.pnwa.org.

Richard Hugo House, 1634 Eleventh Ave., Seattle, WA 98122, (206) 322-7030, www.hugohouse.org.

Seattle Arts & Lectures, 105 S. Main St., Suite 201, Seattle, WA 98104, (206) 621-2230, www.lectures.org.

West Virginia

National Association of Science Writers, P.O. Box 890, Hedgesville, WV 25427, (304) 754-5077, www.nasw.org.

Wisconsin

Associated Church Press, 1410 Vernon St., Stoughton, WI 53589, (608) 877-0011, www.theacp.org.

National League of American Pen Women, 3557 East Blackhawk Dr., Milton, WI 53563, (608) 868-7208, www.americanpen women.org.

Wisconsin Fellowship of Poets, 3709 Zwerg Dr., Madison, WI 53705, www.wfop.org.

Wisconsin Regional Writers Association, 510 W. Sunset Ave., Appleton, WI 54911, www.wrwa.net.

Wisconsin Romance Writers of America, Milwaukee Public Library, 814 W. Wisconsin Ave., Milwaukee, WI 53233, www.eclectics.com/WisRWA.

Woodland Pattern Book Center, 720 Locust St., Milwaukee, WI 53212, (414) 263-5001, www.woodlandpattern.org.

Writers' Place, 122 State St., Suite 607, Madison, WI 53705, (608) 255-4030.

Wyoming

Western Writers of America, 209 E. Iowa, Cheyenne, WY 82009, www.westernwriters.org.

Wyoming Writers, P.O. Box 818, Thayne, WY 83127, (307) 883-4573, www.wyowriters.org.

Organizations in Canada

Here are some writing organizations located throughout Canada: Contact the organizations to find their locations closest to you.

Alberta

Writers' Guild of Alberta, Percy Page Centre, 11759 Groat Rd., Edmonton, AB T5M 3K6, (800) 665-5354, www.writers guild.ab.ca.

British Columbia

Federation of BC Writers, P.O. Box 3887, Stn Terminal, Vancouver, BC V6B 2Z3, (604) 683-2057, www.bcwriters.com.

Periodical Writers Association of Canada, (250) 383-0667, www.islandnet.com/~pwacvic.

Writers' Union of Canada, Box 45052, Ocean Park RPO, Surrey, BC V4A 9L1, (604) 535-8288, www.writersunion.ca.

Manitoba

Manitoba Arts Council, 525-93 Lombard Ave., Winnipeg, MB R3B 3B1, (204) 945-2237, www.artscouncil.mb.ca.

Manitoba Writers' Guild, 206-100 Arthur St., Winnipeg, MB R3B 1H3, (888) 637-5802, www.mbwriter.mb.ca.

New Brunswick

Writers Federation of New Brunswick, P.O. Box 37, Station A, Fredericton, NB E3B 4Y2, (506) 459-7228, www.sjfn.nb.ca/com munity_hall/W/Writers_Federation_NB.

Newfoundland and Labrador

Writers Alliance of Newfoundland and Labrador, P.O. Box 2681, St. John's, NF A1C 5M5, (709) 739-5215, www.writers alliance.nf.ca.

Nova Scotia

Playwrights Atlantic Resource Centre, P.O. Box 269, Guysborough,

NS B0H 1N0, (902) 533-2077, www3.ns.sympatico.ca/parcoffice.

Writers' Federation of Nova Scotia, 1113 Marginal Rd., Halifax, NS B3H 4P7, (902) 423-8116, www.writers.ns.ca.

Ontario

Canadian Association of Journalists, Algonquin College, 1385 Woodroffe Ave., B224, Ottawa, ON K2G 1V8, (613) 526-8061, www.eagle.ca/caj.

Canadian Authors Association, Box 419, Campbellford, ON K0L 1L0, (705) 653-0323, www.canauthors.org.

Canadian Book Marketing Centre, 2 Gloucester St., Suite 301, Toronto, ON M4Y 1L5, (416) 413-4930.

Canadian Literary and Artistic Association Inc., Commerce Court W., Suite 4900, Toronto, ON M5L 1J3, (416) 862-7525.

Canadian Poetry Association, P.O. Box 340, Station B, London, ON N6A 4W1, (519) 660-0548, www3.sympatico.ca/cpa.

Canadian Society of Children's Authors, Illustrators & Performers, 104-40 Orchard View Blvd., Toronto, ON M4R 1B9, (416) 515-1559, www.canscaip.org.

Canadian Science Writers' Association, P.O. Box 75, Station A, Toronto, ON M5W 1A2, (800) 796-8595, www.sciencewriters.ca.

Canadian Writers' Foundation Inc., 1 Nakota Way, Ottawa, ON K2J 4E9, (613) 825-0333, www.canauthors.org/cwf.

Centre for Investigative Journalism, Carleton University, St. Patrick's Bldg., Room 324, Ottawa, ON K1S 5B6.

Crime Writers of Canada, 3007 Kingston Rd., Box 113, Toronto, ON M1M 1P1, (416) 782-3116, www.crimewriterscanada.com.

League of Canadian Poets, 920 Yonge St., Suite 608, Toronto, ON M4W 3C7, (416) 504-1657, www.poets.ca.

Ottawa Independent Writers, P.O. Box 23137, Ottawa, ON K2A 4E2, (613) 841-0572, www.oiw.ca.

Outdoor Writers Association of Canada, RR 1, Parry Sound, ON

P2A 2W7, (705) 746-9440.

Periodical Writers Association of Canada, 54 Wolseley St., Suite 203, Toronto, ON M5T 1A5, (416) 504-1645, www.pwac.ca.

Playwrights Guild of Canada, 54 Wolseley St., 2nd Floor, Toronto, ON M5T 1A5, (416) 703-0201, www.playwrightsguild.ca.

Writers' Circle of Durham Region, P.O. Box 323, Ajax, ON L1S 3C5, (905) 259-6520, www.wcdr.org.

Writers Guild of Canada, 366 Adelaide St. W., Suite 401, Toronto, ON M5V 1R9, (416) 979-7907, www.writersguildofcanada.com.

Writers' Trust of Canada, 40 Wellington St. E., Suite 300, Toronto, ON M5E 1C7, (416) 504-8222, www.writerstrust.com.

Writers Union of Canada, 40 Wellington St. E., 3rd Floor, Toronto, ON M5E 1C7, (416) 703-8982, www.writersunion.ca.

Prince Edward Island

PEI Writers' Guild, Box 1, 115 Richmond St., Charlottetown, PEI C1A 1H7, www.peiwriters.ca.

Quebec

Canadian Literary and Artistic Association Inc., 1981 Ave., McGill College, Montreal, QC H3A 3C1, (514) 847-4512.

Literary Translator's Association of Canada, SB 335 Concordia University, 1455, boul. de Maisonneuve ouest, Montréal, QC H3G 1M8, (514) 848-8702, www.attlc-ltac.org.

Quebec Writers' Federation, 1200 Ave. Atwater, Montreal, QC H3Z 1X4, (514) 933-0878, www.qwf.org.

Saskatchewan

Saskatchewan Writers Guild, P.O. Box 3986, Regina, SK S4P 3R9, (306) 791-7743, www.skwriter.com.

Speculative Fiction Canada, 303-2333 Scarth St., Regina, SK S4P 2J8, www.sfcanada.ca.

CHAPTER SIXTEEN

Grants, Fellowships, and Prizes

S everal thousand organizations exist throughout the U.S. to award money to writers in the form of grants, fellowships, or prizes. Publicly or privately funded, many operate on a national level. Many more exist on the state and local level.

Grants are a way to stay solvent through lengthy projects. Fellowships offer opportunities for career-enhancing education that freelance writers may not otherwise get, since they have no chance at paid leaves of absence. Contests and awards can offer not only recognition for a job well done, but also money to do the next job well, too.

While there are thousands of organizations offering financial support, these programs are anything but a free ride. It takes hard work and skill to be accepted. Much like selling an article or a book, getting a grant, fellowship, or award means having a good idea, doing superior work, and then searching for the appropriate market. You'll need to find catalogs and directories, then study the listings to find ones whose funding interests match your creative interests.

Grants and Fellowships

Many grants have strict eligibility requirements. Some organizations allow you simply to apply. Others require nominations from a member of the organization. Grants from state and local arts councils, for instance, require recipients to live in the state or locality.

The more money in question, the tougher the competition for it. Some of the biggest have rather high hurdles to face even before you apply, such as having a number of years of professional experience, a book previously published, or a set number of articles published in literary magazines.

Every organization approaches the application process differently. Generally, the process involves these steps:

1. Get the details on any changes concerning the deadline, eligibility, and application process by calling, writing, checking their Web site, or sending an e-mail. Be sure to follow exactly any details as far as manuscript preparation or display of published works. And find out if the deadline is when the application must be postmarked or when it must be at their door. You may need to send your application by overnight delivery to ensure on-time arrival.

2. Send in your application, which usually will include samples of your published work and may include an essay or letter of explanation about your plans for future work.

3. Wait for your application to be screened by a committee that chooses finalists. (In some cases there are multiple screening levels or semifinals.)

4. Finalists will often be interviewed before the final decision, especially for higher-paying awards and fellowships.

Grant application is often framed as a mysterious art best left to experienced practitioners. But in many cases, all the bells and whistles you can muster in a grant application won't make much difference. The quality of your work as viewed by the judges is the primary criterion.

With most grants, selection committees must wade through hundreds or thousands of applications for a handful of awards. Other, more specialized programs may only have a handful of applicants.

Like submitting your work for publication, applying for foundation grants and fellowships means getting your share of rejections. Program administrators advise writers not to be discouraged by an initial rejection. Many writers go on to find acceptance elsewhere or even from the same program in later years.

For a more comprehensive and updated listing, visit www.Writers Market.com, or look for the volume entitled *Grants and Awards Available to American Writers*, published by the PEN American Center, 568 Broadway, New York, NY 10012. Phone: (212) 334-1660, E-mail: pen@pen.org, Web site: www.pen.org. Be sure to visit each organization's Web site or request complete submission guidelines before submitting your work.

Contests

There are more contests available to writers than you probably realize. Like grants and fellowships, winning a contest is not necessarily easy. In order to create the best "luck" for yourself, make sure you consider these things before submitting your work. Winning a contest is subjective so there are no guarantees, but there are things you can do to put yourself in a position to compete.

1. **Make sure it's your personal best.** Sending the short story you wrote three years ago for a class assignment is probably not the best idea. Read over your work multiple times for common spelling and grammar mistakes. Then read it again to make sure that it is clear and the word choice perfect. After all, what's the point of submitting subpar work?

2. **Understand the categories.** Many competitions group different genres or types of writing together. This is so each entry can be judged by the best person in that category. Find out which categories are offered, then define your entry. Choosing the wrong category is easy to do, but often results in a poor— and ultimately unfair—judgment of your work.

Fellowship, Grants, & Contests for Writer: A Sampling

There are numerous fellowships, grants, and contests available for writers if they take the time to look for them. Do some research to find opportunities to get recognition for your work. Six such opportunities are listed below, but keep in mind that a deadlines, requirements, and contact information can change. For the most up-to-date and complete guidelines, contact the organization, check their Web sites, or consult a directory like *Writer's Market* or www.WritersMarket.com.

The Pulliam Journalism Fellowships, The Indianapolis Star, Web site: www.indys-tar.com/pjf, Prize: $6,500, Deadline: March 1
Offered annually as an intensive ten-week summer "training school" for college students with firm commitments to, and solid training in, newspaper journalism.

Wallace Stegner Fellowships, Creative Writing Programs, Stanford University, Web site: www.stanford.edu/dept/english/cw/, Prize: Living stipend and required workshop tuition, Deadline: Applications only accepted from September 1 through December 1
Offered annually for a two-year residency at Stanford for emerging writers to attend the Stegner workshop to practice and perfect their craft under the guidance of the creative writing faculty.

Investigative Journalism Grant, Fund For Investigative Journalism, Web site: www.fij.org, Prize: Grants of $500 to $10,000, Deadline: Varies
Offered three times per year for original investigative newspaper and magazine stories, radio and television documentaries, books, and media criticism. The Fund also offers an annual $25,000 FIJ Book Prize in November for the best book chosen by the board during the year.

McKnight Advancement Grant, The Playwrights' Center, Web site: www.pwcen-ter.org, Prize: $25,000, Deadline: February 6
Offered annually to a Minnesota playwright whose work demonstrates exceptional artistic merit and potential. The grants are intended to significantly advance

recipients' art and careers, and can be used to support a wide variety of expenses. Applicant must have had a minimum of one work fully produced by a professional theater at the time of application.

L. Ron Hubbard's Writers of the Future Contest, Web site: www.writersofthefuture.com, Prize: Quarterly awards of between $500 and $4,000, Deadline: January 1, April 1, July 1, October 1.
Offered for unpublished work to reward and publicize new speculative fiction writers. Open to new and amateur writers who have not professionally published a novel or short novel. Eligible entries are short stories or novelettes (under 17,000 words) of science fiction or fantasy.

Independent Publisher Book Awards, Independent Publisher magazine, Web site: www.independentpublisher.com, Prize: $500 and a trophy to one book in each of 10 categories, Deadline: April 15
Offered annually to all members of the independent publishing industry to recognize exemplary independent, university, and self-published titles. Books are accepted in fifty-two subject areas.

To find more fellowship, grant, and contest opportunities that might suit you, check *Writer's Market* or www.writersmarket.com for lists and details.

(Source: Writer's Market 2004)

3. **Stay within the word limit.** Nothing will disqualify your work faster than exceeding a predetermined word limit. (When entering poems, double-check the number of stanzas allowed.) Many competitions have a maximum word count, and contest judges make sure the winning entries adhere to the guidelines. This is especially the case now that computers have made it so easy to follow this rule. Using the word count function on your computer (in Microsoft Word, you'll find the function under Tools), cut your story until it's within the parameters set by the contest. And remember to leave a little breathing room: If you're ten words over the limit, cut twenty-five just to be safe.

4. **Adhere to contest rules.** If a contest calls for a double-spaced entry, don't submit it single-spaced. If it asks for your name and address to appear in the top right corner, make sure that's where your information appears. Don't include your own illustrations when the contest guidelines state, "No artwork accepted"—your entry will be discarded.

   Your work must conform to fonts and formats, as well as other contest guidelines. Make sure it's your words and phrases that stand out, not a sloppy submission.

5. **Send in the right amount.** There's nothing more disappointing to a contest sponsor than reading a good entry and finding out that the entrant didn't include the right payment. Generally, these entries are eliminated. And what if you send in more money than you're supposed to? Don't expect a refund. It often costs a large company more than the amount of the reimbursement check to send a refund. Similarly, don't send a partial payment. If you owe the contest $10 per entry, and you send $40 for five entries, it's likely that only your first four entries will be sent to a judge.

6. **Stick with the details.** Before you hit the print key for the last time, give your manuscript one more read-through. Do all the characters' actions make sense? Is your timing off? Did you use "oversees" when you meant "overseas"? These small details are easy to miss during the editing process but stick out like a sore thumb when a judge is combing through your entry for the first time. Make sure your manuscript is perfect, then send it out. If you find a mistake weeks later, don't try to send in a revised version or an entirely new entry. Many times the entry is already mixed in with multiple others, or perhaps it's been processed and sent to the judge already. Either way, resolve to make your writing even better for the next competition.

7. **Before you close that envelope, double-check every part of**

your entry: **Is the word count correct (and under limit) on your manuscript?** Have you submitted your work in the preferred format? Is your entry form correctly filled out, with the right fee attached? Have you included the right amount of postage? Checking these details now will save you grief later on. Also, don't include any irrelevant material with your entry—such as résumés, photos, business cards, or multiple copies of one entry—unless required by the rules. Doing so will only cause extra work for the judges or competition workers, which can bode poorly for you and your entry.

8. **Ease those worries**. You can easily ensure that your manuscript is submitted to the correct address by the deadline. While at the post office, ask for a receipt or postal number in order to track your entry. This will let you know when (and if) your entry has made it to the competition department. This function is also helpful when submitting entries via e-mail. If you're using Microsoft Outlook, you'll find this gadget under File> Preferences>Mail>Sending. Another option is to enclose a self-addressed stamped envelope with your submission. However, don't expect a contest judge to send your SASE back if the rules state that entries can't be acknowledged.

9. **Mail early. First of all, you can bypass all those expensive "express delivery" services by simply mailing your entry early.** This will also give you time to add more postage or change the address if your envelope is returned to you. Second, judges often read the first few entries with enthusiasm and excitement. Don't wait until the judge is reading his 300th entry only days before his final deadline. Judges receive many entries. Why force yours to compete with the other one hundred people who also waited until the last minute?

10. **Be patient**. Remember that running a contest takes time. The contest entries must be received and processed before the judges

even get to take a look at your work. Then, after they've made their decision, the final results have to be compiled by the sponsor or organizers of the contest before being announced. Trying to contact the contest via mail, e-mail, or phone will only slow down the process, and most likely aggravate whomever you manage to reach. Frequently, the contest is so large that the status of your entry (or entries) is nearly impossible to determine. Save yourself—and contest organizers—some grief.

Even if you take all of this into consideration, know that every judge looks for different things in a manuscript. So don't worry if you can't find your entry on the list of prize winners. All judging is subjective. Next year's judges might be more keen on your word usage and writing style. It's also possible that other entries had tighter writing, clearer character descriptions, and fewer grammatical mistakes than yours. Rework your manuscript to make it better for the next contest.

A final thing to be aware with contests is that many will want to buy one-time rights or first rights for your manuscript. But some ask (and require) all rights, which means that your stellar entry becomes property of the contest sponsor. If that's the case, you can never enter that same piece of work in another contest, publish it, or use part of the material verbatim in any other way. Relinquishing all rights is only worth it when the prize or recognition is higher than average. Think twice before making your decision.

Making the Most of Winning

Once reassured that, yes, it is your manuscript in the winner's circle, you might be tempted to believe an award equals a free ticket to publication. This is not the case. There are so many contests in today's writing world that a winning entry won't automatically lead to publication, nor will it ensure large cash prizes in other contests. You can, however, take steps to keep your entry from fading in the minds of editors. Here's what to remember if you want to go from contest winner to oft-published writer:

1. **Embrace feedback.** Many contests offer winning recipients (or sometimes every entrant) feedback from one of the contest judges. These contests are excellent to enter, since advice from someone who's made it in your field is priceless. If comments are made on your entry, study them. Note common mistakes you make throughout a writing piece. Check for spelling or grammatical mistakes you might have passed over during a final read. Make a mental note to fix these problems in future manuscripts.

2. **Market yourself.** You won or placed in a contest because your writing was good. Now let the world know. Mention the contest on your Web site, to contacts in the publishing business, and in future queries to publishers. State the contest name and, if the number's impressive, how many entrants you beat. If the contest is split into various categories, mention which category claims you as the top winner. Bottom line: Winning a contest is hard work. Your friends and family aren't the only ones who will be impressed.

3. **Keep in touch.** If you know the name of your judge, keep his name and profession in the back of your mind. Is he a book publisher? Remember to send him the book proposal that's been sitting on your desk. Does he work for a magazine? Think of an article idea and send it to his attention. Perhaps the contest sponsor is a certain magazine or publishing house—talk yourself up among other editors in that organization. By querying someone who's familiar with the contest you've entered and won, you'll spark a light of familiarity with an editor or agent.

   Another bonus to keeping in touch: You may be included in future updates. For example, *Writer's Digest* often keeps track of the writing kudos received by past winners. This is the perfect opportunity for free press if you're lucky enough to score a writing contract or finish a manuscript down the road.

4. **Understand where you stand.** If you didn't win, take a look at the winning entries. (They're often published in a booklet, which you'll be able to purchase from the contest sponsor.) What did they do differently? Take a look at the judges—do they have professional experience in your specific genre? Multiple factors go into choosing a contest winner, so don't beat yourself up if you didn't happen to make it this time. It's the feedback that'll be most helpful to you.

After winning one contest, there's no guarantee that you can start living off future contest prize awards. But you can narrow the playing field by analyzing the elements of future contests. First, research the judges of each contest. They should have professional experience in whatever niche they're judging. Secondly, approximate how many entries are submitted to the contest. An easy way to do this is to see how many entries were submitted last year. Placing out of fifty entries is easier than placing out of three hundred entries.

Also, check to see if the contest accepts published and nonpublished work. If the contest only accepts one or the other, chances for a level playing field are better. Contests that are open only to members of a specific organization also help narrow the field. Finally, look for contests that accept manuscripts in various categories. By entering your fiction manuscript in a strictly-fiction category, your entry will do better than when placed in a general contest with entries from multiple fields all vying for one award.

Finding fellowships, grants, and contests that are a good fit for your writing is possible, but don't be discouraged if they are hard to find. Keep checking sources, such as *Writer's Market* or www.WritersMarket.com for possibilities. Talk to other writers you know and see if they have any suggestions or contacts. The effort you put into locating possible sources of extra money for your work will be well worth it if you put the same amount of effort into the work you submit. Like submitting to an agent or editor, don't give up simply because you've been rejected once. Persevere until you get the award you've been hoping for.

Appendix A: Pricing Guide

As a group, writers are underpaid. Surveys by organizations such as the Author's Guild and the National Writers Union show that income growth for most writers lags behind that of most other professions. The question for you, then, is how do you maximize your earning potential either as a full-time or a part-time writer? In actuality, freelance writing is similar to other creative fields like art, photography, and music. You can either earn hobby rates or you can earn a professional wage. The difference is in how seriously you take your work.

Freelancers who command top dollar are experienced professionals who have spent years perfecting their skills either as freelancers or as writers employed in journalism, advertising, public relations, or publishing. Beyond being talented writers, they are reliable professionals who respect deadlines and have mastered the fine details of running an independent business. They are especially good at marketing themselves. A freelancer, like any independent business person, must also set goals and develop a business plan. The plan doesn't have to be as formal as those for bigger businesses, but at the very least you have to decide what writing skills you have to sell, who might buy them, and how you will prove that you are the best person for the job.

Why Are You Writing?

Before you can figure out how much to charge for your work, first figure out why you are writing: Do you want to make writing your full-time occupation? Do you want to write for fun and are you holding onto your day job? Do you want to earn enough with your writing to break even, meeting all the expenses of setting up an office? Or do you want only to earn enough to pay for your computer, rent, or food?

The answers to those questions will help you decide how to set prices in this business of writing. If writing is your livelihood, you may well have to pay for your own IRA, Social Security taxes, and health insurance, in addition to office expenses, food, shelter, and clothing. If you're writing to scratch an itch, any payment you receive may seem like play money.

Or maybe your goal is to practice your art—to write poetry or the great American novel. If this type of writing is more your idea of success, you may want to structure your freelance career in a way that affords you time for your art. Many writers spend half their week churning out freelance work or technical writing so that they can use the rest of their time in more creative pursuits.

While producers of other products can check out the competition's prices at malls and markets, writers are lonely souls, left to negotiate individually with publishers and clients. Joining a writers group can broaden your perspective on pay rates, particularly a national group, such as the Editorial Freelancers Association or the National Writers Union, which publish data about how much their members earn for jobs. Reading books like *Writer's Market*, which annually publishes lists of pay scales for dozens of types of writing, can also help you determine what to charge. Joining an e-mail list allows you to simply post your rates and ask plugged-in counterparts, "Am I charging enough?"

Freelancers find most of their work networking with other writers, editors, and potential clients. Other good leads come through e-mail and/or hard-copy queries, or networking through Chambers of Commerce and similar organizations. But the best referrals come from satisfied clients who tell others about your work.

As is the case in most professions, beginning writers also earn less than those who have been in the business longer. In addition, asking for more money is never easy. Some clients may be more willing to negotiate with writers who have already produced materials that meet their needs, but many are not willing to do so when dealing with a new freelancer. To get your feet wet, you may have to settle for less—at first. The trick is to raise your prices as your reputation grows. Remember: The best client is one who is willing to pay you more than once.

If you don't wish to merely accept whatever pay scale is offered, you can use the formulas on these pages to help determine an hourly rate that can cover your bills and earn you a profit as a writer.

Calculating Your Expenses

Any business has to make enough money to cover expenses. The worksheet on page 298 will help you figure out your overhead costs and other expenses. Overhead for a writing business typically comprises a computer, office supplies, fax, telephone, and office space.

This formula assumes you "expense" your computer equipment in one year, meaning you will write the total off as a business expense in one year. If you plan to use the equipment several years, you can depreciate its value over several years. For example, if you plan to keep your computer three years, then your expense for one year would be $1,600 divided by 3, or $534. Divide this figure by 12 to find the monthly cost.

Taxes are high for freelancers, because you pay yours and the employer's portion of Social Security taxes. Estimate 50 percent of your income going to the government; the figure may be a bit high, but it's better to have too much than too little money ready to send the government at the end of each quarter. In the table below, we estimated an annual income of $30,000, so the tax bill would be about $15,000. That divided by 12 is $1,250 of taxes each month.

You may have other expenses—renting an office, for example. In the table below, "other" expenses can include dues for professional associations, seminar fees, subscriptions, advertising/promotion, travel, and licenses.

Hourly Rate Calculation

It is important to know the hourly rate you need to earn in order to meet your needs. Follow these steps to calculate what your earnings must be in order for you to be a successful freelance writer.

1. **Covering Expenses.** To figure out how much you'll have to earn per hour to pay for expenses, first decide how much time you'll have to devote to writing per month. To calculate the break-even hourly rate, divide your monthly expenses by the number of hours

you plan to work. In the example below, if you can work 160 hours each month on your writing, the hourly rate would be $1,488/160 = $9.50 per hour.

Consider this your bare minimum hourly rate, because it does not include any remuneration for your expertise or any profit. If you use this figure to give an estimate for a job, you'd be valuing your time and talent at zero.

2. **Setting Fees.** One way to make sure you are paid market rates is to estimate how much a company would pay an employee to do similar work. Remember that a company may also pay for health insurance, retirement funds, unemployment insurance, vacation time, holidays, etc. These costs can range from 25 to 45 percent of an employee's annual salary, depending upon which perks the employee gets and where she lives. You can call companies to find actual costs for each of the benefits you need, or just use a 35 percent estimate to get a rough estimate.

- Estimated yearly salary: $30,000 divided by 2,000 (40 hours per week for 50 weeks) equals an hourly pay rate of $15. (This formula assumes you will take two weeks of vacation a year. Adjust the formula as needed.)
- Adding fringe benefit costs of 35 percent ($5.25) gives you an hourly rate of $20.25.

Monthly Expense Calculation	
Computer ($1,600/12 months)	$134
Printer: ($200/12 months)	$17
Telephone	$35
Office Supplies	$25
Postage	$15
Taxes	$1,250 (estimate)
Other ($144/12 months)	$12
TOTAL	$1,488

Monthly Expense Worksheet	
Computer (divided by 12)	$
Printer: (divided by 12)	$
Telephone	$
Office Supplies	$
Postage	$
Taxes (50% of gross)	$
Other (divided by 12)	$
TOTAL	

- Add to this amount your minimum rate to cover overhead ($9.50) and you have a total hourly rate of $29.25.
- In addition, you might want to add another 10 to 20 percent of profit ($3.50) for a total hourly fee of $32.75.

A rate of $30 or more an hour may be high for a particular type of writing or may be quite reasonable depending on your level of experience, the perceived value of your work, and the prevailing rates available to the client. In determining the prices you will charge for various types of work you must first conduct research. This includes talking to other writers about what they charge.

When calculating the hours you invest in your work you also need to consider the time spent writing queries and making calls to find jobs, billing, filing tax returns, driving to the post office, shopping for office supplies, and maintaining your computer. To be successful, at least one-fifth of your time should be spent marketing yourself. Your hourly rate for all these activities needs to be recouped somewhere—either in higher fees or additional hours that you bill your clients.

None of the above calculations include reimbursement for expenses for specific jobs, such as travel, overnight mail, or long-distance telephone calls. These should be added to the bill and paid by the client. It's best to have a written contract spelling out what work you are expected to do at what rate.

Project Rates

An alternative way of pricing is to charge by the project. The advantage of project pricing is that if you work quickly, you can earn a high hourly rate. If you quote a price of $300 for a piece, and manage to turn it around in three hours, well, you do the math. If you decide to work more slowly, that's your option, too. But with a project rate, you've set your ceiling and a client probably won't pay you more.

The disadvantage of accepting a project price is that if you estimate too low, you may discover you could have earned better wages elsewhere. You can always try negotiating for more, but you'll have to convince your client why your original estimate was wrong, which is difficult and, if it's your fault, embarrassing.

Some clients will tell you the pay rate up front. Others may ask what you charge. If asked, don't be evasive. It's not very professional to show uncertainty about something as basic and important as your price. Since they're asking, feel free to quote your full fee. Remember, you can always adjust downward but it's hard to negotiate upward after you have already quoted a price.

Seasoned writers have an easier time figuring out an acceptable price for a project. Almost by instinct they can discern the amount of time and effort that will go into a project. Beginners typically fare better by focusing on an hourly fee. This way they not only learn which types of projects are best suited for them, but they also can keep better track of the gains they make in skill and efficiency. Unfortunately, most clients want a fixed price, especially if they are not familiar with your work. The solution is to negotiate a set price based on the number of hours you expect to spend on the project. If you are going to earn a set fee it is important to detail up front precisely what the work will entail. Once you have talked this over with the client or editor, estimate how many hours you expect to spend on the project including research, interviews, editing, and proofreading. (It helps to look at similar projects completed for the client in the past.) Then multiply the number of hours by your hourly rate to get the amount of money you expect to earn.

When starting out as a freelance writer you won't be able to com-

Fee Worksheet	
Employee's estimated yearly salary	$
Divide by hours worked (2,000 for 40 week for 50 weeks)	/2,000
Employee pay rate	$
2,000 Estimated employee hourly rate	$
Plus fringe benefit cost (add 35%)	+$
Plus your minimum rate to cover overhead	+$
Plus 10%-20% profit (.1 to .2 x hourly rate)	+$
Your hourly rate	$

mand the same fee as someone with several years of experience. This does not mean, however, that you are at the mercy of the client. If you are qualified as a writer, then you are producing a professional product and should be compensated fairly. Decide early on the lowest figure you will accept and stick to it.

Early in your career you might not make out as well charging by the project. But as you gain experience—enabling you to work faster and to estimate your time better—you will do quite well. Publications and most other businesses are time sensitive. To your pleasant surprise, clients and editors will be willing to pay you more for getting work done more quickly. As your proficiency and efficiency improve you will, in effect, earn more money for less work.

Keep Track of Time

Keeping track of how long it takes to finish a project might feel as if you're attaching a meter to your mind. But it is vitally important, whether you are charging by the hour or by the project. By keeping good records for specific types of projects, you will eventually discern patterns. You can use the insight you gain to improve your work flow, cut out unnecessary steps, and set fees that maximize your income while still keeping you competitive. Even so, many writers do not closely track how much time they spend on a project. Even if they know how much time they spend at the keyboard, they often underestimate the hours spent researching, interviewing, billing, and corresponding with their clients.

It need not be this way. Keeping track of your time is not as much effort as you might think. And the payoff far outweighs the investment of time you put into it. The insight you gain into your work habits can help you better use your time in the future—giving you more free time down the road. You will also improve your ability to accurately bid your services.

One easy method is to watch the clock and keep a log book by your computer or in your briefcase. Some people even use a stopwatch. They simply start the watch when they begin work, turn it off whenever they step away, and turn it on again when they resume work. The watch keeps an accurate tally of their cumulative time.

Ironically, it's sometimes the small projects that reveal the most about our work habits. Bigger projects get spread over weeks or even months, making it harder to get a clear picture of all the work involved. A small project that lasts just a couple days is easier to track and analyze. You might be surprised by what you learn.

With a record of time invested in a job, you can examine hard data to estimate how much you think you should earn on a project. You can use the data in asking for more money on the next project. Use the chart on page 304 to track your hours per project. In the column labeled "Notes," include anything that made the job easier or harder than expected.

Negotiating for More

GOOD

INEXPENSIVE   FAST

Few of us like to haggle over the price of goods or services. When you land a writing job, however, you are in a good negotiating position: You have something that your client wants.

A good rule to consider in wrangling over fees is to consider the three points on the triangle at left. Most people want things done well, inexpensively, and fast. But most times, they will only get two of the three. For example, you might be able to write something cheaply and fast, but you probably won't be able to do it well. Or you can do it fast and make it good, but it won't be inexpensive. By this reasoning, if a client asks for a quick turnaround time, you should expect to be paid extra for it.

Once you work with a client or editor, and prove you can deliver, it will be easier to negotiate for more money. While many editors are understandably reluctant to invest large amounts in unknown writers, they may be able to find more in their budgets for someone they have come to know and trust.

It may be easier for beginning writers to quote a range of pay they would like to earn. You could tell the client the job would cost between $100 and $200, for example, depending on how much time it involves. If you can do it for less, they may be grateful for a smaller bill and be more willing to give you another assignment. But never undervalue your work, for if you do, you can be sure that others will, too.

Negotiation doesn't have to be confrontational. After all, an editor often doesn't hold the purse strings, and may be sympathetic to polite requests for more money. Before you ask for more (or ask to retain certain rights to resell your work), decide which things you sincerely want and which you can give up. First, state everything that you would like. Then be prepared to adopt a position that gets you most of what you want. If you've kept a log of how long previous projects have taken and what types of work they entailed, your arguments will be more persuasive. Be realistic, however. A publication that pays ten cents a word is hardly likely to increase that tenfold.

Simply repeating the project price might prompt the client to increase it. Here's a true story: A young woman from Kentucky moved to New York City and was offered a job working in the computer department of a large publishing firm. Used to working for minimum wage, she could not believe it when the interviewer offered her a salary of $50,000. "Fifty-thousand dollars?" she repeated incredulously. Whereupon the company increased the offer to $55,000. Today she makes closer to $70,000. While most writers don't make the wages that computer specialists do, repeating the pay may be a successful negotiating ploy.

Keep in mind that business people talk money all the time, and writing is a business. If you ask for more, usually the worst that could happen is you'll be told no. At that point it's up to you to decide whether you'll take the job or move on.

Time Tracker Worksheet					
Job Name	Date	Notes	Hours of Work	Project Payment	Hourly Rate

Raising Your Rates

A freelancer, like any business person, eventually faces the day when he needs to raise prices. Maybe it is because inflation has cut into your profit margin or your living standard. Perhaps you feel the value of your services has increased. Or maybe you have discovered that you have been pricing your services below the market value. In any of these cases don't be reluctant to ask for what you think is fair and justified.

Other businesses consistently raise their rates. Price increases are a fact of life. So don't keep your prices artificially low when an increase is justified. Underpricing your services can produce an image that you lack the skill and experience to command professional fees. It can also suggest that your work is of lower quality.

If you do decide to raise your rates, avoid being erratic. If you change prices often—whether raising or lowering them—you may create the impression that you have no basis for your fee. When you do raise your price, make the increases small and base the change on a sound business decision you can justify. Keep in mind that an increase of just a few percent in your overall price can raise your profit margin substantially.

Of course you don't always have to raise your rates to bring in extra income. If you really can't justify a rate increase, examine your work for instances where you give services to clients for free. While you don't want to "nickel and dime" your clients with petty fees, neither do you want to give away vital services, especially when the client receives a direct benefit. If you keep good track of your time, you can also look for ways that you may be wasting time. Improving your work habits can have the same effect as raising your rates. By being more efficient you can increase your earning potential.

You can also base your price on speed of delivery. If you are asked to turn a project around in half the time, charge extra for this value-added service. Chances are you have to put other projects on hold and work extra hard to accomplish a last-minute request. Be fair, but charge extra for the added effort. Most businesses and consumers realize the added value of convenience, which is why we pay more for quick oil changes, overnight shipments, and eyeglasses that are ready "in about an hour."

If you are questioned about a price change, explain how you have incorporated extra value into your services, and how your work has helped the client win business or helped a publication gain readership. Explain how your fee is a bargain given the benefits provided or the service received.

As a final word, consider this: A client who does not want you to earn a fair wage is not a client worth having. Is it worth losing some low-profit clients in return for earning extra income from your more profitable clients? Raising your prices may be a way to do a profitable business in a forty-hour week—to work smarter instead of working longer hours.

Sample Fees

The following prices are culled from the 2004 *Writer's Market* survey and represent a range of prices charged by freelance writers across North America. Use the prices only as general guidelines because the fees writers charge can vary greatly depending on location, size, complexity of the project, and the writer's own experience or expertise. The prices do not include additional expenses that are typically paid by the client. You can learn more about the going rates charged in your area by networking with other writers or by joining professional writers organizations near you. The benefits you receive will likely be more than offset the annual fees charged by most groups.

Advertising, Copywriting, and PR
Copyediting: $25 to $120 per hour, $120 per 1,000 words
Copywriting: $33 to $120 per hour, $250 to $750 per project

News release: $23 to $100 per hour, $75 to $1,000 per project

Speechwriting: $30 to $100 per hour, $2,700 to $6,000 per 30-minute speech

Audiovisual

Copyediting: $40 to $85 per hour

Film script for business: $40 to $125 per hour, $1,500 to $3,500 per project

Radio commercials/PSAs: $70 to $85 per hour

Radio editorials: $50 to $70 per hour

Screenplay: $48,700 to $91,500 per screenplay

TV commercial/PSA: $60 to $85 per hour

TV movie: $200 to $500 per run minute

TV news feature: $70 to $100 per hour

TV scripts: $70 to $150 per hour, $1,200 minimum per project

Book Publishing

Abstracting and abridging: $30 to $35 per hour

Book proposal consultation/writing: $30 to $60 per hour, $500 to $5,000 per project

Book query critique: $45 to $55 per hour, $30 per page

Book query: $120 to $500 per project, $120 low per project, $200 average per project

Book writing: $5,000 to $150,000 advance against royalties

Children's book: $4,900 average advance against royalties

Content editing: $20 to $75 per hour

Copyediting: $17 to $75 per hour

Ghostwriting: $25 to $80 per hour

Indexing: $2.35 to $8 per page

Manuscript evaluation and critique: $45 to $65 per hour

Proofreading: $16 to $45 per hour, $1 to $3 high per page

Research: $30 to $75 per hour, $500 per day

Rewriting: $30 to $75 per hour

Translation: 6¢ to 12¢ per target word, $7,000 to $10,000 per book

Business and Government

Annual reports: $40 to $150 per hour, $3,000 to $15,000 per project

Brochures/fliers: $28 to $150 per hour, $500 to $5,000 per project

Business plan: $35 to $150 per hour

Catalogs: $40 to $150 per hour, $2,000 to $2,500 per project

Corporate periodicals, writing: $40 to $125 per hour, $72 average per hour; $2 per word

Editing/copyediting: $27 to $100 per hour, $4 per page

Grant proposal: $15 to $100 per hour

Letter: $35 to $150 per hour, $200 to $1,200 per project

Newsletters: $1,000 to $3,800 per project (4 pages), $750 per page

Research: $30 to $100 per hour

Writing seminars: $65 to $200 per hour, $1,000 to $3,500 high per project

Computer and Technical

Computer manual writing: $40 to $125 per hour

Online editing: $28 to $120 per hour

Technical writing: $40 to $110 per hour

Web page writing/editing: $25 to $120 per hour, $50 to $300 high per page

Magazines and Trade Journals

Book/arts reviews: $20 to $650 per project

Column: $200 to $575 per project

Content editing: $35 to $55 per hour, $2,000 to $6,500 per issue

Copyediting: $18 to $55 per hour, $40 average per hour

Events column: $50 to $150 per column

Fact checking: $15 to $20 per hour

Feature articles: $100 to $3,000 per project

Proofreading: $25 to $40 per hour

Newspapers

Book/art reviews: $20 to $250 high per review

Copyediting: $17 to $35 per hour

Feature story: $50 to $1,500 per project

Local Column: $10 to $175 per column

Obituary: $35 to $75 per story

Proofreading: $22 to $28 per hour

Stringing: $150 to $300 high per story

Resources for Pricing Guides

These books and Web sites can help you as you determine your rates.

Web Sites

Brenner Books (www.brennerbooks.com). Brenner Books publishes books and articles on pricing for writers, graphic designers, and other publishing professionals.

National Writers Union (www.nwu.org). In a section for members, includes a database of magazine rates paid to NWU members.

Society for Technical Communication (www.stc.org). The STC publishes a survey for members detailing salaries and benefits in the U.S. and Canada.

WritersMarket.com (www.writersmarket.com). Offers members a link to the detailed results of its annual rate survey.

Anne Wallingford, WordSmith (www.aw-wrdsmth.com). Anne Wallingford's Freelancer's FAQs offers useful information about setting fees, taxes, and other aspects of finance.

Books

Writer's Market (Writer's Digest Books), edited by Kathryn S. Brogan. Includes typical pay rates, updated annually, for a variety of writing and publishing work. Writer's Market Deluxe Edition includes access to WritersMarket.com, the regularly updated online component of the book.

The Wealthy Writer (Writer's Digest Books), by Michael Meanwell. Includes suggested pricing for high-paying freelance writing work.

Appendix B: Resources for Writers

This comprehensive section includes books, Web sites, magazines, and newsletters that can help you develop and perfect your skills as a writer, no matter what the genre or form.

Books for Writers

Go to any bookstore, and you're likely to be overwhelmed by the number of writing books on the shelves. Here you'll find descriptions of some of the strongest books on writing technique, creativity and inspiration, and style.

The Art and Craft of Feature Writing, by William E. Blundell (New American Library). He practiced his craft at The Wall Street Journal. Now Blundell gives you the benefit of his knowledge, guiding you from the initial steps of gathering information for a story.

The Art and Craft of Playwriting, by Jeffrey Hatcher (Story Press). The author offers practical and creative insights, using classical and modern works to illustrate his points.

The Art and Craft of Poetry, by Michael J. Bugeja (Writer's Digest Books). If poetic skill can be taught, this book can do it, or at least get you started. The step-by-step format shows you how to conceive and capture ideas. The basics of voice, line, stanza, meter, and rhyme are all explored, along with forms, formats, and modes of expression.

The Associated Press Stylebook and Libel Manual (Addison-Wesley Publishing). Maybe you know that "Dumpster" is a trademark and should rightfully be capitalized. But what about the other five thousand entries in this journalist's bible? Few people will ever master the AP's convoluted rules for numerals, but with this quick reference you can avoid common mistakes.

Bird by Bird: Some Instructions on Writing and Life, by Anne

Lamott (Anchor Books). Written in an often hilarious conversational tone, this step-by-step survival guide covers all aspects of the writer's life, from how to deal with writer's block to budgeting your time.

The Chicago Manual of Style (University of Chicago Press). A weighty reference for writers, editors, and proofreaders alike. Full of essential advice, such as how to format your manuscripts to impress an editor.

The Complete Book of Scriptwriting, by J. Michael Straczynski (Writer's Digest Books). This book doesn't cover a lot on technique. What it does offer is a detailed look at how to turn good writing into marketable scripts, whether it's for film, television, radio, animation, or stage.

The Complete Guide to Magazine Article Writing, by John M. Wilson (Writer's Digest Books). From writing compelling leads to the good use of quotes, this book is full of step-by-step instructions from an experienced writer and editor.

Complete Guide to Writing Fiction and Nonfiction, and Getting it Published, by Pat Kubis (Prentice-Hall). This helpful book offers advice on research, article writing, and interviewing, in addition to discussing plot, viewpoint, character, dialogue, setting, and style. It takes you from the fundamentals of writing simply to preparing a complete manuscript.

Creating Poetry, by John Drury (Writer's Digest Books). A new poet continually strives to see life from new angles and reshape language. This book understands that and can help you find your own voice.

The Elements of Style, by William Strunk and E.B. White (Allyn and Bacon). One of the most essential and well-read style books ever written. It's so short, there's no reason not to read it cover to cover. Chances are your editor owns a copy, so you might as well know what's in it, too.

Find It Fast: How to Uncover Expert Information on Any Subject, by Robert I. Berkman (HarperCollins). The hardest part of research is deciding where to begin. This book is a road map that helps you get the most out of libraries, business sources, government documents, and the Internet. This book should be the first step in any research process.

Find It Online: The Complete Guide to Online Research, by Alan M. Schlein (Facts on Demand Press). This is an essential tool for journalists, researchers, and freelance writers who need to know how to do comprehensive and reliable research in hundreds of disciplines. Includes tips and search strategies from dozens of information experts.

Formatting & Submitting Your Manuscript, 2nd edition, by Cynthia Laufenberg and the Editors of Writer's Digest Books (Writer's Digest Books). Using dozens of examples, this book teaches readers how to properly prepare attention-getting submissions. Sample query letters, book proposals, cover letters, outlines, and novel synopses show readers how to put together winning submission packages for all types of writing.

Handbook for Freelance Writing, by Michael Perry (NTC Business Books). There's no need to starve while honing your creative writing skills. Perry shows you how to put together a successful freelance career that can pay the bills. He offers insights on researching markets, writing query letters, and working with editors.

How to Write a Book Proposal, 3rd edition, by Michael Larsen (Writer's Digest Books). If you have the talent and a sound book idea, Larsen can show you how to get your proposal seriously considered by a top agent or publisher. An agent himself, Larsen has placed manuscripts with more than one hundred publishers. His book takes you through each step of the process.

How to Write: Advice and Reflections, by Richard Rhodes (William Morrow and Company). Full of inspiring and practical advice from a Pulitzer prize-winning author. Rhodes isn't afraid to open his mind and bare his heart. Nor is he afraid to talk about his own struggles to write well.

How to Write and Sell Your First Novel, by Oscar Collier, with Frances Spatz Leighton (Writer's Digest Books). This book presents the success strategies of two dozen published authors to help you navigate today's complicated market.

How to Write Irresistible Query Letters, by Lisa Collier Cool (Writer's Digest Books). This is a must read for anyone who wants to enter the magazine market. Before you get to write a great article you first have to write a killer query letter.

The Insider's Guide to Writing for Screen and Television, by Ronald B. Tobias (Writer's Digest Books). A practical guide that teaches how the film industry works. All-star interviews transport you behind the scenes to see how directors and actors look at scripts.

Magazine Writing That Sells, by Don McKinney (Writer's Digest Books). No freelancer should bypass the advice of this former editor of the Saturday Evening Post and McCall's. McKinney shows you how to write enticing query letters and leads that capture the reader's interest. Each step of writing and selling your work is covered.

On Writing, by Stephen King (Pocket Books). King offers a memoir with vivid tales of how he grew from a mischievous boy who loved to read, to a janitor raising a family in a trailer, and, ultimately, to one of our era's most respected writers.

On Writing Well, by William Zinsser (HarperPerennial). Full of the principles and practices that are necessary for good writing. This book stems from a course Zinsser taught at Yale. He turns his lessons into an inspiration for anyone who writes.

The 38 Most Common Fiction Writing Mistakes (and How to Avoid Them), by Jack M. Bickham (Writer's Digest Books). Short and to the point, this book distills decades of writing experience into one easy-to-read volume. Don't write fiction without it.

The Wealthy Writer, by Michael Meanwell (Writer's Digest Books). This book gives thorough information about the highest-paying freelancing opportunities many writers overlook. It offers writers the instruction they need to break into new freelancing markets and how to write effectively for those markets. Meanwell also includes valuable tips for freelancers on how to run their own writing business from marketing themselves to outsourcing work.

The Well-Fed Writer: Financial Self-Sufficiency as a Freelance Writer in Six Months or Less, by Peter Bowerman (Fanove Publishing). Bowerman offers helpful insight on how to earn money from corporate clients. He uses an easy-to-read style to show independent writers how they can better market themselves. His commonsense tips and personal anecdotes show beginning freelance writers how to forge ahead.

Write Faster, Write Better, by David A. Fryxell (Writer's Digest Books). This book teaches writers of all forms how to save time with careful organization, diligent planning, and smart research. Fryxell walks readers through every step of the writing and publishing process, offering timesaving techniques that can help all writers.

The Writer's Digest Writing Clinic, edited by Kelly Nickell (Writer's Digest Books). Using real-life manuscripts, query letters, book proposals, novel synopses, etc., this book shows readers how to properly edit their own work. The book also includes information on how to start a critique group, find an existing critique group, and get the most out of such a group.

Writer's Market, by Kathryn S. Brogan (Writer's Digest Books). Probably the single greatest tool for beginning and experienced writers. This annual directory contains up-to-date lists of several thousand magazine and book publishers broken down by subject category. Articles and features lend important advice from editors, agents, and published authors.

Writing and Illustrating Children's Books for Publication: Two Perspectives, by Berthe Amoss and Eric Suben (Writer's Digest Books). This book offers a self-instruction writing course that guides you through the process of creating a publishable manuscript. Reading lists, editing checklists, and case studies of actual experiences make this a valuable tool.

Writing for Story: Craft Secrets of Dramatic Nonfiction by a Two-Time Pulitzer Prize Winner, by Jon Franklin (Atheneum). With a title this long it better live up to its billing. Unlike authors who focus on style and grammar, Franklin offers a valuable lesson in building a nonfiction story, starting with an outline.

You Can Write Children's Books, by Tracey E. Dils (Writer's Digest Books). This helpful collection of guidelines will help you get your book in print. This book covers all the steps from inspiration to publication.

Web Sites for Writers

Hundreds of sites on the Internet exist to provide valuable information exclusively for writers, but nearly all are also trying to sell something. Imagine that! After all, they can't pay for computer time by giving away information. In many cases the free advice or information is a hook to draw your interest. Here's a hint to keep you from paying for more than you should: If you "shop" around enough sites, you'll find enough free information that you'll feel less compelled to pay for information that comes with the cost of a membership or newsletter.

This is not to say that you should reject all commercial offers. There are good services available online for a fee. Just be careful. More important, be selective. And look around a lot first, so you don't end up paying for something you could have gotten free.

If you are not familiar with writers resources online, check out the sites listed below. They offer a lot of free information and advice, and most provide links to hundreds of other Internet sites.

Absolute Write (www.absolutewrite.com): Offers writing instruction in all areas and keeps tabs on upcoming contests and deadlines. Also delivers two free e-newsletters, one specifically on markets.

American Society of Journalists and Authors (www.asja.org): Offers news about the latest terms and negotiations in the world of newspapers and magazines, provides information on contracts and freelancing.

BookWire (www.bookwire.com): Provides industry news, access to literary journals and reviews, and an expansive directory of book sites around the world. Sponsored by R.R. Bowker Co.

Copyright and Fair Use (http://fairuse.stanford.edu): Contains regulations, judicial opinions, current legislation, and overviews of copyright law and fair use. Sponsored by Stanford University.

Publishers Lunch (www.publisherslunch.com): Offers insider information on the publishing industry, job information, etc. Also offers free-sign up for a daily newsletter on the industry and a weekly newsletter covering the latest book deals.

Sensible Solutions (www.happilypublished.com): Offers advice on marketing your work, looking for a publisher, and self-publishing.

Writers Club (America Online, keyword: Writers): Provides online workshops and a wide range of information, including the basic steps to becoming a writer, how to get the most from writers conferences, how to work with editors, and how to handle rejection.

Writer's Digest (www.writersdigest.com): Features daily market updates, a searchable database of writer's guidelines, and an online ranking of places to get published.

Writers Market (www.writersmarket.com): Offers up-to-date contact information for thousands of editors and agents, along with interviews, valuable insights, and how-to articles for writers.

Writers Write (www.writerswrite.com): Provides articles, reviews, job listings, online communities, chat and discussion boards, live events, and a writers guidelines database.

Writing Resources (http://owl.english.purdue.edu): Provides online workshops, PowerPoint presentations on all aspects of writing, and links to a wide variety web pages covering all aspects of writing. Sponsored by Purdue University's Online Writing Lab.

WritersNet (www.writers.net): Features articles, online discussions and a directory of agents.

Additional Web Sites by Genre

Niche and specialized writing Web sites abound. To help you get started, here are some popular sites broken down by genre:

Children's

Canadian Children's Book Centre: www.bookcentre.ca

Children's Book Council Online: www.cbcbooks.org

Children's Literature Web Guide: www.ucalgary.ca/~dkbrown

Write4Kids.com: www.write4kids.com

Purple Crayon: www.underdown.org

Society of Children's Book Writers and Illustrators: www.scbwi.org

Crime/Mystery

American Crime Writers League: www.acwl.org

ClueLass: www.cluelass.com

Crime Writers of Canada: www.crimewriterscanada.com

Mysterious Home Page: www.cluelass.com/MystHome

Mystery Writer's Forum: www.zott.com/mysforum

Mystery Writers of America: www.mysterywriters.org

Sisters in Crime: www.sistersincrime.org

Horror

DarkEcho Horror: www.darkecho.com

Horror Writer's Association: www.horror.org

International Horror Guild: www.ihgonline.org

Humor

Creating Comics: www.members.shaw.ca/creatingcomics

Humor and Life:
www.geocities.com/SoHo/Gallery/4111/menu.html

HumorLinks: www.humorlinks.com

Stand-Up Comedy FAQ: www.faqs.org/faqs/comedy-faq/hack

Journalism

American Journalism Review: www.ajr.org

Newslink: http://newslink.org

American Society of Journalists and Authors: www.asja.org

Columbia Journalism Review: www.cjr.org

National Press Club: http://npc.press.org

Playwriting and Scriptwriting

Done Deal: www.scriptsales.com

Hollywoodlitsales: www.hollywoodlitsales.com

Internet Theatre Bookshop: www.stageplays.com

New Dramatists: www.newdramatists.org

Playbill On-Line: www.playbill.com

Playwrights on the Web: www.stageplays.com/writers.htm

Playwriting Seminars: www.vcu.edu/artweb/playwriting

Screenwriters Homepage: http://home.earthlink.net/~scribbler

Screenwriters Online: www.screenwriter.com

Screenwriters Utopia: www.screenwritersutopia.com

Studio Systems: www.studiosystemsinc.com

Wordplay: www.wordplayer.com

WriteMovies.com: www.writemovies.com

Writers Guild of America: www.wga.org

Poetry

Academy of American Poets: www.poets.org

Aha! Poetry: www.ahapoetry.com

Poetic Voices: www.poeticvoices.com

Poetry Daily: www.poems.com

Poetry Today Online: www.poetrytodayonline.com

Rhyming Dictionary: www.rhymezone.com

Romance

Cata-Romance: www.cataromance.com

Gothic Journal: www.gothicjournal.com

Romance Central: www.romance-central.com

Romance Novels and Women's Fiction:
www.writepage.com/romance.htm

Romance Writers of America: www.rwanational.org

Romantic Times: www.romantictimes.com

Science Fiction

Broad Universe: www.broaduniverse.org

Science Fiction and Fantasy Workshop:
  www.burgoyne.com/pages/workshop
Science Fiction and Fantasy Writers of America: www.sfwa.org
Science Fiction Resource Guide: www.sflovers.org/SFRG
SF Site: www.sfsite.com
Science Fiction Writers of Earth: www.flash.net/~sfwoe
Spicy Green Iguana: www.spicygreeniguana.com

Technical Writing

Internet Resources for Business and Technical Writers:
  www.english.uiuc.edu/cws/wworkshop/writers'%20resources.htm
Write Place Catalogue:
  http://leo.stcloudstate.edu/catalogue.html#business

Magazines and Newsletters for Writers

Trade magazines provide a great means of getting up-to-date information on the writer's world. A good writers magazine provides articles that inspire creativity or help us to solve problems. Some great magazines and newsletters are included with the cost of membership to the writers organizations listed on previous pages. Some of these include *American Writer*, from National Writers Union, and *Novelists' Ink*, an excellent publication from the group Novelists Inc. Many more magazines and newsletters offer advice online.

The magazines listed below are among the most established and respected publications available to writers through subscription. All are reasonably priced, at about $15 to $40 per year. Each contains articles to help make you a better writer, or to help make your life as a writer a little easier.

American Journalism Review: Covers topics related to both print and broadcast journalism. Monthly publication. University of Maryland, 1117 Journalism Bldg., College Park, MD 20742, (800) 827-0771, www.ajr.org.

Byline: Presents articles on the craft and business of writing, including columns on writing poetry, fiction, nonfiction, and children's literature. Monthly publication. P.O. Box 5240, Edmond, OK 73083, www.bylinemag.com.

Canadian Writer's Journal: Lists markets, contests, awards, and writers guidelines, and features poetry, articles, and reviews. Quarterly publication. P.O. Box 1178, New Liskeard, ON Canada P0J 1P0, (705) 647-5424, www.cwj.ca.

Children's Book Insider: Information for new and experienced writers of children's literature. Monthly newsletter. 901 Columbia Rd., Ft. Collins, CO 80525, (800) 807-1916, www.write4kids.com.

Creativity Connection: Features author profiles, how-to articles, and conference/workshop listings for writers and small publishers. Quarterly newsletter. University of Wisconsin at Madison, Department of Liberal Studies and the Arts, 610 Langdon Street, Rm. 715, Madison, WI 53703, (608) 263-6320, www.dcs.wisc.edu/lsa/writing/creativity_connection.htm.

Cross and Quill: This organizational newsletter profiles members of the Christian Writers Fellowship, and provides writing instruction, advice from editors and professional writers, etc. Bimonthly newsletter. Christian Writers Fellowship International, 1624 Jefferson Davis Rd., Clinton, SC 29325, (864) 697-6035, www.cwfi-online.org.

The Editorial Eye: Specializes in standards and practices for writers, editors, and publication managers. Monthly newsletter. 66 Canal Center Plaza, Suite 200, Alexandria, VA 22314, (800) 683-8380, www.eeicommunications.com/eye.

Freelance Success: Marketing and management strategies for veteran freelance writers. Weekly e-newsletter. 32391 Dunford St., Farmington Hills, MI 48334, (877) 731-5411, www.freelancesuccess.com.

Hellnotes: Your Insider's Guide to the Horror Field: The name says it all. A weekly e-newsletter. 4212 Derby Lane, Evansville, IN 47715, www.hellnotes.com.

Hollywood Scriptwriter: Offers practical advice and guidance from working professionals. Bimonthly publication. P.O. Box

10277, Burbank, CA 91510, (310) 530-0000, www.hollywood scriptwriter.com.

Locus: The Newspaper of the Science Fiction Field: Offers insight and news of interest to writers and publishers in the science fiction field. Monthly publication. P.O. Box 13305, Oakland, CA 94661, (510) 339-9198, www.locusmag.com.

Network Journal: Specializes in news about women writers. Bimonthly publication. International Women's Writing Guild, P.O. Box 810, Grand Station, New York, NY 10028, (212) 737-7536, www.iwwg.com.

Novelists' Ink: Offers up-to-date information about the business of publishing, plus "how-to" articles. Monthly newsletter. Novelists Inc., P.O. Box 1166, Mission, KS 66222, www.ninc.com.

Poets & Writers: Offers commentary, interviews with authors, information on grants, and lists of awards. Bimonthly publication. 72 Spring St., Suite 301, New York, NY 10012, (212) 226-3586, www.pw.org.

Publishers Weekly: The leading news magazine covering book publishing and bookselling worldwide. Weekly publication. 360 Park Ave. S., New York, NY 10010, (800) 278-2991, www.publishersweekly.com.

Script: Covers both the craft and business of screenwriting, plus interviews with screenwriters, agents, managers, attorneys, and filmmakers. Bimonthly publication. 5638 Sweet Air Rd., Baldwin, MD 21013, (888) 245-2228, www.scriptmag.com.

Science Fiction Chronicle: Cover many aspects of the genre, from mainstream publishing to gaming and fan activities. Bimonthly publication. P.O. Box 022730, Brooklyn, NY 11202, www.dna-publications.com/sfc.

SFWA Bulletin: Offers insight and news from the Science Fiction and Fantasy Writers of America. Quarterly publication. P.O. Box 10126, Rochester, NY 14610, www.sfwa.org.

Small Press Review: Contains book reviews, columns, tips for getting published, and news on the small press and small magazine industry, including start-ups. Bimonthly publication. P.O. Box

100, Paradise, CA 95967, (800) 477-6110, www.dustbooks.com.

Speechwriter's Newsletter: Practical advice on speech writing in the business, government, and education sectors. Monthly publication. Ragan Communications, 316 N. Michigan Ave., Suite 300, Chicago, IL 60601, (800) 878-5331, www2.ragan.com.

Talking Agents: Examines the world of literary agents from a writer's point of view. Monthly newsletter. Agent Research & Evaluation,. 25 Barrow St., New York, NY 10014, (212) 924-9942, www.agentresearch.com.

Writer's Digest: Features interviews, expert instruction, inspiration, and information on every aspect of the writing life. Monthly publication. 4700 E. Galbraith Rd., Cincinnati, OH 45236, (513) 531-2222, www.writersdigest.com.

Writers Guild of America East Newsletter: News and information on the broad range of activities and services of interest to writers, including advice on contract negotiations. Bimonthly newsletter. 555 W. 57th St., Suite 1230, New York, NY 10019, (212) 767-7800, www.wgaeast.org.

Writing That Works: Offers techniques on business writing and communications in print and on the web. Monthly publication. 7481 Huntsman Blvd., #720, Springfield, VA 22153, (703) 643-2200, www.writingthatworks.com.

Written By: Covers the art, craft, and business of writing in Hollywood. Monthly publication. Writer's Guild of America West, 7000 W. 3rd St., Los Angeles, CA 90048, (800) 548-4532, www.wga.org.

Appendix C: Publishers and Their Imprints

The publishing world is constantly changing and evolving. With all of the buying, selling, reorganizing, consolidating, and dissolving, it's hard to keep publishers and their imprints straight. To help you make sense of these changes, we offer this breakdown of major publishers (and their divisions)—who owns whom and which imprints are under each company umbrella. Keep in mind that this information is constantly changing. We have provided the Web sites for each of the publishers so you can continue to keep an eye on this ever-evolving business.

SIMON & SCHUSTER
(Viacom, Inc.)
www.simonsays.com
Simon & Schuster Audio
  Pimsleur
  Simon & Schuster Audioworks
  Simon & Schuster Sound
    Ideas
Simon & Schuster Children's Publishing
  Aladdin Paperbacks
  Atheneum Books for Young
    Readers
  Little Simon®
  Margaret K. McEldeiry Books
  Simon & Schuster Books for
    Young Readers
  Simon Pulse
  Simon Spotlight®
Simon & Schuster Adult Publishing

  Atria Books
  The Free Press
  Kaplan
  Pocket Books
  Scribner
  Simon & Schuster
  Simon & Schuster Trade
    Paperback
Simon & Schuster Interactive
Simon & Schuster International
  Simon & Schuster Australia
  Simon & Schuster Canada
  Simon & Schuster UK

HARPERCOLLINS
(subsidiary of News Corp.)
www.harpercollins.com
HarperCollins General Books Group
  Access Press

Amistad Press
Avon
Ecco
Eos
Fourth Estate
Harper Design International
HarperAudio
HarperBusiness
HarperCollins
HarperEntertainment
HarperLargeprint
HarperResource
HarperSanFrancisco
HarperTorch
Perennial
PerfectBound
Quill
Rayo
ReganBooks
William Morrow

HarperCollins Children's Books Group

Avon
Greenwillow Books
HarperCollins Children's
  Books
HarperFestival
HarperTrophy
Joanna Cotler Books
Laura Geringer Books
Tempest

HarperCollins Australia

Angus & Robertson
Flamingo
4th Estate

HarperBusiness
HarperCollins
HarperReligious
HarperSports
Voyager

HarperCollins Canada

HarperFlamingoCanada
Perennial Canada
HarperCollins UK
Collins
Collins Education
4th Estate
Thorsons/Element
Voyager Books

Zondervan
Inspino
Vida Publishers
Zonderkidz

RANDOM HOUSE, INC.

(Bertelsmann AG) www.ran
domhouse.com

Ballantine Publishing Group

Ballantine Books
Ballantine Reader's Circle
Del Rey
Del Rey/Lucas Books
Fawcett
Ivy
One World
Wellspring

Bantam Dell Publishing Group

Bantam Hardcover

Bantam Mass Market
Bantam Trade Paperback
Crimeline
Delacorte Press
Dell
Delta
The Dial Press
Domain
DTP
Fanfare
Island
Spectra

Crown Publishing Group
Bell Tower
Clarkson Potter
Crown Business
Crown Publishers, Inc.
Harmony Books
Prima
Shaye Areheart Books
Three Rivers Press

Doubleday Broadway Publishing Group
Broadway Books
Currency
Doubleday
Doubleday Image
Doubleday Religious
    Publishing
Main Street Books
Nan A. Talese

Knopf Publishing Group
Alfred A. Knopf
Anchor
Everyman's Library

Pantheon Books
Schocken Books
Vintage Anchor Publishing

Random House Adult Trade Publishing Group
The Modern Library
Random House Trade Group
Random House Trade
    Paperbacks
Strivers Row Books
Villard Books

Random House Audio Publishing Group
Listening Library
Random House Audible
Random House Audio
Random House Audio Assets
Random House Audio
    Dimensions
Random House Audio Price-
    less
Random House Audio Roads
Random House Audio Voices

Random House Children's Books
BooksReportsNow.com
GoldenBooks.com
Junie B. Jones
Kids@Random
Magic Tree House
Parents@Randorn
Seussville
Teachers @Random
Teens@Random

Knopf/Delacorte/Dell Young

Readers Group
Alfred A. Knopf
Bantam
Crown
David Fickling Books
Delacorte Press
Dell Dragonfly
Dell Laurel-Leaf
Dell Yearling Books
Doubleday
Wendy Lamb Books

Random House Young Readers Group
Akiko
Arthur
Barbie
Beginner Books
The Berenstain Bears
Bob the Builder
Disney
Dragon Tales
First Time Books
Golden Books
Landmark Books
Little Golden Books
Lucas Books
Mayer Shaw
Nickelodeon
Nick, Jr.
pat the bunny
Picturebacks
Precious Moments
Richard Scarry
Sesame Street Books
Step into Reading
Stepping Stones
Star Wars
Thomas the Tank Engine and Friends

Random House Direct, Inc.
Bon Appétit
Gourmet Books
Pillsbury

Random House Information Group
Fodor's Travel Publications
Living Language
Prima Games
Princeton Review
Random House Español
Random House Puzzles & Games
Random House Reference Publishing

Random House Large Print Publishing

Random House Value Publishing

Random House International
Areté
McClelland & Stewart Ltd.
Plaza & Janés
Random House Australia
Random House of Canada Ltd.
Random House Mondadori
Random House South America
Random House United Kingdom

Transworld UK
Verlagsgruppe Random House
Waterbrook Press
Fisherman Bible Study Guides
Mercer Books
Waterbrook Press

PENGUIN GROUP (USA), INC.
(Pearson plc) www.penguinput nam.com
Penguin Putnam, Inc. (Adult)
Ace Books
Avery
Berkley Books
Diamond Books
Jam
Prime Crime
Boulevard
Dutton
Gotham
G.P. Putnam's Sons
Blue Hen Putnam
HPBooks
Jeremy P. Tarcher
Jove
NAL
New American Library
Penguin
Perigee
Plume
Portfolio
Riverhead Books (paperback)
Viking
Penguin Putnam Books for

Young Readers (Children)
AlloyBooks
Dial Books for Young Readers
Dutton Children's Books
Firebird
Frederick Warne
G.P. Putnam's Sons
Grosset & Dunlap
Planet Dexter
Platt & Munk
Philomel
Phyflis Fogelman Books
PaperStar
Planet Dexter
Platt & Munk
Playskool
Price Stem Sloan
PSS
Puffin Books
Viking Children's Books

AOL TIME WARNER BOOK GROUP
www.twbookmark.com
Warner Books
Aspect
Mysterious Press
Time Warner AudioBooks
Warner Business Books
Warner Faith
Warner Forever
Warner Vision
Little, Brown and Co. Adult Trade Books
Back Bay Books

Bulfinch Press
Little, Brown and Co.
Children's Publishing
   Megan Tingley Books

Mirasol/libros
North Point Press
Sunburst Paperback

HOLTZBRINCK PUBLISHERS (Germany)
www.vhpsva.com
St. Martin's Press
   Griffin
   Minotaur
   St. Martin's Press Paperback & Reference
   St. Martin's Press Trade Division
   Thomas Dunne Books
   Truman Talley Books
   Whitman Coin Books & Products
Tor Books
   Forge Books
   Orb Books
Henry Holt & Co.
   Henry Holt Books for Young Readers
   John Macrae Books
   Metropolitan Books
   Owl Books
   Picador USA
   Times Books
Farrar Straus & Giroux
   Faber and Faber
   FSG Books for Young Readers
   Hill and Wang

Appendix D: Glossary of Publishing Terms

Advance: A sum of money a publisher pays a writer prior to the publication of a book. It is usually paid in installments, such as one-half on signing the contract; one-half on delivery of a complete and satisfactory manuscript. The advance is paid against the royalty money that will be earned by the book.

Agent: A liaison between a writer and editor or publisher. An agent shops a manuscript around, receiving a commission when the manuscript is accepted. Agents usually take a 10 to 15 percent fee from the advance and royalties, and 10 to 20 percent if a co-agent is involved, such as in the sale of dramatic rights.

All rights: See chapter twelve.

Anthology: A collection of selected writings by various authors or a gathering of works by one author.

Assignment: Editor asks a writer to produce a specific article for an agreed-upon fee.

Auction: Publishers sometimes bid for the acquisition of a book manuscript that has excellent sales prospects. The bids are for the amount of the author's advance, advertising and promotional expenses, royalty percentage, etc. Auctions are conducted by agents.

Avant-garde: Writing that is innovative in form, style, or subject, often considered difficult and challenging.

B&W: Abbreviation for black and white photographs.

Backlist: A publisher's list of its books that were not published during the current season, but that are still in print.

Bimonthly: Every two months.

Bin: A sentence or brief paragraph about the writer. It can appear at the bottom of the first or last page of a writer's article or short story or on a contributor's page.

Biweekly: Every two weeks.

Boilerplate: A standardized contract. When an editor says "our standard contract," he means the boilerplate with no changes. Writers should be aware that most authors and/or agents make many changes on the boilerplate.

Book packager: Draws all elements of a book together, from the initial concept to writing and marketing strategies, then sells the book package to a book publisher. Also known as book producer or book developer.

Business-size envelope: Also known as a No. 10 envelope, it is the standard size used in sending business correspondence.

Byline: Name of the author appearing with the published piece.

Category fiction: A term used to include all various labels attached to types of fiction. See also genre.

Chapbook: A small booklet, usually paperback, of poetry, ballads, or tales.

Circulation: The number of subscribers to a magazine.

Clean copy: A manuscript free of errors, cross-outs, wrinkles, or smudges.

Clips: Samples, usually from newspapers or magazines, of your published work.

Coffee-table book: An oversize book, heavily illustrated.

Column inch: The amount of space contained in one inch of a typeset column.

Commercial novels: Novels designed to appeal to a broad audience. These are often broken down into categories such as Western, mystery, and romance. See also genre.

Commissioned work: See assignment.

Concept: A statement that summarizes a screenplay or teleplay—before the outline or treatment is written.

Confessional: Genre of fiction essay in which the author or first-person narrator confesses something shocking or embarrassing.

Contact sheet: A sheet of photographic paper on which negatives are transferred so you can see the entire roll of shots placed together on one sheet of paper without making separate, individual prints.

Contributor's copies: Copies of the issues of magazines sent to the author in which the author's work appears.

Cooperative publishing: See copublishing.

Copublishing: Arrangement where author and publisher share publication costs and profits of a book. Also known as cooperative publishing. See also subsidy publisher.

Copyediting: Editing a manuscript for grammar, punctuation, and printing style, not subject content.

Copyright: A means to protect an author's work. See chapter twelve.

Cover letter: A brief letter, accompanying a complete manuscript, especially useful if responding to an editor's request for a manuscript. A cover letter also may accompany a book proposal. A cover letter is not a query letter.

Creative nonfiction: Nonfiction writing that uses an innovative approach to the subject and creative language.

CV: Curriculum vita. A brief listing of qualifications and career accomplishments.

Derivative works: A work that has been translated, adapted, abridged, condensed, annotated, or otherwise produced by altering a previously created work. Before producing a derivative work, it is necessary to secure the written permission of the copyright owner of the original piece.

Desktop publishing: A publishing system designed for a personal computer. The system is capable of typesetting, some illustration, layout, design, and printing—so that the final piece can be distributed and/or sold.

Docudrama: A fictional film rendition of recent newsmaking events and people.

Dramatic poetry: Poetry written for performance as a play. It is one of the three main genres of poetry (the others being lyric poetry and narrative poetry).

Eclectic: Publication features a variety of different writing styles or genres.

Electronic submission: A submission made by modem or on computer disk.

E-mail: Electronic mail. Mail generated on a computer and delivered over a computer network to a specific individual or group of individuals. To send or receive e-mail, a user must have an account with an online service, which provides an e-mail address and electronic mailbox.

Erotica: Fiction or art that is sexually oriented.

Experimental: See avant-garde.

Fair use: A provision of the copyright law that says short passages from copyrighted material may be used without infringing on the owner's rights. See chapter twelve.

Feature: An article giving the reader information of human interest rather than news. Also used by magazines to indicate a lead article or distinctive department.

Filler: A short item used by an editor to "fill" out a newspaper column or magazine page. It could be a timeless news item, a joke, an anecdote, some light verse or short humor, puzzle, etc.

First North American serial rights: See chapter twelve.

First-person point of view: In nonfiction, the author reports from his or her own perspective; in fiction, the narrator tells the story from his or her point of view. This viewpoint makes frequent use of "I," or occasionally, "we."

Formula story: Familiar theme treated in a predictable plot structure—such as boy meets girl, boy loses girl, boy gets girl back.

Frontlist: A publisher's list of its books that are new to the current season.

Galleys: The first typeset version of a manuscript that has not yet been divided into pages.

Genre: Refers either to a general classification of writing, such as the novel or the poem, or to the categories within those classifications, such as the problem novel or the sonnet. Genre fiction describes commercial novels, such as mysteries, romances, and science fiction. Also called category fiction.

Ghostwriter: A writer who puts into literary form an article, speech, story, or book based on another person's ideas or knowledge.

Gift book: A book designed as a gift item. Often small in size with few illustrations and placed close to a bookstore's checkout as an "impulse" buy, gift books tend to be written to a specific niche, such as golfers, mothers, etc.

Glossy: A black and white photograph with a shiny surface as opposed to one with a nonshiny matte finish.

Gothic novel: A fiction category or genre in which the central character is usually a beautiful young girl, the setting an old mansion or castle, and there is a handsome hero and a real menace, either natural or supernatural.

Graphic novel: An adaptation of a novel in graphic form, long comic strip, or heavily illustrated story, of forty pages or more, produced in paperback form.

Hard copy: The printed copy of a computer's output.

Hardware: All the mechanically-integrated components of a computer that are not software. Circuit boards, transistors, and the machines that are the actual computer are the hardware.

High-lo: Material written for newer readers, generally adults, with a high interest level and low reading ability.

Home page: The first page of a World Wide Web document.

Honorarium: Token payment—small amount of money, or a byline and copies of the publication.

How-to: Books and magazine articles offering a combination of information and advice in describing how something can be accomplished. Subjects range widely from hobbies to psychology.

Hypertext: Words or groups of words in an electronic document that are linked to other text, such as a definition or a related document. Hypertext can also be linked to illustrations.

Illustrations: May be photographs, old engravings, artwork. Usually paid for separately from the manuscript. See also package sale.

Imprint: Name applied to a publisher's specific line or lines of books (e.g., Avon is an imprint of HarperCollins).

Interactive: A type of computer interface that takes user input, such as answers to computer-generated questions, and then acts upon that input.

Interactive fiction: Works of fiction in book or computer software format in which the reader determines the path the story will take. The reader chooses from several alternatives at the end of a "chapter," and thus determines the structure of the story. Interactive fiction features multiple plots and endings.

Internet: A worldwide network of computers that offers access to a wide variety of electronic resources.

Kill fee: Fee for a complete article that was assigned but which was subsequently cancelled.

Lead time: The time between the acquisition of a manuscript by an editor and its actual publication.

Libel: A false accusation or any published statement or presentation that tends to expose another to public contempt, ridicule, etc.

List royalty: A royalty payment based on a percentage of a book's retail (or "list") price.

Literary fiction: The general category of serious, nonformulaic, intelligent fiction.

Little magazine: Publications of limited circulation, usually on literary or political subject matter.

Lyric poetry: Poetry in which music predominates over story or drama. It is one of the three main genres of poetry (the others being dramatic poetry and narrative poetry).

Mainstream fiction: Fiction that transcends popular novel categories such as mystery, romance, and science fiction. Using conventional methods, this kind of fiction tells stories about people and their conflicts with greater depth of characterization, background, etc., than the more narrowly focused genre novels.

Mass-market: Nonspecialized books of wide appeal directed toward a large audience. Smaller and more cheaply produced than trade paperbacks, they are found in nonbookstore outlets, such as supermarkets.

Memoir: A narrative recounting a writer's (or fictional narrator's) personal or family history.

Midlist: Those titles on a publisher's list that are not expected to be big sellers, but are expected to have limited sales. They are usually written by new or unknown writers.

Modem: A device used to transmit data from one computer to another via telephone lines.

Monograph: A detailed and documented scholarly study concerning a single subject.

Multimedia: Computers and software capable of integrating text, sound, photographic-quality images, animation, and video.

Multiple submissions: Sending more than one poem, gag, or greeting card idea at the same time.

Narrative nonfiction: A narrative presentation of actual events.

Narrative poem: Poetry that tells a story. One of the three main genres of poetry (the others being dramatic poetry and lyric poetry).

Net royalty: A royalty payment based on the amount of money a book publisher receives on the sale of a book after booksellers' discounts, special sales discounts, and returns.

Network: A group of computers electronically linked to share information and resources.

New Age: A "fringe" topic that has become increasingly mainstream. Formerly, New Age included UFOs and occult phenomena. The term has evolved to include more general topics such as psychology, religion, and health, but emphasizing the mystical, spiritual, or alternative aspects.

Newsbreak: A brief, late-breaking news story added to the front page of a newspaper at press time or a magazine news item of importance to readers.

Nostalgia: A genre of reminiscence, recalling sentimental events or products of the past.

Novelization: A novel created from the script of a popular movie, usually called a movie "tie-in" and published in paperback.

Novella: A short novel, or a long short story; approximately 7,000 to 15,000 words. Also known as a novelette.

On spec: An editor expresses an interest in a proposed article idea and agrees to consider the finished piece for publication "on speculation." The editor is under no obligation to buy the finished manuscript.

One-time rights: See chapter twelve.

Outline: A summary of a book's contents in 5–15 double-spaced pages; often in the form of chapter headings with a descriptive sentence or two under each one to show the scope of the book. A screenplay's or teleplay's outline is a scene-by-scene narrative description of the story (10–15 pages for a ½-hour teleplay; 15–25 pages for a one-hour teleplay; 25–40 pages for a 90-minute teleplay; 40–60 pages for a two-hour feature film or teleplay).

Over-the-transom: Describes the submission of unsolicited material by a freelance writer.

Package sale: The editor buys manuscript and photos as a "package" and pays for them with one check.

Page rate: Some magazines pay for material at a fixed rate per published page, rather than per word.

Parody: The conscious imitation of a work, usually with the intent to ridicule or make fun of the work.

Payment on acceptance: The editor sends you a check for your article, story, or poem as soon as he decides to publish it.

Payment on publication: The editor doesn't send you a check for your material until it is published.

Pen name: The use of a name other than your legal name on articles, stories, or books when you wish to remain anonymous. Simply notify your post office and bank that you are using the name so that you'll receive mail and/or checks in that name. Also called a pseudonym.

Photo feature: Feature in which the emphasis is on the photographs rather than on accompanying written material.

Plagiarism: Passing off as one's own the expression of ideas and words of another writer.

Proofreading: Close reading and correction of a manuscript's typographical errors.

Proposal: A summary of a proposed book submitted to a publisher, particularly used for nonfiction manuscripts. A proposal often contains an individualized cover letter, one-page overview of the book, marketing information, competitive books, author information, chapter-by-chapter outline, two to three sample chapters, and attachments (if relevant) such as magazine articles about the topic and articles you have written (particularly on the proposed topic).

Prospectus: A preliminary written description of a book or article, usually one page in length.

Pseudonym: See pen name.

Public domain: Material that was either never copyrighted or whose copyright term has expired.

Query: A letter that sells an idea to an editor. Usually a query is brief (no more than one page) and uses attention-getting prose.

Release: A statement that your idea is original, has never been sold to anyone else, and that you are selling the negotiated rights to the idea upon payment.

Remainders: Copies of a book that are slow to sell and can be purchased from the publisher at a reduced price. Depending on the author's book contract, a reduced royalty or no royalty is paid on remainder books.

Reporting time: The time it takes for an editor to report to the author on her query or manuscript.

Reprint rights: See chapter twelve.

Roundup article: Comments from, or interviews with, a number of celebrities or experts on a single theme.

Royalties, standard hardcover book: 10 percent of the list price on the first 5,000 copies sold; 12 ½ percent on the next 5,000; 15 percent thereafter.

Royalties, standard mass paperback book: 4 to 8 percent of the list price on the first 150,000 copies sold.

Royalties, standard trade paperback book: No less than 6 percent of list price on the first 20,000 copies; 7½ percent thereafter.

Scanning: A process through which letter-quality printed text or artwork is read by a computer scanner and converted into workable data.

Screenplay: Script for a film intended to be shown in theaters.

Self-publishing: In this arrangement, the author keeps all income derived from the book, but he pays for its manufacturing, production, and marketing.

Semimonthly: Twice per month.

Semiweekly: Twice per week.

Serial: Published periodically, such as a newspaper or magazine.

Serial fiction: Fiction published in a magazine in installments, often broken off at a suspenseful spot.

Series fiction: A sequence of novels featuring the same characters.

Short-short: A complete short story of 1,500 words maximum, and around 250 words minimum.

Sidebar: A feature presented as a companion to a straight news report (or main magazine article) giving sidelights on human-interest aspects or sometimes elucidating just one aspect of the story.

Simultaneous submissions: Sending the same article, story, or poem to several publishers at the same time. Some publishers refuse to consider such submissions.

Slant: The approach or style of a story or article that will appeal to readers of a specific magazine. For example, a magazine may always use stories with an upbeat ending.

Slice-of-life vignette: A short fiction piece intended to realistically depict an interesting moment of everyday living.

Slides: Usually called transparencies by editors looking for color photographs.

Slush pile: The stack of unsolicited or misdirected manuscripts received by an editor or book publisher.

Software: The computer programs that control computer hardware, usually run from a disk drive of some sort. Computers need software in order to run.

Style: The way in which something is written—for example, short, punchy sentences or flowing narrative.

Subsidiary rights: All those rights, other than book publishing rights included in a book contract—such as paperback, book club, movie rights, etc. See chapter twelve.

Subsidy publisher: A book publisher who charges the author for the cost to typeset and print her book, the jacket, etc., as opposed to a royalty publisher who pays the author.

Synopsis: A brief summary of a story, novel, or play. As part of a book proposal, it is a comprehensive summary condensed in a page or page and a half, single-spaced.

Tabloid: Newspaper format publication on about half the size of the regular newspaper page, such as The Star. These are not usually considered hard journalism.

Tagline: A caption for a photo or a comment added to a filler.

Tearsheet: Page from a magazine or newspaper containing your printed story, article, poem, or ad.

Teleplay: A play written for or performed on television.

TOC: Table of Contents.

Trade: Either a hardcover or paperback book; subject matter frequently concerns a special interest. Books are directed toward the layperson rather than the professional.

Transparencies: Positive color slides, not color prints.

Treatment: Synopsis of a television or film script (40–60 pages for a two-hour feature film or teleplay).

Unsolicited manuscript: A story, article, poem, or book that an editor did not specifically ask to see.

Vanity publisher: See subsidy publisher.

Work-for-hire: See chapter twelve.

World Wide Web (WWW): An Internet resource that utilizes hypertext to access information. It also supports formatted text, illustrations, and sounds, depending on the user's computer capabilities.

YA: Young adult books.

Index

Copyright, 160–161,
212–213
Copyright Act, 205–206
Corporations, selling to,
178–192
Correspondence course,
188, 261–262
Courses. See Education
Cover letter, 133
Create Your First
Web Page in a
Weekend, 196
Credit-checking tips,
238–239
Critique groups, 251,
253–255
Crowley, Pat, 23–24

D

Da Capo Press, 37
Dams, Jeanne M.,
133–134
Dark Wing, The, 128

E

Easy Web Page
Creation, 196
E-books, 198–200
Editorial Freelancers
Association, 181, 252
Education, 188
college programs,
259–261
correspondence
courses, 188,
261–262
online courses,
188, 191
See also
Organizations for
writers

Electronic books. See E-
books
Electronic rights,
205–207
Emotions, 32, 76–77
E-query, 101,
196–197, 201
Evanovich, Janet, 128
Expenses, 243–246, 297

F

Fair use, 214
Federal government
research information,
62–63
Fees. See Pricing
guide; Rates
Fellowships, 285–289
Fiction
growth in, 14–15
selling, 128–158
See also Short fiction
Follow-up interview
questions, 79–80
Freelancers, 231
advertising and public
relations, 180,
182–183
copyediting and
proofreading, 186–188
finding opportunities,
179–180
ghostwriting, 191–192
indexing, 189
job banks and
agencies, 181
pricing guide,
295–308
resources for, 183–184
technical writing, 184
See also Writers
Freewriting, 31–32

G

Gay fiction, 14
Ghostwriting, 191–192
Grants, 285–289
Graywolf Press, 37

H

Hourly rate, 297–299
Hunt, Walter C., 128

I

Ideas
emotions and, 32
finding market for,
33–39
freewriting and, 31–32
generators for, 26–32
lists, 32
narrowing, 27
news stories and,
30–31
personal experiences,
29–30
recognizing, 22–24
researching, 54–72
uncovering new,
24–26
Income. See Pricing
guide; Writing, busi-
ness of; Rates
Incorporating, 239
Independent
contractor, 184
Independent Publisher
Book Awards, 289
Indexing, 189–191
Individual Retirement
Account (IRA),
239–240
Insurance, 241–242
Internet